3.00

K. Loganburne
3820 Gordon Hd Rd.

NEW

INTERNATIONAL

ILLUSTRATED

ENCYCLOPEDIA
OF ART

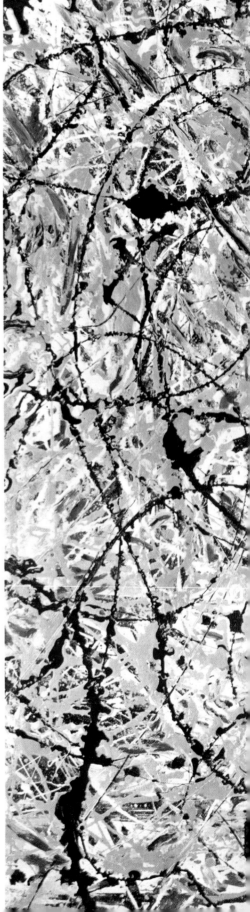

General Editorial Consultant
Sir John Rothenstein, C.B.E., Ph.D., LL.D.

NEW
INTERNATIONAL
ILLUSTRATED
ENCYCLOPEDIA
OF ART

Volume 2
(Architectural Terms —
Baroque Art and Architecture)

GREYSTONE PRESS / NEW YORK • TORONTO • LONDON

Title page illustrations: Page 2 (top left) maiolica plate (sixteenth century) produced in Lyons, France; (bottom left) detail from Pierre-Auguste Renoir's *By the Seashore* (1883), Metropolitan Museum, New York; (right) detail from Jackson Pollock's *Undulating Paths* (c. 1950), Galleria d'Arte Moderna, Rome. Page 3 (left) Favrile glass vase (c. 1900) by Louis Comfort Tiffany, Museum für Kunst und Gewerbe, Hamburg, Germany; (top right) Bajokwe dance mask from the Congo region of Africa, Musée Royal de l'Afrique Centrale, Tervuren, Belgium; (bottom right) painting of the Japanese actor Danjuro (eighteenth century).

PICTURE ACKNOWLEDGEMENTS: Anderson / Andi / Arsphoto / Art Institute of Chicago / Australia House, London / Australian News and Information Bureau / Bagatti-Valsecchi / Bevilacqua / Blauel / Bodleian Library, Oxford, England / British Museum, London / Carpinacci / Ciccione / Cirani / The Cleveland Museum of Art / The Cooper Union Museum, New York / Crocellá / De Antonis / De Biasi / De Giovanni / Dimt / Directorate General of Antiquities, Baghdad, Iraq / Dixson Collection, Sydney, Australia / Dulevant / Elettra Cliché / Favole / Ferruzzi / Fototeca Storica Nazionale / Frassi / Freeman / French Tourist Office / Gallerie dell'Accademia, Venice, Italy / Giancolombo / Gilardi / Giovetti / Giraudon / Hinz / I. G. D. A. / I. G. D. A.-Andi / I. G. D. A.-S. E. F. / I. L. P. / Irifoto / Louvre, Paris / Mairani / Mandel / Martile / Marzari / M. A. S. / Mascherpa / Mauritshuis, The Hague, The Netherlands / Mella / Mercurio / Montesahara / Museum of Fine Arts, Boston / Museum of Modern Art, New York / National Gallery, London / National Gallery of South Australia, Adelaide / Dagli Orti / Pedone / Perogalli / Philadelphia Museum of Art / Popper / Prato / Publifoto / G. P. Putnam's Sons / Sacchi / Scala / S. E. F. / Sperryn's Limited / Splendid Color / Springhetti / Stadtmuseum, Munich, Germany / Statens Museum for Kunst, Copenhagen, Denmark / Stoedtner & Klemm / Strada / Tavanti / Titti / Tomsich / Villani / Vogenbeck / Wadsworth Atheneum, Hartford, Connecticut / Wallace Collection, London / Whitney Museum of American Art, New York.

Library of Congress Catalog Number: 67-24201
Designed by Harold Franklin
MANUFACTURED IN THE UNITED STATES OF AMERICA

(right) Mosque of Selim II, Edirne, Turkey. View of the exterior from the west, showing the *dome* and the *minarets*. Constructed between 1570 and 1574, the mosque is the work of the great Ottoman architect, Sinan. The plan of the mosque is octagonal, with emphasis on solid, massive walls and a low, wide dome, counterbalanced by the four tall, slim minarets.

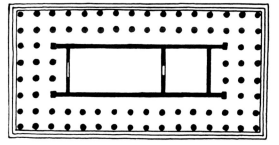

(below) Plan of a *dipteral* temple so-called because of the two rows of columns which surround the sanctuary

Diaper. A geometrical, repeated pattern of stylized flowers, individually framed in either a square or a rhombus, forming an over-all decorative design. Diapers are common features of early Gothic art, and were often painted or carved as wall decoration in churches. There is a diaper carved in relief in Westminster Abbey, London.

Dipteral (Greek, *dipteros:* two-winged). A term applied in Greek architecture to temples having a double range of columns on each of their sides, as for example the Temple of Zeus Olympus (the Olympieion) at Athens (174 B.C.-A.D. 132).

Dogtooth Molding. An architectural molding on which the ornamentation takes the form of a series of pyramidal, toothlike projections. Each projection is carved to resemble four or more leaves joining at the central apex of the pyramid. Dogtooth moldings were used extensively in England during the thirteenth century, particularly to frame archways.

Dome. A hemispherical structure placed like an inverted bowl over a square, round, or polygonal compartment. Such structures were built in a number of ancient cultures and by the Romans —notably for the Pantheon (c. A.D. 120). After

Byzantine capital in church of San Vitale (sixth century A.D.); Ravenna, Italy. Above this capital, and partially repeating its shape and basket-weave pattern, is the *dosseret*, which supports the arch.

the decline of Rome the dome continued to be an important feature of Byzantine architecture, but it was little used in western Europe until the Renaissance. Then it was most frequently used in church architecture; the word "dome" comes from the Latin *domus* (house; roof).

The dome is most commonly placed over a square space, and there are three possible construction methods. One type, the pendentive dome, has a diameter equal to the diagonal of the square and it is supported on four inverted spherical triangles (pendentives) attached to the corners of the square. A second type is the dome on pendentives, which begins like the pendentive dome but has a smaller diameter, equal to the length of one of the sides of the square. The third type of dome differs from the other two in that it is supported on arches or series of arches (squinches) thrown across each angle of the square; this structure forms an octagon on which an eight-sided dome may be raised.

There is often a vertical window-pierced wall

Egg and dart ornament.

(drum) placed between a dome and its support to give it greater height and to admit light. Some domes have circular openings at the top, usually surmounted by a small turret (lantern). (See illustrations on pages 216 and 217)

Donjon. The word *donjon* was a French derivation from the Latin *dominus*, meaning a lord or master, and thus came to mean the dwelling of a lord. In medieval architecture, it was applied to the keep or central fortress of a castle. Among many examples are those of the Château Gaillard, Les Andelys (1196-1198), by Richard Coeur-de-Lion, and in the castle at Caerphilly, Wales (1267-1277).

Entablature in the Greek Doric Style.

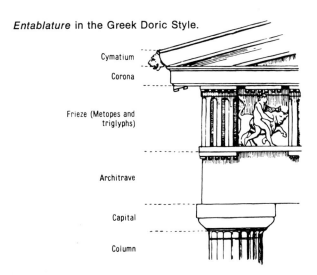

Dormer (Latin, *dormitorium:* a sleeping room). An extension projecting vertically from a sloping roof and incorporating a window; its function is to admit light into a room or space under a roof. The triangular vertical sides of a dormer are known as "cheeks," and its roof may be either flat or ridged.

Dosseret. A square block, widening toward the top, placed on the capital of a Byzantine column in order to support the voussoirs of the arches above it. (See illustration on this page)

Dripstone. A molding in masonry that projects over a door or window to divert rainwater from the façade. The term is normally applied only to Gothic or Tudor architecture.

Drum. A vertical window-pierced wall between a dome and its support to give added height and admit light.

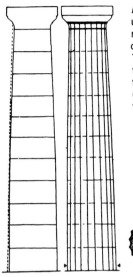

Doric column, showing the use of *entasis* or the enlargement of the central segments or *drums* of the column shaft. This swelling creates an optical illusion which makes the column appear straight (here illustrated by the dotted line).

Echinus. The convex molding that supports the abacus of the Greek Doric capital; also known as ovolo.

Egg and Dart, Egg and Tongue. The enrichment of an ovolo molding, which alternates egg shapes with carved arrowheads or tongues, on cornices, capitals, and the like. (See illustration on facing page)

Elizabethan Style. Early Renaissance architecture of the Elizabethan period (1558-1603) in England. The style resulted from an amalgam of the native Perpendicular Gothic and Italian Renaissance and Flemish traditions.

Engaged Column. A column attached to and partly built into a wall, leaving from one-half to three-quarters of its depth exposed.

Entablature. The upper part of an order of architecture, supported by columns and consisting of an architrave, a frieze, and a cornice. The cornice is divided into two sections: the corona (lower part) and the cymatium (upper part). (See illustration on facing page)

Entasis. In Classical architecture, entasis is the slight swelling of a column shaft, which counteracts the optical illusion that, from a distance, gives straight lines the appearance of curving inward. (See above)

Epistyle. A synonym for architrave.

Exedra (Greek: outdoor seat). In Greek architecture, a semicircular recess or alcove with raised seats, used for disputations by the learned. In the Roman era the term came to refer to any semicircular or rectangular recess with benches, and later it was also applied to an apse or niche in a church.

Extrados. The outer curve of an arch.

Façade. The face or external elevation of a building. (See below and on page 220)

Facing. The outer surface of a wall. (See illustration on page 220)

Fanlight. The window, usually semicircular in shape, that is placed above a door. It derives from the custom of late Georgian builders of dividing the panes by glazing bars radiating from the center, like the veins of a fan. Fanlights of this period were often of great beauty.

Fascia (Latin, *facies:* a face). A term used in Classical architecture to describe the flat surfaces of the architrave, particularly in the Ionic and

Façade, church of St. Pierre (1130); Angoulême, France.

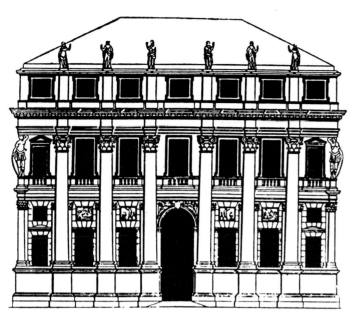

Façade of a sixteenth century palace showing the giant order, characterized by the *pilasters* that extend over two stories, the ground floor and the *piano nobile*, up to the *cornice*. Between the cornice and the roof is the *attic*.

Sacrificial altar of Dionysius; Theater of Dionysius, Athens. At the center of the relief decoration on the altar is the mask of Dionysius, over which an intricately carved *festoon* is hung. Conventionalized *rosettes* complete the ornamental scheme.

(above) Stone *facing*, decorated in low relief, from a façade of the Greek Hellenistic era.

Corinthian orders. Fasciae were executed in marble, stone, or wood. The term is also applied to a band of wood that conceals the ends of the rafters of a roof. Fascia further denotes the nameplate above the front of a shop.

Federal Style. In United States architecture, the name given to the Neo-Classic style employed in the late eighteenth and early nineteenth centuries, shortly after the establishment of a Federal government.

Festoon. A carved, molded, or painted ornamental garland of foliage. flowers, and sometimes fruit suspended in a loop between two points. (See above)

(below) *Finials.* Left: Thirteenth century. Right: Fifteenth century.

Flamboyant window tracery from the late Gothic period. In the continual search for a vivid expression of architectural elements, the relatively simple outlines of earlier medieval window design gave way to such flame-like forms as these. The *keystone,* seen at the top, crowns the arch.

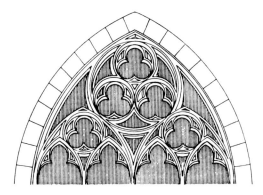

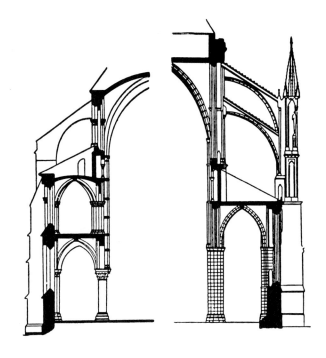

(above) Gothic tracery (thirteenth century) using *trefoil* patterns; Maulbronn, Württemberg, Germany. Here the trefoil pattern is in the shape of a clover leaf.

(right) Sectional views of two uses of the *flying buttress*. The example on the left, with a vaulted second or triforium level and a relatively small clerestory level, is from the Early Gothic period. The example on the right is from the late thirteenth century, and by the use of superimposed flying buttresses the aisle and clerestory levels have been considerably heightened.

Fillet (French: a little thread). A narrow, flat molding. Fillets are used particularly as dividers between two other, more elaborate moldings. The term is also applied to the space between two flutings on the shaft of a column, and, as an alternative to listel, to the uppermost member of a cornice.

Finial. The ornamental feature, usually of stone, surmounting a spire, pinnacle, or buttress, and at the apex of a gable or canopy. The finial offered opportunities for lavish and fantastic invention and was designed particularly elaborately during the era of Flamboyant Gothic. Examples can be

seen on the tombs of Edmund Crouchback, Westminster Abbey, London (1296); Edward II. Gloucester Cathedral (late fourteenth century); and on the Palais de Justice, Rouen, France (1493-1508). (See illustration on facing page)

Flamboyant. The last phase of French Gothic architecture (fifteenth century), so called because of its characteristic wavy, flame-like patterns of window tracery. (See illustration on facing page)

Flèche. A small, slender wooden spire on the ridge of a roof.

Fluting. The shallow, concave grooves cut vertically into the shafts of Classical columns. The

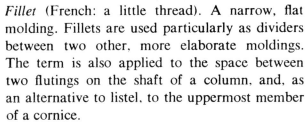

(left) Gothic style of *gable* roof, with *crockets* along the line of the roof and a *finial* at the apex. Below is *trefoil* design.

(right) A Renaissance building with the *gable* end as the street façade, here decorated with elaborate scroll work to give the impression of a triangular shape.

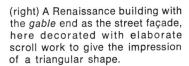

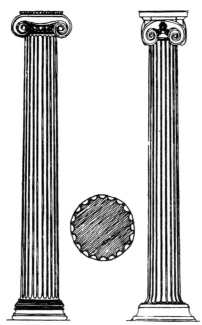

(above) Ionic columns, Attic (left) and from Asia Minor (right), showing *fluting*. The view of the cross-section of the column shows the shallow grooves cut into the shaft. Characteristic of the Ionic style is the *volute*, a scroll-like form at the top of the column.

(below) Ceiling fresco including grotesques; Uffizi Gallery, Florence. The use of such decorative figures, initiated by the ancient Romans, was revived in the fifteenth century and again in the mannerist period of the sixteenth. Both natural and geometric motifs are included in this elaborate ceiling.

term fluting is also applied to similar decorative concepts in pottery and furniture. (See left)

Flying Buttress. A piece of masonry in the form of an arch that starts from a detached pier and abuts against a wall to help take the thrust of the vaulting. The flying buttress was most extensively used in Gothic architecture. (See illustration on page 221)

Foils. In Gothic tracery, small arch openings, separated by cusps. Trefoil, quatrefoil, cinquefoil, and multifoil indicate the number of arc openings in a group. (See illustration on page 221)

Folly. An architectural extravaganza created for visual rather than utilitarian purposes. Follies are associated with the Picturesque movement in England, and were most popular in the late eighteenth and early nineteenth centuries. Inspired by the ruins of classical buildings, follies were designed to enhance the picturesque and romantic elements of a landscape. Although most often in the Gothic style, they can be Greek, Roman, or Chinese in design. Examples include the earliest dated folly by Sanderson Millar in Edgehill, Warwickshire (1746), and the Chinese Pagoda in Kew Gardens, England.

Gargoyle. The pipe that drains the gutter runs through this grotesque creature's mouth.

Half-timbering on façade of Shakespeare's birthplace; Stratford on Avon, England. In this English Renaissance house a rich surface is created through the contrast of the light plaster and dark beams. Half-timbering was often combined with thatched roofs and small leaded window-panes.

(above) Exterior *galleries* on the apse of the church of Santa Maria della Pieve; Arezzo, Italy. These galleries, also serve as *loggie* since they open out on a principal square of the town.

(below) Detail of iron *grille* at the Scaliger Tombs (fourteenth century); Verona, Italy. The main decorative motif here is a quatrefoil rose design, similar to the Gothic rose window, while the leaves along the top are more naturalistic.

(left) Interior, church of Santa Gada (medieval); Disentis, Switzerland. In this example of a *hall church,* the spatial simplicity of the three apses is combined with profuse fresco decoration. The ceiling was lowered after the completion of the church.

(below) Basilica of St. Demetrius (begun fourth century A.D., restored 1926-1948); Salonika, Greece. Behind the railing may be seen the *iconostasis* a closed screen decorated with icons, which served to separate the sanctuary from the area of the congregation.

(above) Two-faced herm of Epicurus and Metrodorus, found during the excavation of the foundations of the porch of the church of Santa Maria Maggiore, Rome. Originally dedicated to Hermes, the herm first appeared in the sixth century B. C.

(right) *Hypostyle* hall in the temple of Ammon; Karnak, Egypt. The construction of such monumental multi-pillared halls as this reached a peak during the eighteenth and nineteenth dynasties at Thebes. The columns originally supported the roof.

Formeret, or Wall Rib. In a medieval vault, the half-rib against the wall.

Frieze. The middle part of the classical entablature, between the architrave and the cornice, it is usually decorated with relief sculpture. The term frieze is also applied to decorative bands in general.

Gable. The triangular wall under a sloping roof. (See illustration on page 221)

Gallery. A covered passage, one side of which is left open. Galleries of this type were often designed both on the exterior and in the interior of Renaissance buildings. The term is also used for the upper story of a church, theater, or movie house, which provides extra seating from

(above) *Lantern* on the Cathedral of Florence, Italy. Designed by Filippo Brunelleschi and executed by Giovanni da Maiano, this Renaissance example of a lantern is surrounded by small lancet windows and flying buttresses.

Lunettes, in a barrel vault.

Megaron; Troy II (third millenium B.C.).

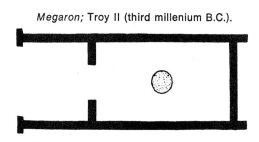

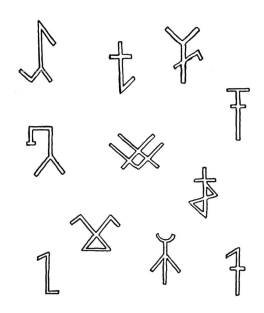

(above) An assortment of *masons' marks.* Marks such as these, which in general derive their calligraphic style from the mason's square, have been found on buildings dating from the twelfth to the eighteenth century.

(below) Tomb of Mausolus at Halicarnassus, according to the Krischen reconstruction (1927). This monumental tomb was provided for Mausolus by his wife Artemisia and his sister, and was designed in the form of a peripteral temple on a high platform. The term *Mausoleum* derives from this tomb.

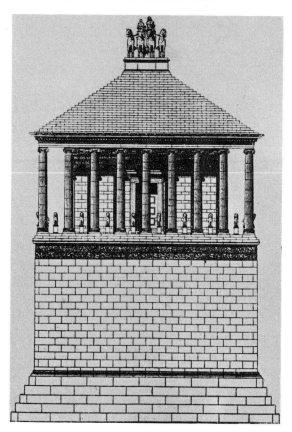

which the congregation or audience can see the events taking place in the lower portion of the building. (See illustration on page 223)

The term gallery is also applied to the wide corridor that was a feature of Jacobean buildings, and to any wide corridor in which works of art are displayed.

Gargoyle. A projecting waterspout, often grotesquely carved, used in Gothic architecture to drain water off a roof. (See illustration on page 223)

Gazebo. A term most commonly applied to a summerhouse, situated at the far end of a garden, and offering an extensive view. A gazebo may also be a lantern or turret located on the roof of a building, or a protruding balcony or window.

Grille. An openwork grating used to fill window openings, or to enclose a shrine or chapel. (See illustration on page 223)

Grotesque (Italian, *grottesco,* from *grotta:* a cave). A fanciful decorative figure representing a human being, an animal, or a combination of the two, often with foliated limbs and other fanciful embellishment. The earliest known grotesques were found in the grottoes of Rome and Pompeii, and these prototypes were widely imitated as decorative devices during the Renaissance. (See illustration on page 222)

Half-timbering. A type of building construction in which the structural elements—posts, rails, and struts—are made of timber and left visible while the spaces between them are filled in with brick or other material.

This style was popular in Northern Europe

Benci di Cione Dami and Simone di Francesco Talenti: *Loggia dei Lanzi* (begun 1376); Piazza della Signoria, Florence, Italy. Fronting on Florence's most famous piazza, this *loggia* reflects the Gothic style in its *groined vaulting* and its clustered *piers.* Yet the large round arches anticipate the spaciousness and balance of Renaissance architecture.

(above) Relief *Medallion* from the Arch of Constantine;
Rome. The scene portrayed here is evidently the successful
conclusion of an imperial lion hunt. The sculptor composed
the figures at the right and left holding horses, and a low-
relief tree overhead, to make a successful transition from
the square grouping of the men to the round medallion.

and England during the Gothic period and the
Renaissance. (See illustration on page 223)

Hall Church. A church in which the nave and
aisles are of equal, or approximately equal,
height. (See illustration on page 224)

Hammerbeam Roof. A type of timber roof, found
only in England, used in late Gothic or Tudor
buildings. To obviate the need for tie-beams
across large halls or church naves, struts are
used to support short cantilevered timbers,
called hammerbeams. These in turn form braces,
which form pointed arches, and a system of
verticalities, carrying the main rafters.

Hammerbeam roofs are sometimes elaborately

(right) Engraved illustration showing the *module* of a Doric
column, from a 1767 French edition of Giacomo Vignola's
Rules of the Five Orders of Architecture. The scale to the
right indicates the proportion of the column diameter to its
height, as well as to the various components of the capital
and the entablature.

carved. Westminster Hall, London (1395-1399),
and St. Stephen's Church, Norwich (1480),
furnish excellent examples.

Header. A brick or stone laid with its end toward
the face of a wall.

Herm (Hermes). The bust of a human figure,
originally representing the Greek god Hermes,
mounted on a square or rectangular pedestal.
The Greeks used these figures as signposts and
boundary markers; later they were used decoratively. (See illustration on page 225)

Herringbone Brickwork. A decorative arrangement of facing bricks in a diagonal pattern.
Herringbone brickwork was sometimes used to
fill in the panels of half-timbered structures. The
term is also applied to similar arrangements of
flooring or paving bricks.

Hexastyle. A portico with a row of six columns.

High Relief. *see:* Relief

Hypocaust. A Roman heating chamber. The
floor of a building was raised on small brick
columns and hot air was circulated through a
system of ducts beneath it.

Hypostyle (Greek *hypo:* under; and *stylos:*
pillar). The name given to a hall or vestibule,

Metope of the Temple of Selinunte showing Perseus killing Medusa (*c.* 570 B.C.), relief sculpture; Museo Nazionale, Palermo, Italy. This archaic Doric *frieze* consists of a horizontal band of alternating *metopes* and *triglyphs*. The triglyph is a block of stone with two vertical grooves, and two half-grooves at the sides. The metope is the inner slab of stone, generally carved in relief.

the roof of which is supported by columns. Hypostyle is used to describe the multi-pillared halls of temples in ancient Egyptian architecture. Examples include those in the temples of Ammon in Karnak, and Ramesseum in Thebes. (See illustration on page 225)

Iconostasis. In the Eastern Church a screen, covered with icons, separating the sanctuary from the remainder of the church.
(See illustration on page 224)

Impost. A block of stone or molding from which an arch springs.

Intercolumniation. The space between columns. In the Doric, Ionic, and Corinthian orders the spacing of columns followed strict rules of proportion, being related to the diameter of the column at the base.

Intrados. The inner curve of an arch.

Jamb. The sides of a door, window, or arch opening.

Jesse Window. In church architecture, a stained-glass window designed to show Christ's descent from the house of David. The genealogy begins with Jesse, the father of David, and culminates in the figure of Jesus, or sometimes the Madonna and Child.

Jesse windows in England include that of the east end of Wells Cathedral, Somerset. A window at the west end of Chartres Cathedral is a French example of the type.

Courtyard of the *Mosque* of Ibn-Tulun at the Qattai; Cairo,
Egypt. Built in A.D. 879 and restored at the beginning of the
twentieth century, this mosque is the first Egyptian example
of Islamic architecture using heavy piers in the arcade
rather than columns. The arches of the arcade narrow
slightly at the bottom in the usual Islamic horseshoe form.
In the foreground at the left is seen the exterior of a dome
on *squinches,* in which the transition from the square plan
of the base to the round plan of the dome has been made
by changing the square into an octagon and then into a
circle. The principal *minaret,* above the arcade at the left,
is surrounded by a spiral staircase.

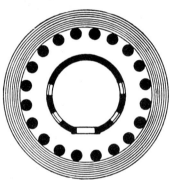

Monopteral temple plan.

Niche.

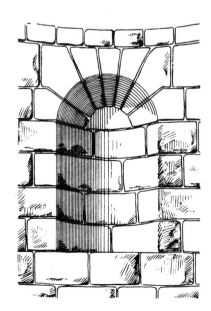

Four-part window of the
Bonaparte palace (sixteenth
century); Ascoli Piceno,
Italy. The *mullions* are the
vertical members of the window at right angles to the
transoms. The line of the sill
is continued along the wall
in a *stringcourse.*

Joist. A wood, metal, or reinforced concrete beam, supporting a ceiling or floor. A joist may extend from wall to wall, or, in a large framed structure, from girder to girder.

Keep. see: Donjon

Keystone. The central stone of an arch or rib vault, sometimes decorated with sculpture. *see:* Boss

Lady Chapel. A chapel within a church dedicated to the Virgin Mary.

Lancet. A tall, slender window, pointed at the top, which is a common feature of thirteenth-century Gothic architecture.

Lantern. A small turret surmounting a roof, dome, or tower. (See illustration on page 226)

Lean-to or Monopitched Roof. A roof having only one slope.

Lierne. A short rib connecting two main ribs in Gothic vaulting.

Lintel. A horizontal beam or stone, which spans an opening.

Loggia. A roofed gallery behind an open arcade or colonnade. (See illustration on page 227)

Long Gallery. In English architecture, a long narrow room in Elizabethan and Jacobean mansions, often extending the entire length of the upper floor. The walls of these galleries were paneled or hung with tapestries, and mullioned windows and ornamental fireplaces were common features.

Long and Short Work. A typical ornamental feature of Saxon architecture in England, commonly applied to the external angles of buildings, particularly towers. In long and short work, vertical slabs of stone were arranged alternatively with horizontal ones. An example is the tower of the tenth-century Earl's Barton Church, Northamptonshire, England.

Lunette. A semicircular or crescent shaped opening in a vault or dome, to admit light. (See illustration on page 226)

Lych Gate (Old English, *lic:* a body). The covered entrance to a churchyard, where a coffin may be placed until a clergyman arrives to perform the burial service.

Machicolation. An opening between a wall and a parapet, supported by corbels, in a fortified building. The projection of the corbels meant that defenders were over the heads of their attackers and could drop missiles without exposing themselves.

Mansard Roof. A roof with a double slope on each side, the lower slope steep and the upper one flat. This type of roof was named for the French architect François Mansart (1598-1666).

Masons' or Pieceworkers' Marks. The individualized marks that the medieval and later stone masons carved on the stones they handled, so that their work could be identified and payment computed. (See illustration on page 226)

Mastaba. In ancient Egyptian architecture, mastaba refers to a low flat-topped tomb, executed in stone in the form of a truncated

Interior of Freiburg Cathedral looking along the *nave* (begun 1235) toward the later Gothic choir (begun 1359); Freiburg, Germany. To the left and right may be seen the arcades and the clustered piers separating the naves from the aisles. Overhead are the ribbed groin vaults of the nave. The absence of a triforium above the aisle arches and below the clerestory windows is characteristic of Gothic architecture of the Upper Rhine.

The Greek theater of Epidaurus, Greece. In front of the colonnaded stage is the semicircular *orchestra*, from which rises the sweeping auditorium in rows of stone blocks. Greek theaters were built so as to take advantage whenever possible of the natural slope of a hillside.

pyramid. It was divided into three rooms, one of which sometimes contained murals. The term also denotes the seat, reserved for the watchman, at the doorway of an Arab dwelling.

Mausoleum. A large, stately, sepulchral monument. The name comes from the tomb of Mausolus, king of Carea (died 352 B.C.) at Halicarnassus. (See illustration on page 226)

Medallion. A circular decorative plaque, resembling a medal, bearing a relief carving, picture, or ornament. (See illustration on page 228)

Megaron. In Greek palaces or private residences, an oblong suite with a porch and great hall. (See illustration on page 226)

Metope. The space between two triglyphs in a Doric frieze, often filled with panels on which relief figures are carved. (See illustration on page 229)

Mezzanine. An intermediate story between two floor levels.

Minaret. A high, narrow tower of a mosque, containing one or more galleries. Minarets are used by the muezzin, or Moslem crier, to announce the call to worship. They vary in shape, but many are square. Some mosques contain a number of minarets, often with rich ornamentation on the upper section.

Modillion. In Greek, Roman, and Renaissance entablatures, an ornamental bracket under the corona of the cornice.

Module (Latin, *modulus:* a measure). In Classical architecture, a unit, normally one half of the diameter of the column at its base, on which the proportions of an order of architecture or building were based. In modern architectural practice, a module is an agreed unit of 4 in. used to determine the proportions of buildings and their components . (See illustration on page 228)

Monastery. A residence for a community of monks.

Monolith. A single stone, often in the form of a free-standing pillar.

Monopteral, Monopteros. A circular temple having a single row of supporting columns and no cella. (See illustration on page 230)

Mosque. The name given to Moslem

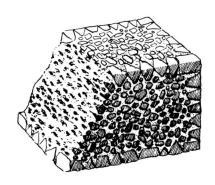
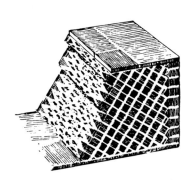

temples, the first of which was built at Mecca, the center of the Moslem religion. Subsequently, all mosques were constructed so that the mihrab, or niche for worship, faced toward Mecca. Near the mihrab was the mimbar, or pulpit, which was topped by a roof in the form of a pyramid. Each temple contained a minaret, from which times of prayer were announced. Early mosques comprised a number of colonnades, in front of which was a rectangular courtyard, with a fountain in the center. As the Islamic empire expanded, mosque architecture became subject to Christian, and in particular Byzantine, influences. A fine example of a mosque is the Great Mosque (*c.* 706-715), Damascus, Syria. (See illustration on page 230)

Mudejar Style. A twelfth- to sixteenth-century Spanish style combining Moslem and Christian features, with a preponderance of the former. Characterized by intricate ornamentation, the Mudéjar style was also widely used in Spain's New World empire.

(right) Five-storied *pagoda* of the Hôryûji; Nara, Japan. Built during the Asuka period (A.D. 552-645), this pagoda served characteristically not only as a place of ritual but also as a symbolic representation of the universe. The construction of the pagoda is ingenious and highly complex. The building is supported by a wooden skeleton on which light walls have been hung. The beams which support the wide overhang of the roofs are connected on the interior to the main skeleton of the building. These beams are shaped with great beauty and are thus important both for their form and function. The wide overhang of the roofs hides the vertical shaft of the building and creates a sense of floating horizontal forms. This sense is augmented by the slight upturn of the roof line at the corners. In this respect Japanese pagodas are considerably more elegant and graceful than Chinese examples.

◄(left) Three Roman systems of facing a concrete wall with small stones (from left to right): *Opus incertum,* using irregular shaped stones; *opus reticulatum,* using small squared stones placed diagonally; *opus spicatum,* using bricks or stones set in a diagonal herringbone pattern.

Mullions. Vertical members dividing a window into a number of lights (glazed sections). (See illustration on page 230)

Mutule. A projecting slab under the cornice in the Doric order of Greek architecture.

Nailhead. In early English architecture, an ornamental motif, consisting of a regularly repeated pattern of small carved projections resembling the heads of nails.

Naos. *see:* Cella

Narthex. In early Christian churches, a vestibule or arcaded porch in front of the main entrance.

Nave. The central aisle of a church, extending from the entrance to the choir. (See illustration on page 231)

Newel. A term used in connection with staircases, to describe the post to which the handrail of the balustrade is secured at each landing or story. The term also refers to the central column around which a circular staircase turns.

Niche. A recess in a wall, often decorated, designed to hold a statue or other object. (See illustration on page 230)

Ornamental motifs: 1) Greek-key or fret; 2) Vitruvian wave; 3) anthemion; 4) chevron; 5) denticulated; 6) arcuated; 7) checkered; 8) billet; 9) nailhead; 10) imbricated; 11) foliated.

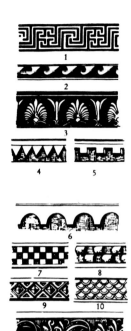

Detail from Byzantine mosaic of Empress Theodora and her court, from the church of San Vitale (sixth century); Ravenna, Italy. A direct development of the Roman technique of *opus tesselatum*, this Byzantine style found vigorous expression in several buildings of Ravenna of the period. The various colors are intrinsic to the stones.

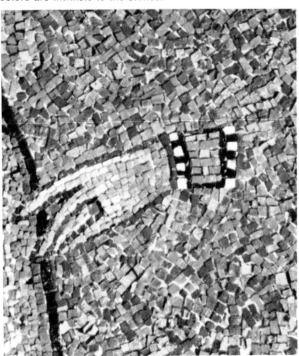

Nymphaeum. In ancient Greece, a sanctury dedicated to the nymphs, usually situated near a spring. Later, in Roman times and after, the term referred to a water garden within a colonnaded courtyard.

Obelisk. A term used most commonly in reference to ancient Egyptian architecture to describe a tall monument, usually monolithic, which tapers toward a pyramid at the top. Executed in stone or granite, and generally square in plan, obelisks were erected in pairs at the doorways of temples. In modern times, they have been transported to Europe and the United States. Well known examples, known as Cleopatra's Needles, originally from Heliopolis, are on the Thames Embankment, London, and in Central Park, New York. The term also denotes copies of obelisks on a smaller scale, made in faience.

Oculus (Latin: eye). A term used in connection with the Classical style of architecture. Oculus refers to the central disc of the spiral scroll of the capital in the Ionic order. The term also denotes any circular window, including the large one found at the west side of a church.

Octastyle. A portico with eight columns.

Opisthodomos. In Greek architecture, a porch or room at the rear of the cella.

Opus Incertum. In Roman architecture, the facing of a concrete wall with small, irregularly shaped stones. (See illustration on page 232)

Opus Reticulatum. In Roman architecture, the facing of a concrete wall with small, square, diagonally placed stones. (See illustration on page 232)

Opus Sectile. A Roman decorative design consisting of large pieces of mosaic set in geometrical patterns.

Opus Spicatum. A Roman masonry design consisting of small bricks set in a herringbone pattern. (See illustration on page 232)

Opus Tesselatum. A Roman mosaic consisting of small, regularly shaped stone cubes (tesserae) used to form patterns or figures. (See illustration on facing page)

Oratory (Latin, *oratorium:* place of prayer). A term used to describe a small, private chapel, building, or room, used for the purpose of worship. An example from Irish architecture is the stone Oratory of Gallerus in Dingle, County Kerry (sixth or seventh century). The term oratory also denotes a number of religious communities, in particular the Order of St. Philip Neri, or the Congregation of the Fathers of the Oratory, founded in Rome in 1564. The term

Palmettes.

is further applied to the faldstool at which churchgoers kneel for prayer.

Orchestra. In Greek architecture, the circular or semicircular space in front of the stage of a theater, where the chorus danced and sang. In modern architecture, the orchestra is the narrow pit in front of and below the level of the stage, reserved for musicians; the term is also applied to the ground-level seats for spectators. (See illustration on page 232)

Orders. see: Orders of Architecture article.

Oriel Window. An upper-story bay window supported on corbels.

Orientation. The placement of a building with reference to the points of the compass.

French rococo paneling. (below) Typical detail. (right) Music Room in the Hôtel de Lauzun (eighteenth century); Paris. This room shows the richly decorative *paneling* characteristic of French rococo style, in which the wood was elaborately carved and gilded.

(above) Sculptured end of a *pew* in the church of Launcells (fourteenth to fifteenth centuries); Cornwall, England. Trefoil and quatrefoil shapes, as well as heraldic motifs, are used in this Gothic carving.

(right) Gothic clustered pier at Ely Cathedral (thirteenth century); Ely, England. (below) Diagram and section of typical Romanesque pier, showing semicircular shafts extending from the square core.

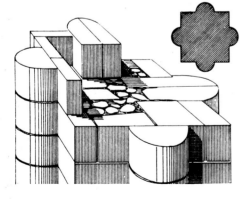

Ornamental Motifs. Among the most commonly used ornamental motifs are: 1. Fret ornament or Greek key pattern; 2. Vitruvian wave; 3. Anthemion, or honeysuckle or palmette ornament, in Greek and Roman architecture; 4. Chevron; 5. Denticulated; 6. Arcuated; 7. Checkered; 8. Billet; 9. Nailhead; 10. Imbricated; 11. Foliated. (See illustration on page 234)

Pagoda. A religious monument, often Buddhist, found most frequently in Burma, China, and Japan. The pagoda originated in India, from the tower built by Kaniska I near Peshawar in the second century A.D. With the rise of Buddhism, the form spread eastward to China and Japan.

The ground floor of the pagoda is usually in the shape of an octagon, which is repeated and gradually diminished in size in the upper stories, so that the whole structure tapers toward a spire. Each story has its own projecting roof and upturned eaves, generally richly carved and colored. Originally, every part of the design had a religious and symbolic significance; the stories, for example, represented the terraces of the mountain of the world.

Examples of pagodas include the 368-ft.-high Shwe Dagon, Rangoon, the most famous in Burma. The whole structure, which is cone-shaped and built of brick, is decorated with gold leaf. A striking Chinese pagoda is the Yüan ming yüan, near Peking, built with porcelain tiles in five colors. Japanese pagodas are distinguished from the Chinese variety by the more graceful curvature of their projecting roofs. They are mostly square in plan, with five stories, as in the pagoda in Yasaka (1618). A western example of the pagoda form can be seen in Chambers' Chinese Pagoda (1861), Kew Gardens, England. (See illustration on page 233)

Palaestra. A public building for the training of athletes.

Palmette. A fan-shaped ornamental motif based on the design of a palm leaf. (See illustration on page 235)

Paneling. The division of a wall, door, ceiling, etc., into a number of compartments, which are often decorated. (See illustrations on page 235)

Pantile. A clay tile, resembling in section a shallow S, which was used extensively in southeast England for roofing, until the nineteenth century. Although this type of tiling is now less widely used, modern techniques of weatherproofing pantiles have been developed, and glazed pantiles are used for decorative purposes.

Parapet (Latin, *parare:* to guard, *pectus:* breast). Originally, the portion of a wall which was battlemented and rose above the roof of a fortress or above the gutter height of a house. The low walls surrounding or edging balconies, platforms, or bridges, are also called parapets.

Paraskenion. A short wing projecting from the *skene* (stage) of a Greek theater.

Parvis. An enclosed area or court in front of a church.

Pavilion. The name originally given to a large tent or moveable dwelling. A pavilion later came to denote a light building or pleasure house, set in spacious gardens, and, in modern usage, refers to a light building on a sports ground. In architecture, the term is applied to the prominent section of a monumental façade, which projects centrally or at both ends.

Pedestal. A base designed to support a statue, vase, or column. Pedestals are usually composed

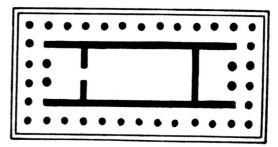

Peripteral temple plan.

Pilaster strip decoration.

(below) Le Corbusier: Swiss Pavilion (1932) at the Cité Universitaire; Paris. Le Corbusier a pioneer exponent of the reinforced concrete *pilotis*, here uses them to raise the main part of the dormitory building. He thus provides a ground floor terrace and parking area.

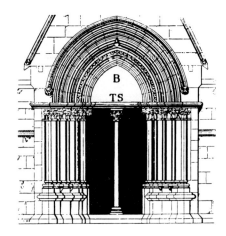

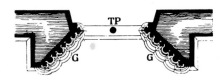

(above) *Portal* of a Gothic church (top) recessed planes of arch (A), typanum (B), lintel (TS); (bottom) plan of decorative colonnettes (G), and single supporting column (TP).

(below) Development of the arch *profile* from the tweltfh to the fifteenth century: 1) eleventh and twelfth centuries; 2) twelfth and thirteenth centuries; 3) thirteenth and fourteenth centuries; 4) fifteenth century. The first three groups show the development from original rectangular simplicity to a variety of complex geometric forms. But during the late Gothic of the fifteenth century the design was again simplified, this time toward a relatively narrow and linear character.

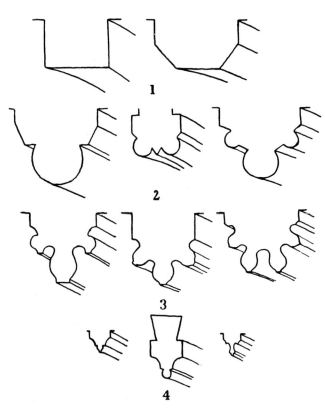

(below) Giovanni Battista Filippo Basile: Teatro Massimo (1875-1897); Palermo, Italy. Monumental buildings during the nineteenth century and the early years of the twentieth were often modeled in the eclectic style after classical prototypes. The central part of Basile's design, with its *dome,* its *pediment,* and its colonnaded *porch* (or portal), is closely reminiscent of the Pantheon in Rome.

of three separate units, the base, the die, and the cap-mold or cornice.

Pediment. In Classical architecture, the triangular segment of wall above the entablature at the end of a building. In Renaissance architecture, pediments might also be bowed or semicircular in shape. In Gothic architecture, these features are called gables.

Pendant (French, *pendre:* to hang). A hanging ornament, widely used in the Decorated and Perpendicular styles of architecture. Pendants were secured to the fanvaulting of buildings during the Late Gothic period. They were also employed in open-timber roofs, being attached to the hammerbeam, or to the lower section of the main rafter. A pendant is also an ornament of precious or semiprecious stones, suspended from a necklace or other item of jewelry.

Pendentive. *see:* Dome

Peripteral, Peripteros. A building surrounded by a single row of columns. (See illustration on page 237)

Peristyle. A range of columns surrounding a building or courtyard.

Perpendicular Style. The final phase of English Gothic architecture (*c.* 1350-1550) characterized by emphasis on vertical lines of window tracery and paneling.

Pew. The name applied in church architecture to a group of raised benches with backs, which are affixed to the ground. Pews are employed for seating worshipers during a service. A single pew may be reserved for a family or party of churchgoers. (See illustration on page 236)

Piano Nobile. An Italian phrase, applied to the main story in a large mansion or palace. Elevated above ground level, the piano nobile comprises the principal suite of reception rooms used for entertaining guests. An example in Rome can be seen in the Palazzo Massimi (1532-1536).

Piazza. A public square surrounded by buildings in an Italian town or city. A piazza is an open area, the closest English equivalent to which is a marketplace or square. It can be of almost any

(right) Hindu goddess sculptured in *high relief* on the portal of the Museum of Kharujaho, India. The strong, somewhat contorted form of this principal figure dominates the profuse activity of the small figures crowding the background. Sculpture of such high relief produces an effect of intensified chiaroscuro, or contrast of light and dark.

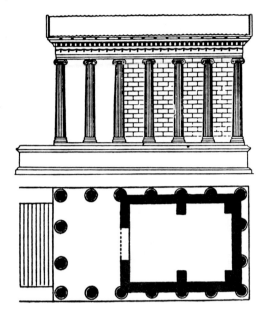

(left) Side elevation and plan of a *pseudoperipteral temple,* showing all of the columns, except those of the portico, to be engaged to the cella wall.

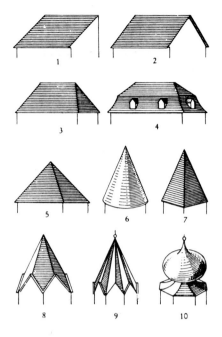

(right) Common *roof* forms: 1) Lean-to; 2) Gabled; 3) Hipped; 4) Mansard; 5) Pyramidal; 6) Conoidal; 7) Pyramidal; 8) Rhomboidal; 9) Folded Rhomboidal; 10) Bulbous or Onion.

shape. although many are square or rectangular. The finest example of a piazza is generally considered to be Gianlorenzo Bernini's elliptical Piazza di San Pietro. Rome (1656-1667).

Pier. A massive piece of masonry as distinct from the more slender column. used as a support. The term may also be applied to the wall between doors, windows, or other openings. (See illustrations on page 236)

Pilaster. A flat, rectangular pier attached to a wall, but decorated as a column, with base and capital.

Pilaster Strip Decoration. In early Christian and Romanesque architecture. a simple exterior wall decoration, consisting of vertical strips resembling pilasters but without bases and capitals; these strips are connected at the top by a series of small arches. (See illustration on page 237)

Pilotis (French: piling). A series of pillars of reinforced concrete rising from an open ground floor to support a multistory structure. Modern architects have made much use of the pilotis construction technique. (See illustration on page 237)

Pinnacle. A small ornamental turret with a steep pyramidal or conical roof. common in Gothic architecture as a crown for buttresses, towers, and parapets.

Piscina. A term used in church architecture to describe a pierced stone basin. employed for washing the chalice and the hands of the priest. The piscina was generally situated in a niche near the altar, and was frequently richly decorated. In Roman times. the term referred to any receptacle containing water, including the public baths.

Pitched Roof. Any sloping roof, however slight the deviation from horizontal. The pitch of a

Rocaille ornament.

Two examples of *rosettes.*

roof is calculated either as the angle from horizontal, or in ratio of maximum elevation from horizontal to width of span.

Plan. A drawing of the horizontal section of a building, also known as "floor plan" or "ground plan."

Plaque. A term used to describe an ornamental or commemorative tablet, most commonly attached to a wall, either inside or outside a building. Plaques may be decorated or unadorned, and are usually executed in porcelain or metal.

Plateresque (Spanish, *platero:* silversmith). An architectural style which evolved in Spain in the late fifteenth and sixteenth centuries. Moorish, Gothic, and Renaissance elements are combined in its ornament, which is elaborate and delicate, and reminiscent of silversmiths' work.

Plinth. The projecting base of a column or building. Plinths can be plain or molded and, when supporting a building, often form a series of steps. A plinth may also be called a podium.

Podium. The continuous base of a column or building. The term is also applied to the platform surrounding the arena of an amphitheater.

Porch. Any projecting structure that provides shelter at the entrance to a building. The term when referring to a veranda or a loggia is a usage confined to the United States. (See illustration on page 238)

Portal. An entrance, often elaborately ornamented, to a building. Some of the most richly decorated portals are found in medieval churches. In a typical medieval portal the splayed jambs are enriched with colonnettes (G), and carry deeply molded arches in a series of recessed planes (A). The arch is filled with a tympanum (B) resting on a lintel (TS), which is supported by a central colonnette (TP). (See illustration on page 238)

Portcullis (French, *porte:* a door, *coulisse:* a groove). A term uniquely applicable in military architecture. A portcullis is a solid frame of wood or iron, designed to move vertically in grooves. Placed at the gates of a fortress, the portcullis could be swiftly lowered in the event of attack.

Portico. A covered colonnaded entrance or vestibule.

Prefabrication. A fast and economical method of building, whereby standardized components are produced in factories. Work on the building site is thus reduced to the assembly of such parts.

Profile. The vertical section of a molding or group of moldings in an architectural feature. Illustrated is the development of the arch profile

Windows of the north transept, cathedral of Notre Dame (second half thirteenth century); Paris: the *rose window* which dominates this group is actually a complex of small stained glass windows filled with scenes of Christian iconography and radiating from the central medallion of Christ in Glory. In medieval art the rose or wheel window was used to symbolize Christ as the sun, or center of the universe.

Rustication.

Alessandro Antonelli: La Mole Antonelliana, Turin, Italy. This massive building, completed in 1900 by Antonelli's son, tapers to a tall spire which, after having been destroyed in 1953, was restored according to the original plan.

from the twelfth to the fifteenth century: 1. eleventh and twelfth centuries; 2. twelfth and thirteenth centuries; 3. thirteenth and fourteenth centuries; 4. fifteenth century. (See illustration on page 238)

Pronaos. The part of a temple in front of the cella.

Propylaeum. A major gateway to a temple or enclosure.

Proscenium. A term used in connection with theaters in ancient Greece. Proscenium denotes the platform, upheld by a series of columns, on which the drama was enacted. It was situated between the fixed scenic background and the orchestra. The term now refers to the arch in front of the stage in a theater.

Prostyle. A portico with a single range of columns in front and no columns on the other sides.

Prothesis. In an early Christian or Byzantine church, the chamber adjoining the sanctuary, used to prepare the bread and wine for the Eucharist.

Pseudodipteral. A temple planned as a dipteral temple, but with the inner range of columns omitted, so that the width of the space between the side colonnades and the cella wall is doubled.

Pseudoperipteral. A temple that appears to be surrounded by one row of columns, but which has its side and rear columns attached to the cella walls. (See illustration on page 240)

Pulpit. Since the birth of Christianity, the term pulpit has generally denoted an elevated platform in a church, mounted by steps, from which a sermon was delivered. Usually situated in the nave, pulpits were also erected in the open air in medieval times. In design and decoration they vary according to the style of the period, but are often elaborately carved. During the eighteenth century, pulpits with three stages were widely used. The term is also applicable to any raised structure, such as an auctioneer's desk, used to address an audience.

Pulpitum. A term used to describe a stone gallery or rood screen, erected in some large churches to divide the ritual choir from the nave.

Pylon (Greek, *pylon:* gateway). A term originally applied to the high tapered gate towers that are found on either side of the ancient Egyptian temple entrances at Karnak and elsewhere. It is now applied to steel latticework towers that carry electricity cables.

Quatrefoil. *see:* Foil

Quoins. Stones or bricks marking the angles of a building; cornerstones.

Rampart. A term used in connection with fortifications to describe a raised mound of earth, set up for the purpose of defense and able to withstand gunfire. The top was sufficiently broad to permit the free movement of troops and equipment. Ramparts were usually topped by stone parapets.

Relief. Sculpture in which the forms are projected from a flat surface, (high- or haut-relief and low- or bas-relief) or depressed beneath it (intaglio). (See illustration on page 239)

Relieving Arch. An arch concealed in the wall

Domenico Indivino, known as Domenico di San Severino (c. 1445-1502): choir *stalls* from the upper church of San Francesco; Assisi, Italy. This example of early Renaissance woodworking shows finely executed carving and gold inlay.

Stilted arch (at the center), whose springing line is well above the impost blocks. The effect is to give added emphasis to the center door.

above a lintel to support the weight of that wall.

Respond. A half-pillar or corbel, built on to a wall that acts as one of the supports of the final arch in an arcade.

Retable. In church architecture, a shelf or shelf-like structure behind an altar, used as a base for such furnishings as the altar cross and candles. The term is also used to describe the frame enclosing painted or carved altar panels.

Reticulated Tracery (Latin, *reticulum:* a small net). Tracery found on stone windows, consisting of identical foiled openings repeated in rows. It is characteristic of fourteenth-century English architecture, the nearest French parallel being flamboyant tracery.

Rib. A band projecting from vaulting.

Ridge. The apex of a sloping roof. Along this crest runs a wooden beam (ridge piece) which is covered by tiles (ridge tiles).

Rocaille. An eighteenth-century Rococo style of ornamentation based on the shapes of rocks or shells. (See illustration on page 240)

Rood Loft or Jube. A raised gallery over the screen (rood screen), which separates the chancel of a church from the nave.

Roof. The most common types of roof are: 1. Lean-to; 2. Gabled; 3. Hipped; 4. Mansard; 5. Pyramidal (Towers); 6. Conoidal; 7. Pyramidal; 8. Rhomboidal; 9. Folded Rhomboidal; 10. Onion or Bulbous. (See illustration on page 240)

Rosette. A circular ornament, the stylized design of which represents a wild rose. (See illustrations on page 240)

Rose Window or Wheel Window. A round window with radiating tracery. This type of window has been used frequently in church architecture, often with dramatic effect, as in the Cathedral

Military trunk (eighteenth century); Marzoli collection, Palazzolo, Italy. The *strapwork* carved on the cover and around the sides of this iron trunk served to increase its strength, and illustrates a type of relief texture that was carried into architectural decoration.

(left) *Stupa;* Sanchi, India. This early example of the architectural type of domed monument constructed by order of the Emperor Asoka in the third century B.C. to house relics of the Buddha. The Stupa is surrounded by a railing and by four ceremonial gateways (toranas).

(below) Front elevation (left) and plan (right) of typical *temple in antis,* whose only columns are the two supporting the entablature and pediment over the entrance. (bottom) Plan of the *Thermae* of Caracalla; Rome. The calidarium, tepidarium, and frigidarium were rooms used for bathing in hot, luke-warm, and cold water.

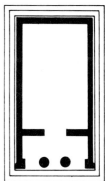

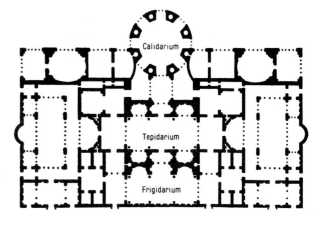

of Notre Dame, Paris. (See illustration on page 241)

Rotunda (Latin, *rotundus:* round). A term applied to a circular building, generally with a domed roof. The most famous example is the Pantheon, Rome (*c.* A.D. 120). A rotunda is usually an independent structure, but the term is also applicable to a feature incorporated in a larger building or complex.

Roughcast. A rough plaster made of lime mixed with gravel and water and applied unevenly to the outsides of buildings.

Rubblework, Roughwalling. A masonry made of rough, irregularly shaped stones.

Rustication. A type of stonework in which the joints are recessed. The surfaces of the blocks may be rough or smooth. (See illustration on page 241)

Sallyport. A protected or concealed gateway to a medieval castle, from which the defenders could make surprise sorties against their enemies.

Scagliola. Plaster colored in imitation of marble.

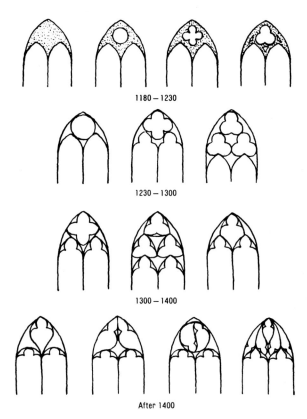

1180 – 1230

1230 – 1300

1300 – 1400

After 1400

(above) *Tracery*, as developed from the twelfth to the fifteenth century. Window design became increasingly more complex with the use of a wider variety of delicate geometric designs.

(below) Two examples of the *triforium*. (left) Romanesque (eleventh century), from St. Benoît sur Loire, France. (right) Gothic (thirteenth century), from Amiens Cathedral, France.

Scotia. In Greek architecture, the concave molding in the base of a column, which casts a strong shadow. *See:* Base

Section (Latin, *sectus:* cut). A view of a building cut by an intersecting plane. It is usually a drawing made on the vertical plane showing the interior.

Sedilia (Latin: seats). In Gothic churches, a row of masonry seats, recessed in the south wall of the chancel, set aside for the clergy.

Segmental Arch. An arch which forms a less than semicircular segment of a circle.

Sexpartite. see: Vault

Shaft. The portion of a column between base and capital; also in medieval architecture, a small column, usually part of a clustered pier, supporting a vaulting rib.

Spandrel. The triangular space between the extrados of an arch and its enclosing frame, or between two arches.

Spiral Staircase. A circular staircase with wedge-shaped treads widening toward their outer ends.

Spire (Anglo-Saxon, *spir:* a stalk). A tall pyramidal structure, surmounting a tower attached to a church. The spire was evolved by the elongation, in the Gothic period, of the comparatively squat pyramidal roof built on Romanesque church towers. Spires are common features of nearly all Gothic and Renaissance churches. (See illustration on page 242)

Splay. The slanted walls of an opening which is wider at one end than the other.

Squinch. see: Dome

Stalls. A range of connected seats in a chancel, for clergy and choir. Often stalls are elaborately carved and have overhanging canopies. (See illustration on page 243)

Steeple. The tower and spire attached to a church. The term steeple can also apply to any structure of great height compared to its length and breadth, such as a tall factory chimney.

Stilted Arch. An arch with its springing line above the line of the imposts. (See illustration on page 244)

Strapwork. A geometrical decorative pattern, usually carved in relief, resembling interlacing or crossed straps. Strapwork was a common decoration on early Renaissance architecture in England, and also on the Continent. It was also (right) Arch of Trajan (A.D. 114); Benevento, Italy. This fine example of the *triumphal arch* was erected by the Roman Senate to celebrate the completion of the Via Traiana, a 200-mile highway over the mountains linking Rome with the port of Brindisi. In addition to the sculptured areas of the arch showing scenes from the life of Trajan, the *attic* surface provides space for a large and imposing inscription.

(below) *Triumphal arch;* Orange, France. Built during the Roman occupation of France, this triple arch includes among its architectural features a pediment and two *attics*. Much of the original relief sculpture has been lost. The triumphal arch was one of the most popular monuments in Roman architecture since it expressed in an impressive manner the power and prestige of the Roman Empire.

The *Teatro Marittimo* at Hadrian's Villa (*c.* A.D. 120), near Tivoli, Italy. In the midst of the huge complex that was the *villa* of the Roman Emperor Hadrian is the so-called *Teatro Marittimo*. A circular *colonnade* surrounds a canal, in the middle of which lies an island with the remains of a once complete little *villa,* where the Emperor could isolate himself from court life.

used as ornamentation on articles such as furniture and bookbindings. (See illustration on page 244)

Stretcher. A brick or stone laid so that its length is parallel to the wall face.

Stringcourse. A projecting band or molding running horizontally along the face of a building, often used to indicate divisions between stories.

Stylobate. In Classical architecture, the top step of a platform on which a colonnade is placed. Frequently, the term is also used for the entire platform, which usually consists of three steps.

Stupa. Name given in Buddhist architecture to a monument of domical shape, surrounded by railings, and with four ceremonial gateways (toranas). The stupa was erected in commemoration of a religious event and was used to contain sacred relics. (See illustration on page 245)

Tabernacle. A recess or receptacle, usually above an altar, to contain the Host. By extension, a place of worship.

Temple. A building designated for religious observances.

Temple in Antis. A temple having from one to four columns (usually two) between the antae at the front. (See illustration on page 245)

Teocalli. A stepped, pyramidal structure, truncated to form a base for a temple. A teocalli is usually square-based and was erected by the pre-Columbian Indians of Mexico and Central America. (See illustration on facing page)

Tepidarium. In the Roman thermae, the hall in which the tepid baths were placed.

Tetrastyle. A portico with four columns.

Thermae (Greek: warm springs). Public bathing establishments, often large and lavishly decorated, which were an important feature of Roman life. Many thermae contained areas for cultural and social activities as well as bathing facilities. Among the most famous thermae is that of Caracalla in Rome (A.D. 211-217), the ruins of which are still extant. (See illustration on p. 245)

Aisle of the church of St. Philibert (eleventh century); Tournus, France. This example of a *groin vault* is one of the first expressions of French Romanesque architecture. The church was constructed with a central nave and two side aisles, all vaulted.

Mayan *teocalli* known as *El Castillo;* Chichén Itzá, Mexico. Each side of this terraced pyramid has a wide ceremonial staircase leading to the massive sanctuary on top, 75 feet from the ground. Also on each side are fifty-two *panels* relating to the Mayan worship of Venus. At certain periodic ceremonies a new teocalli would be built over the core of an earlier one.

Tholos. A small, circular Greek temple; the term is also applied to the dome of a circular building.

Tierceron. In Gothic vaulting, a subordinate rib between main ribs.

Torus. A large rounded convex molding used principally in the bases of columns.

Trabeated. A type of construction based upon beams rather than upon arches. The architecture of ancient Egypt and Greece is trabeated.

Tracery. The decorative pattern formed in the upper part of a Gothic window through the use of molded stone bars (mullions and transoms). The most elaborate tracery was produced during the fifteenth century. (See illustration on p. 246)

Transept. The part of a cruciform church that projects at right angles to the major section of the building (nave and choir). The place of intersection is called the crossing, and the sections of the transept on either side of the crossing are called transept arms.

Transoms. The horizontal wooden or stone bars in a window.

Trefoil. see: Foil

Tribune Gallery. The raised platform at one end of a Roman basilica. The tribune gallery was a feature of some early Christian churches, but in the thirteenth century it was superseded by the triforium.

Triforium. In large churches, a narrow arcaded

passage or gallery above an aisle, usually between the nave arches and the clerestory windows. (See illustration on page 246)

Triglyphs. In the Doric entablature, regularly spaced blocks on the frieze. The triglyph decoration consists of two vertical grooves flanked by half-grooves.

Triumphal Arch. A monumental structure pierced by one or more arched gateways and often richly decorated with relief sculpture and bearing an inscription. The triumphal arch originated in Rome as a memorial to emperors and generals who were victorious in battle. In church architecture, the triumphal arch is the one which gives access to the chancel. (See illustrations on page 247)

Trophy. A Renaissance decorative motif representing a group of military weapons. The motif was inspired by the Roman custom of erecting a victory memorial consisting of some of the vanquished enemy's battle equipment.

Tudor Arch. see: Arch

(left) *Ziggurat* known as *al-Mela-wiyya* (ninth century); Samarra, Iraq. This seven-story high monumental ziggurat was designed as a minaret and encircled with a spiral ramp. It became the model for other Islamic structures in the Mesopotamian region. Commonly referred to as the "Tower of Babel," the ziggurat has served as an archetype of the biblical tower in later European art.

(right) Various types of vaults. The first two are false vaults in which large horizontal rows of stone are corbeled out to meet each other. The other twelve examples are true vaults: 1) Barrel vault, with a continuous arch (Romanesque); 2) Cross or groined vault, resulting from the intersection of two barrel vaults (of Roman origin); 3) Quadripartite rib vault in which ribs divide the vault into four parts (Gothic); 4) Sexpartite vault with a transverse rib (Gothic); 5) and 6) Stellar vaults (Late Gothic); 7) Fan or conoidal vault, with radiating ribs (Late English Gothic); 8) Net vault, common in hall churches (Late German Gothic); 9) Honeycomb vault (Gothic of northern Germany); 10), 11), and 12) Coved vaults (Renaissance). ▶

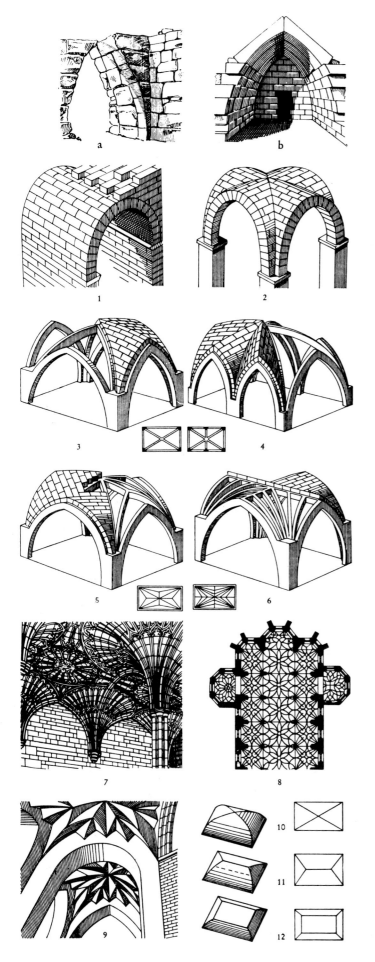

Tympanum. In a pediment, the triangular surface bounded by the sloping and horizontal cornices. In medieval architecture, tympanum refers to the space between the lintel and the arch of a doorway. Both types of tympanum are usually richly decorated.

Vault. An arched stone or brick covering over any space. Prior to the development of vaulting, a vault-like effect was achieved by placing layers of stones in two walls successively closer together until they met ("false" vaulting, illustrations *a* and *b*). The various types of true vault include: 1. Barrel vault; 2. Cross or groined vault; 3. Quadripartite rib vault; 4. Sexpartite vault; 5. and 6. Stellar vault; 7. Fan or conoidal vault; 8. Net vault; 9. Honeycomb vault; 10., 11., and 12. Coved vault. (See left and illustration on page 248)

Villa. In the original Latin meaning, a villa was a large country estate comprising the main house with the surrounding farm buildings and accommodation for the laborers. The remains of many such villas have been found throughout the countries formerly included in the Roman Empire. During the Renaissance, the term was applied to any large country mansion occupying its own grounds. Today the term is used for a somewhat pretentious suburban or rural house. (See illustration on page 248)

Volute. The spiral scroll that is the main form of decoration in the Ionic capital. The volute is also a characteristic feature of the Corinthian and Composite orders of architecture.

Voussoirs. The wedge-shaped stones of which an arch is built.

Wall Rib. see: Formeret

Westwork or Westblock. A construction, at the west end of some medieval Dutch and German churches, usually consisting of a towered, multistory central gallery with staircase towers on either side.

Ziggurat (Assyrian, *ziqquratu:* height or pinnacle). Towers built near groups of temples in ancient Chaldea, Assyria, or Babylonia, between about 3500 B.C. and 500 B.C. Constructed in the form of pyramids, ziggurats originally consisted of only one story, but the number of stages gradually increased, until in Neo-Babylonian times there were seven, beneath a temple at the summit. Each stage contained a flat terrace, and was painted in a different color, with white or

(above) Ictinus and Callicrates: Parthenon (447-432 B.C.); Acropolis, Athens, Greece. Erected under Pericles' order and with Phidias as master sculptor, this temple to Athena has come to epitomize the Greek ideal of proportion through its trabeated balance of verticals and horizontals. Much of the sculpture originally in the Parthenon is now in the British Museum, London.

(left) Le Corbusier; Notre Dame du Haut (1950-1955); Ronchamp, France. The Swiss architect has treated this church in part as a sculpture. He plays curved surfaces against planes in the outer walls, and perforates them with an irregular fenestration. The white and colored light that penetrates the thick, rough concrete relieves the massive power of the forms.

(right) Frank Lloyd Wright: Interior of the Solomon R. Guggenheim Museum (1959); New York. In place of the traditional gallery composed of connecting rectangular rooms, Wright designed the exhibition area along a continuous, spiraling ramp, from which the visitor may experience the internal organization of space as he moves from picture to picture. ►

blue at the top, symbolizing the sky. Built with mounds of brick, the towers were mounted by stairs leading directly to the summit, in earlier instances, and later by means of a continuous spiral ramp. Primarily religious in purpose, the ziggurats may also have been used as observatories. Examples include the ziggurat at the White Temple, Warka (c. 3500-3000 B.C.), with one stage, rectangular in plan, and the one at Khorsabad, of which four stories remain. Probably the most famous ziggurat is the structure in Babylon, known as the "Tower of Babel." Set on a square base, it has a spiral ramp which makes seven turns around the central core. (See illustration on page 250)

Architecture

The term "architecture" is derived from the Greek *architekton* (Latin: *architectura*); the term generally is used to mean the art or science of constructing buildings for human use. Strictly, however, a building should be called a piece of "architecture" only when designed specifically with a view to aesthetic effect. John Ruskin in his *Seven Lamps of Architecture* remarked: "Architecture is the art which so disposes and adorns the edifices raised by man . . . that the sight of them contributes to his mental health, power and pleasure." In this respect architecture proper transcends man's need for shelter and material security and becomes an expression of

(left) Guarino Guarini: Cupola of the church of San Lorenzo (1668-1687); Turin, Italy. The central octagon of this design is cleverly formed by the intersection of sixteen ribs, between which are niches with windows. These windows provide added decorative elements as they are interspersed at various levels throughout the dome. During this period an elaborate phase of the Baroque developed in Turin under such architects as Guarini and Filippo Juvarra.

(right) Roman aqueduct (second century A.D.); Segovia, Spain. Segovia, in north-central Spain, boasts one of the finest Roman aqueducts. This impressive structure, built in the time of the Emperor Trajan, is still used to carry water on two tiers of arches, 182 feet high, from the Río Frío, half a mile away. The rugged masonry of the piers and the arches, which made possible the spanning of large spaces without intervening supports, rhythmically work together as both a practical and aesthetic expression. ▶

his artistic, religious, magical, and other non-practical activities. A building can appeal aesthetically in a number of ways, the most important being through the relative proportions of its constituent parts, the internal organization of space, the interior and exterior treatment of the wall surfaces and wall space, the fenestration (arrangement and distribution of windows on the wall space), the ornamentation when specifically suited to its position and purpose, the relation of window space to wall space, and the relation of one story to another.

The history of architecture is the history of man shaping space for a specific purpose. In the erection of a building to enclose space for human use there are two main considerations—structure and materials. As architecture developed, three basic structural methods evolved. The first was the trabeated (or post-and-lintel) system, where two posts support a horizontal member, as for example in Greek architecture. Next came the more advanced arcuated system of the Roman and Gothic periods, in which the use of the arch made possible the spanning of large spaces without intervening supports, and also conveniently transferred the weight of the superstructure through the columns or piers to the ground. The third method came into use in modern times with the introduction of the cantilever principle, pre-cast concrete, and the internal skeleton of steelwork from which the walls could be hung, especially as they were no longer required to support the roof. The materials used in early periods were mostly clay, wood, and stone, but later artificial building materials such as brick and concrete were almost universally adopted when it was learned how to manufacture them.

It is important to remember that, even though

◀ (left) Pagoda of Flowers; Canton, China. The design of this wooden, many-tiered Chinese temple is not only highly decorative but also rich with symbolic religious meaning. Canton, a major city of southern China, served for centuries as an important point of contact between the Chinese and Western cultures.

(below) Ludwig Mies van der Rohe (born 1886): Apartment building in Lafayette Park housing development (1956-1957); Detroit, Michigan. The architecture of Mies van der Rohe is noted for the refined simplicity and classical restraint of forms. He established a new style of modern architecture by thinking of a building in terms of space rather than as a solid, geometrical mass. He realized this new idea by turning walls into windows and reducing the supporting structure to steel and reinforced concrete beams.

the historical approach to the evolution of architecture is the clearest and most logical one, the building of edifices for human use has largely been formulated by six basic factors: geographical, geological, climatic, religious, magical, and social. These are the factors which account for the various modes of the structures mankind has erected.

The origins of architecture are obscure. Probably the first type of actual building took the form of crude huts fashioned to satisfy primitive man's need for shelter from the elements and to

(left) Cathedral of Notre Dame (1163-1250); Paris. An early masterpiece of French Gothic architecture, this cathedral was one of the first to use flying buttresses to reinforce the high walls. The original supports were later replaced by the slender, spidery buttresses circling the apse.

(right) Temple of Parsvanatha (eleventh century); Khajuraho, India. The Jain religion called for a profuse arrangement of small roofed cells around a courtyard, each cell containing a seated holy figure. This imposing structure was one of six Jain temples in a huge complex. The richly carved, horizontally oriented exterior reliefs counteract the vertical thrust of the central tower. ▶

protect him from the incursions of wild beasts and human foes. These were purely functional structures built from the materials at hand, such as rough stone, tree trunks, clay, and the like. The earliest surviving structures which can strictly be termed architecture are probably the Sumerian temples, dating from the fourth millennium B.C., which were built for religious purposes on complicated geometrical plans.

Architecture has developed throughout the world, creating a permanent yet varied record of the conditions under which people have lived. In countries such as India, China, and Japan, the architecture showed little or no major influence from other civilizations. Consequently, the architecture of each of these countries has, until comparatively recent times, retained a consistent and individual stylistic character of its own.

Western architecture has, for the most part, evolved through many phases and styles, exhibiting a continuous development which moves progressively from the achievements of Egypt, Greece, and Rome, through the periods of Early Christian, Romanesque, Gothic, and Renaissance architecture, to the later years of the nineteenth century when, largely as a result of the discovery of new materials and building techniques, a new form of architecture emerged.

The "Modern Movement" rescued architecture from the monopoly of stylistic revivals which had characterized nineteenth-century buildings in Europe and elsewhere. Strongly supported by the growth of the factory systems and the facilities of the machine age, it developed rapidly in the hands of a number of outstanding pioneer architects, such as Louis Sullivan and Frank Lloyd Wright in America, Walter Gropius in Germany, Le Corbusier in France, and the engineer-architect Pier Luigi Nervi in Italy, to mention only a few of the most important.

see: entries for specific architects, buildings, countries, periods, schools, and sites

◄ (left) Casa de Pilatos (begun 1492); Seville, Spain. The slender columns of this residential courtyard, an elegant example of the late Mudéjar style, support arches so delicately carved as to offset the appearance of weight. The influence of Moorish art remained in Spain through the works of Moslem artists — this style became known as Mudéjar art. Here it also successfully combined Gothic forms with a lace-like adaptation of Renaissance detail.

(right) Giuseppe Arcimboldi: *Composite Head;* Castello Sforzesco, Milan, Italy. What appears at first to be simply an unusual arrangement of flowers and fruit becomes on second glance a human portrait. Arcimboldi was not only gifted in this kind of proto-surrealistic fantasy, but also excelled as a more conventional portraitist, and as a producer of court spectacles.

Architrave
See: Architectural Terms

Archivolt
See: Architectural Terms

Arcimboldi, Giuseppe (c. 1527-1593)
Italian painter born in Milan. Arcimboldi, although able to paint in the conventional styles of his day, as seen in his work for the Cathedral, Mi-

lan, between 1549 and 1558, specialized in weird, fantastic, and symbolic paintings, often of human forms composed of vegetables, flowers, or fish. There seems to be no precedent for this type of painting in Italian art, nor did he inaugurate a new tradition: his style was strictly peculiar to himself. However, Jan Bruegel is known to have admired and imitated some of Arcimboldi's work, and the Surrealists have cited him as a forerunner of their fantastic style.

Between 1549 and 1558 Arcimboldi worked

(left) Arent Arentsz: *Fishermen;* Louvre, Paris. Arentsz responded to the taste of his time for such outdoor genre scenes as this. He showed a feeling for the serene Dutch landscape and for the naturalistic treatment of the landscape figures.

(right) Guillaume de Pierre de Marcillat (1475-1529): *Honorius III Approves the Order of Saint Francis,* stained glass window in the church of San Francesco; Arezzo, Italy. This French painter has introduced into the art of stained glass spatial and compositional elements of contemporary Renaissance mural painting. The artist displayed a remarkable control of design both in the figures and in the use of perspective. ▶

in the Cathedral, Milan, and designed tapestries for the Cathedral, Como. He became court painter to the Habsburgs in Prague (1562-1587), displaying remarkable imaginative and technical ability in portraiture, stage design, and festival decoration.

Typical examples of Arcimboldi's use of animal and vegetable forms to compose a symbolic human form are *A Fantastic Man*, Accademia Carrara, Bergamo, Italy, and *Still Life Composed of a Human Face*, Pinacoteca, Cremona, Italy. Other important examples of his allegorical style are *Fire* (1566) and *Water*, Kunsthistoriches Museum, Vienna, part of a series of the Four Elements. Arcimboldi also executed a series of allegories of the Four Seasons, Museo Martinengo, Brescia, Italy.

Arden Quin, Carmelo (born 1913)
Uruguayan abstract painter, born in Rivera. After studying in Brazil he came into contact with nonrepresentational art through the lectures of Torres-Garcia in Montevideo in 1935 and through his friendship with Vieira da Silva and Arpad Szenes in Buenos Aires in 1941.

The founder of the Madi movement in 1944, Arden Quin has exhibited his "irregularly framed" pictures in Buenos Aires, Rio de Janeiro and, since 1948, in Paris. His theories have been tempered since his first visit to Paris in 1948-1950 by the ideas of Piet Mondrian, Kasimir Malevich, and Georges Vantongerloo.

Arena
See: Architectural Terms

Arentsz (Arentz), Arent (1585/86-1635?)
Dutch painter, born in Amsterdam. Arentsz, sometimes called Cabel, worked throughout his life in his native city, painting mainly scenes of outdoor life with animated figure groups in a manner similar to that of Hendrik Avercamp.

A typical example of Arentsz' work is *Fishermen and Peasants*, Rijksmuseum, Amsterdam. He is also represented in the Louvre, Paris, and in the National Gallery, London.

Arezzo
The capital of Arezzo Province in Tuscany, Italy, south of Florence, birthplace of Petrarch, Giorgio Vasari, and Pietro Aretino. Originally an Etruscan town, Arezzo was famous for its terra cotta and pottery and, under the Romans, for its red clay Arretine vases. In the late Middle Ages it was a notable center of learning and the arts.

Although parts of the town were badly

damaged during World War II, the walls, built in 1320 by Guido Tarlati di Pietramala, its warrior bishop, and reconstructed by Cosimo I de'Medici in 1541-1568, still stand. During the rebuilding of the walls the bronze statues of *Minerva* and the *Chimera*, now in Florence, were discovered.

There are many noteworthy buildings to be found in Arezzo:

In the Piazza San Francesco stands the church of San Francesco, a fine example of late Italian Gothic style begun in 1322 and never completed. Inside is the fresco cycle by Piero della Francesca, *The Story of the True Cross*. There are also frescoes by Spinello Aretino and an *Annunciation* by Luca Signorelli.

The twelfth-century Romanesque church, Santa Maria della Pieve, stands near the Palazzo dei Tribunali and the Palazzo della Fraternità, begun in the Gothic style in 1375 and completed in 1460 in the

Renaissance style by Antonio Rossellino. who was also the sculptor of the *Virgin* in the tympanum. A colonnade designed by Vasari is behind the church.

Near Santa Maria della Pieve is the restored fourteenth-century Palazzo Pretorio. The citadel. designed by Antonio da Sangallo. is surrounded by a park. The cathedral near it was begun in the thirteenth century, and completed in 1511 but its façade is a work of the twentieth century. Here are found frescoes by Piero della Francesca and terra-cotta reliefs by Andrea della Robbia.

The fourteenth-century Palazzo Comunale stands beside the cathedral, and nearby is the thirteenth-century Gothic church of San Domenico with a *Crucifix* by Cimabue. Vasari's house, with frescoes by the master, still stands. The Renaissance church of the Santissima Annunziata is by Bartolommeo della Gatta and Antonio da Sangallo. There is also the church of Santa Maria in Gradi, built by Bartolommeo Ammanati, and the Badia, a thirteenth-century abbey enlarged by Vasari, with his altarpiece *St. George* on the high altar. Santa Maria delle Grazie is notable for its portico by Benedetto da Maiano.

The remains of the Roman Amphitheater contain a famous collection of Roman vases and Stone and Bronze Age objects. The Palazzo della Dogana houses a museum of medieval art and a picture gallery with works by Spinello Aretino, Luca Signorelli, and Vasari, and ceramics by Maestro Giorgio as well as ivories, enamels, medals, and coins.
see: Arretine Ware

Argos

Ancient Greek city in the eastern Peloponnese, near which was situated the Temple of Hera, one of the oldest and most important religious sites of the Greek civilization. Little of artistic or archaeological importance remains at Argos itself, which was destroyed by Ibrahim Pasha in 1825 during the Greek wars of independence. Five miles from the town, however, and three miles from Mycenae is the site of the Argive Heraeum, a complex of buildings which was excavated between 1854 and 1895.

The first Temple of Hera on this site was said to be founded by Phoroneus in *c.* 1750

B.C. This was destroyed by fire in 423 B.C. and a new temple was erected near the site of the old by Eupholemos. Particularly notable among the sculptures executed by Polyclitus for the new temple was the 18-ft.-high seated statue of Hera. executed in gold and ivory. The statue no longer exists, but a detailed description of it survives in the writings of Pausanias.

Enough fragments of the temple were salvaged during the excavations to reconstruct a detailed model for the building and its surroundings. It was found that in addition to the temple there were at least ten other buildings on the site, most of them used for administrative purposes. Excavations below the foundations of the old temple indicated the existence of an organized religion long before the foundation of Mycenae. and votive offerings from both new and old temples illustrate the successive artistic styles from Middle Minoan to Roman.

Argunov, Ivan Petrovich (1727-after 1797)

Russian painter, born a serf on the lands of Count Sheremetev, near Moscow. Argunov was encouraged by the Sheremetev family to take up painting. He was active mainly in St. Petersburg.

Argunov was an academic painter, skilled in suggesting depth and volume in his work. His paintings include *Princess Lobanova-Rostovkaia,* now in the Russian Museum in Leningrad, and *Cleopatra* (1750), Rumyantzev Muzei, Moscow. *see:* Russian Art and Architecture

Aristides of Thebes

Greek painter of the fourth century B.C. No works by Aristides have survived. but ancient sources claim that he excelled in the rendering of expression. He is known to have painted one of the battles of Alexander the Great, and it is reported that Attalus I, King of Pergamon (Pergamum), 241-197 B.C., paid an enormous sum for a work by Aristides. *see:* Greek Art and Architecture

Arles

A town of southeast France. standing on the left bank of the Rhone River. An important Roman settlement and the principal residence of the Emperor Constantine. it declined under the Visigoths and was plundered by the Saracens in 730.

but emerged as a free city, capital of the kingdom of Arles, in the tenth century, remaining so until its submission to Charles I of Anjou in 1251.

Notable Roman remains include the amphitheater, Les Arènes, built on the model of the Colosseum with a capacity of 25,000 and still used for bullfights; the theater, constructed in the first century B.C. with a capacity of 7,000, of which only the stage and a few columns remain; and the Roman cemetery, known as the Aliscamps, one of the most famous burial places of the Roman Empire, consisting of a long avenue lined with tombs. Many sarcophagi found here are preserved in a former Gothic church, now the Museum of Christian Art.

The Cathedral of St. Trophime dates from the seventh century but has often been restored and is now mainly Romanesque. The twelfth-century portal, with sculptures representing *Christ in Majesty*, and the cloisters, are considered to be the finest in Provence. The seventeenth-century Hôtel de Ville contains the town library. There is also a museum of Provençal culture, founded by the poet Frédéric Mistral (1830-1914).

The yellow house in which Vincent van Gogh lived, and which he so often painted, was in Arles. Van Gogh's painting of the Aliscamps is now found in the Kröller-Müller Museum, Otterlo, The Netherlands.

The "Venus of Arles," discovered in the theater in 1651, is now in the Louvre, Paris.

Armature

A rigid skeleton or framework, usually metal, used to support wax, clay, or plaster in modeling. In modern direct-metal sculpture, an armature of wire or sheet metal may be welded or soldered together and then coated with bronze, copper, nickel-silver, steel, or lead and then melted and fused with the armature by the heat of an arc-welding machine or an oxyacetylene torch. Armatures are used also to support the weight of glass in stained-glass windows.

Sculptured figure of *St. Peter*, from the left jamb of the main portal of the church of Saint Trophime (second half of the twelfth century); Arles, France. This rather austere Provençal church concentrates its wealth of firmly-modeled sculpture around the "triumphal arch" of its doors and on the principal piers of its cloisters.

Armitage, Edward (1817-1896)

English painter, born in London. Armitage specialized in historical and mythological subjects and religious scenes.

In 1836 Armitage went to Paris, where as a pupil of the historical painter, Paul Delaroche, he assisted in the execution of the large fresco series known as the *Hemicycle* in the École des Beaux-Arts. He studied in Rome from 1849 to 1851 and visited the Crimea during the Crimean War, making a number of sketches which were later used for paintings of military subjects.

Following his return to England, Armitage was commissioned to decorate several churches and public buildings, notably the Houses of Parliament, for which he executed the large frescoes of the *Thames* (1852) and *The Death of Marmion* (1854). He frequently exhibited his work at the Royal Academy, was elected a member in 1872, and became a Professor at the Royal Academy Schools in 1875, his lectures being published in the United States in 1883.

An example of Armitage's easel painting is *The Remorse of Judas* (1866), Tate Gallery, London, and work in Burlington House, London.

Armor

From the earliest times man has had to use his ingenuity to protect his body from his enemies. The history of defensive armor goes back into the mists of time. It was not long before the wearer found pleasure in embellishing what was at first a dire necessity, and body armor early became a vehicle of artistic skill. Personal wear has always been a source of pride and self-advertisement. Primitive man strove to impress and terrify his opponent with frightful faces painted on his shield and towering plumes on his head. It is only very recently that arms and armor have ceased to be a recognized branch of applied art and become purely functional in form.

Body armor was not only embellished by every means at hand, but care also was taken to make the forms pleasing to the eye. For instance, the shapes and outlines of Gothic armor show how very sensitive its designers were to changes in taste. In this respect Gothic and Renaissance armor have much in common with Gothic and Renaissance architecture and furniture.

First comes the shield, which, being movable,

(below) Proto-Etruscan helmet (eighth century B.C.); Museo delle Antichità, Turin, Italy. This example from the iron age shows an early type of crested casque with rows of bronze rivets.

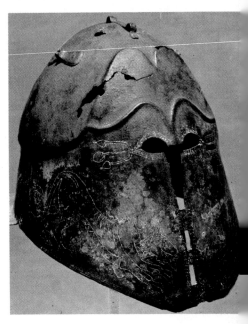

(left) Greek helmet in Corinthian style (fifth century B.C.); Museo Poldi-Pezzoli, Milan, Italy. (below) Etruscan helmet (sixth to fifth century B.C.); Museo Poldi-Pezzoli, Milan, Italy.

Japanese helmet (fifth to sixth century A.D.), bronze and gilt; National Museum, Tokyo. This type of bowl-shaped helmet, together with a mail suit, was worn by mounted warriors of the Kofun period of prehistoric Japan. The perforated brim once completely encircled the helmet, and was attached with rivets.

could be made to protect all parts of the body except the back. It offered a broad surface to decorate, and often the early forms of this decoration are highly significant. using complicated patterns with stylized representations of birds and animals which only the practiced eye of the ethnologist can recognize today. Early man had used the materials available to him, such as the skins of animals. wood. rope. and other vegetable derivatives. Even bones and teeth were pressed into the service of defense. With the discovery of the malleability of metals a new era began. which is with us still. Classical antiquity used arms of bronze, and later of iron. Homer's *Iliad* makes many references to the magnificence of armor and equipment worn in the siege of Troy. as when Hephaestus produced the armor and especially the shield of Achilles at the request of his mother. Etruscan armor is often very decorative. Copper and bronze are comparatively soft and easy to work. and the metal was embossed into various designs, often showing in

relief combats of warriors or mythical beasts. The *hoplite,* or heavy armed soldier of Hellenic times. wore a helmet of bronze which had a large globular skull topped with a curving plume of dyed horsehair; the face was protected by flat cheek-pieces projecting from the helmet at the sides. and there was a narrow nasal (nose guard). like a peninsula, between them. The cuirass (*thorax*) was a breastplate made in two parts, back and front. joined by braces over the shoulders; there were greaves or leg armor to protect the shins; the shield was generally large and circular. made of wood covered with a flat plate of bronze. often engraved or gilded. Smaller crescent-shaped shields were used by the more lightly armed.

From the earliest times there was a conflict between the desire for safety or to impress. and the need for agility in combat. Mobility is in itself a useful defense. It was. therefore necessary to guard against armor becoming too unwieldy. The Roman gladiator wore heavy armor in the

Etruscan suit of armor as seen on the *Mars of Todi;* Museo Gregoriano Etrusco, Rome. Late Etruscan armor was influenced both by the Hellenistic style and by that of the Italic peoples. The *thorax* here shows the early form of mail in which oblong pieces of metal are joined together by thongs.

siderable. One of the earliest forms of mail was of very small, oblong plates of metal, which were joined together by thongs. This type of mail is depicted in Assyrian sculptures of the eleventh century B.C. and was still being used by the Tibetans against the British Expedition of 1904. Textile armor cannot be stronger than its weakest point, and a great improvement was made when mail was formed of circular links of iron. This counteracted the weakness of the thongs which formed the structure of lamellar mail (mail made up of small joined plates), and when these rings were riveted, instead of merely having their ends butted together, it gave great strength to the whole structure. Interlinked mail is represented on the Trajan Column in Rome and on other Roman monuments. Although tedious to make, it did not wear out, and it gradually superseded armor of other kinds. In Europe mail remained in use until the sixteenth century, and

arena because he only needed to wear it for a short time, but the standardized equipment of the Roman legionary showed a compromise between the two needs. The Roman soldier wore a round helmet and a cuirass *(lorica)* of overlapping pieces of metal or leather which left his arms and legs comparatively free, except for greaves on the shins. His shield, usually rectangular, was prominently decorated with the sign of his legion, and was made to a standardized size so that it could be used to form the combined defense of the *testudo,* in which shields were overlapped to form a shieldwall. The Roman general wore an embossed cuirass of bronze and a crested helmet.

A new form of defense came with the invention of mail. It is not known who devised it first, but its textile nature gave great flexibility and permitted all movements of the body and limbs, although its aggregate weight was con-

(right) Equestrian armor of Cardinal Ascanio Maria Sforza (late fifteenth century); Armeria Reale, Turin, Italy. The horse, protected by the chamfron on its head to the crupper on its hindquarters, is almost as fully armored as the rider.

◄ (left) Half-armor of an English pikesman (c. 1630); Armories, Tower of London, England. This type of armor had been in use in England since the reign of Queen Elizabeth I, during which the English defeated the Spanish Armada (1588) and became a leading European power.

in Asia, almost to the present day.

In the Bayeux Tapestry, which illustrates the incidents preceding and during William of Normandy's invasion of England in 1066, the Duke is shown wearing a conical helmet with a nasal over a hood of mail, a sleeved shirt of mail (hauberk) with long skirts divided in the center, front and back, for riding, and mail leggings on his shins. This armament continued with little change for 250 years, apart from minor improvements, such as the introduction of the great

barrel-shaped helm, mail extensions to protect the hands, and a shortening of the skirts of the hauberk.

Mail, however, had certain disadvantages. It could not protect the body from bruising unless it was heavily padded underneath, and if the mail was pierced, links might be driven into the wound and make it septic. The final success of the smith in forging iron plates on the anvil brought about the gradual replacement of mail by plate armor. It was a slow process which

Italian helmet (early fifteenth century) Museo Poldi-Pezzoli, Milan, Italy. Renaissance designers modeled this so-called barbute style of sallet helmet after the Corinthian pattern of the Greeks. The simple, rounded forms served to deflect the blows of the attackers.

covered the whole of the fourteenth century in Europe. but by the end of that century a mán who could afford it could clothe himself from head to foot in an armor of articulated plates, designed to cover him completely and still allow movement of the limbs.

On account of its aggregate weight. plate armor was essentially the equipment of the horseman. for the burden was transferred to a large extent to the horse which carried him. The footsoldier had to content himself with less, and as armor was always expensive, he had as a rule to rely on his master to equip him, or on looting the battlefields.

Mention has been made earlier of the shield. The long, kite-shaped shields carried by the Norman warriors depicted in the Bayeux

Tapestry, show various simple designs of birds and animals. These decorations, however, represented an individual, possibly even casual choice, and did not carry the same significance that the science, or art, of heraldry was to bring about. Heraldry was directly derived from the feudal system of the early Middle Ages. Compositions involving creatures or combinations of certain colors became strictly personal and were codified in a rigid system that was hereditary. A man was immediately recognizable by the heraldic "arms" he wore. A son bore the arms of his father on his shield, on his surcoat and in the form of the crest upon his helmet. and in miniature upon many parts of his accoutrements. The kite-shaped shield of Norman times was followed by a shorter, broader shield. tapering to a point at the bottom. This shape was dictated by the rider's position in the saddle. with the horse's neck rising in front of him.

The surcoat was a garment of linen or other textile worn over the armor and often made as conspicuous as possible. The leader had to be recognized by the men he led. The splendor of his equipment took the place of modern badges

Italian helmet with visor, of a type sometimes known as "sparrow-beak," (late fifteenth century); Museo Poldi-Pezzoli, Milan, Italy. This closed style of helmet, fitted securely around the head and neck, was less likely than the one-piece helmet to be dislodged in battle.

or rank, and the armorer became an important member of society, receiving large sums of money and even civil honors for his skill. The knight was probably more of a peacock in the fourteenth century than he has ever been before or since.

Mail did not lend itself to decoration, but it was brightened by inserting rows of brass links among the steel ones. From the fourteenth century onward it was a common practice to finish the ends of sleeves or shirts of mail with four or five rows of brass links. Sometimes there were insertions of lozenges or other patterns. This was very commonly done with Indian mail, though Indian mail, as distinct from European mail, is often composed of links with their ends butted together, and is consequently easily torn apart.

The gradual addition of pieces of plate to the mail, beginning with the great helm and hollow bosses over the vulnerable joints of the knees and elbows, and gradually spreading over the whole body, made armor very heavy. Attempts were made to find substitutes for iron, notably by the use of *cuir bouilli* (leather boiled in oil). Leather is much lighter than iron, and in the process of manufacture it could be molded to any shape required. In the fourteenth century the shoulders and knees were sometimes protected by leather molded in the form of lions' heads or decorative foliage. These details, and also the helmets themselves, were often gilded or made of brass. The gauntlets of the Black Prince in Canterbury Cathedral are made of copper gilt. At the same time, the hip-belt, which carried a sword on the left side of the wearer and a dagger on the right, became a very decorative adjunct, consisting of a series of plaques, horizontally linked together, resembling the finest work of goldsmiths. Much ingenuity was used to make sword-hilts, chapes (scabbard tips), scabbards, and all other adjuncts highly decorative. Often architectural details of gables and crockets appear, and enamel was freely used. The tombs of the Scaliger family at Verona, Italy, show three equestrian figures wearing the armor of the fourteenth century. Two of them, Can Grande and Mastino, show the family crest of a mastiff (*cane*) both on the top of their great helms and on their horses' heads. The heraldic

bearing of the family, a ladder (*scala*), though it might appear at first sight not to offer many possibilities, is used very cleverly as a decoration all over the textile caparisons (coverings for the horses).

An alternative to mail was armor made of overlapping scales. It is illustrated in Roman sculpture and in manuscripts of the later Middle Ages, and it persists for a long time in the representations of the Eastern Empire. In Poland it survived into the eighteenth century, but it was heavy and had not the advantage of a homo-

Italian suit of armor from the Missaglia armorers of Milan (fifteenth century); Santuario della Grazia, Mantua, Italy. Milan was one of the principal Renaissance centers of armor-making, and its products were widely used. The left pauldron (at the shoulder) and the left couter (at the elbow) are shaped for use in combat by jousting.

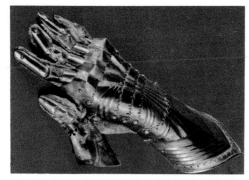

(above) German gauntlet (fifteenth century); Coira Castle, Sluderno, Italy. Metal plates that cover the back of the hand, and circlets that extend the warrior's protection to his fingers, illustrate the functional elegance of the Gothic style.

(above) Marks of celebrated Italian and German armorers, often punched beside the guild mark of the armorer's town. 1) The Negroli family; 2) and 3) The Missaglia family; 4) The Piccinino family; 5) Konrad Treytz the Elder; 6) Michel Witz the Elder; 7) Helmschmied Coloman.

geneous structure like mail. In the form of the brigandine, a body garment consisting of small metal plates riveted to a leather foundation generally covered with velvet, on which the heads of the rivets made a decorative pattern, it was much worn in western Europe as an informal substitute for plate armor.

The large area of a horse's body makes it extremely vulnerable. Once unhorsed an armored man-at-arms was at a great disadvantage. Before the battle of Barnet in 1471, the Earl of Warwick and his brother deliberately slew their horses in sight of their men to show that they had no intention of retreating if the battle went against them. Both were killed. Attempts were made to protect the horse like his rider, at first with a mail trapper, which was very heavy, and later with steel plate or leather molded to fit the body. A horse's armor, or bard, as it was called, consisted of a chamfron for the head, a crinet for the neck, a peytral for the chest, and a crupper for the hindquarters. The whole was often covered with a rich and voluminous caparison extending to the horse's fetlock. These "housings" were often of the richest materials, colored silk or velvet, with the owner's heraldic

(right) Italian breastplate and backplate (second half of seventeenth century), iron with ornament in gilt bronze; Armeria Reale, Turin, Italy. Once the property of the counts of Carmagnola, this richly overlaid suit seems designed for dress rather than battle use.

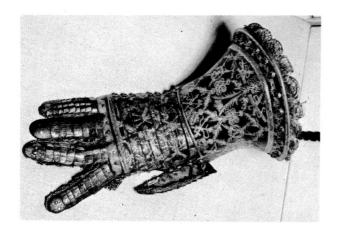

Dress gauntlet executed with gold and silver ornamentation for the son of Philip II of Spain; Victoria and Albert Museum, London. Designed for dress or parade use, such intricately decorated armor as this was restricted to the nobility by the costliness of its workmanship. In this kind of detail the armorer's craft becomes almost a jeweler's art.

Waffensammlung in Vienna is also rich in armor from this time to its disuse in the seventeenth century.

The outlines of Gothic armor show the most subtle shapes, carefully thought out to present a slippery, glancing surface to an opponent's blow, mobile on the right, or striking side of the body, and built up as a more solid protection on the left. The tulip-shaped vambraces covering the lower arms from elbow to wrist, the delicate tapering of the cuffs of the gauntlets, the pointed sabatons, or shoes, and a little later, the piercing of the edges and chiseling of surfaces—all aimed at making a man's armor a pleasure to see. This type of armor has come to be called Gothic because of the effects it borrowed from the lines of late Gothic architecture, with its details of cusps and finials. Gothic armor had a great vogue in Germany, where the smiths of Augsburg and Nuremberg produced some of the most

arms prominently displayed on them, and were hung with bells and topped with plumes.

At the end of the fourteenth century the riot of form and color became more subdued. Mail had become secondary to plate, which now sheathed the wearer from head to foot in shining steel. Pleasure began to be taken in the smooth surface of the metal itself, and surcoats, tabards (cloaks), and other decorative accessories were often discarded. The shield fell into disuse for horsemen, although it continued to be used for infantry and parade. The great helm was abandoned (except for the tournament) and replaced by the lighter basinet or sallet helmet, which had a movable visor. When the beauty of the metal itself was understood, its form became an object of close attention.

Apart from helmets and a few shields, very little armor has survived from the Middle Ages of a date earlier than the fifteenth century. The pagan custom of burying chieftains with their personal possessions was discontinued, except on a much smaller scale, by their Christian successors. The funeral "achievements" of the Black Prince (Edward, Prince of Wales, died 1376), preserved in Canterbury Cathedral, are the most important of such survivals which have not deteriorated by burial in the ground. From the middle of the fifteenth century, armor has survived to an increasing extent. The armory of Count Trapp in the castle of Churburg, near Merano, Italy, is the most complete example of an armory representing the wear of successive generations of one family from the end of the fourteenth century. The Imperial Habsburg

Venetian helmet (fifteenth century); decorated with lion's head and acanthus leaves in gilt bronze; Bargello, Florence, Italy. These decorative additions enhanced the helmet's picturesque quality. This helmet may have been used for dress or parade use, and was perhaps worn by a victorious Venetian soldier of fortune.

(above) Venetian helmet (fifteenth century); Museo Poldi-Pezzoli, Milan, Italy. This is an ornate example of the burgonet, with cheek-guards and an extended peak.

(right) German infantryman's breastplate (fifteenth century), the work of a Milanese shop; Trapp-Sluderno Collection, Sluderno, Italy. The simple, cartoon-like shape of the embossed head enlivens this armor decoratively without impairing its functionality.

(below) Examples of halberds; Museo Poldi-Pezzoli, Milan, Italy. 1) Swiss (fifteenth century); 2) and 3) German; 4) and 5) Italian; 6) Swiss. The last five are from the sixteenth century, and show a more elaborate design than the first.

satisfying armor that has ever been made. In Italy the armorers of Milan produced armor of blunter and rounder forms, with smoother surfaces. The Milanese were recognized masters of their craft and earned a deservedly high reputation throughout Europe. Kings, princes, and those who could afford their products hastened to buy them, and there was a brisk export trade to England, Scotland, France, and Spain. It is this armor of the fifteenth century which we see painted with loving care by the Italian artists of the period and the illuminators of medieval manuscripts. The latter may have enjoyed depicting it for the attractive way in which it could enhance their pages, but the absurd claim that armor was seldom worn because of its weight and unwieldiness is not borne out by the inventories of armories and the account rolls recording its sale and purchase.

Armor of steel was difficult to make, and the guilds which specialized in the processes of manufacture tended to concentrate it in certain geographical centers. Families who passed on their skill from one generation to another became famous as armorers. The centers were usually near the mines from which the ore came. Milan became famous for its production of armor in the fourteenth century, the family of Missaglia being the most important. In the next century the South German towns of Augsburg, Nuremberg, Landshut, and a little later Innsbruck, reached a high standard of skill. Their work can be recognized not only by the marks the makers stamped upon their products, as goldsmiths do upon their wares, but also by characteristic individual forms.

It is not generally known that the art of etching originated with the armorers. It probably came about from the casual marks bitten by rust on the steel surface, from which someone conceived the idea of making patterns on armor with acid. The patterns were drawn by a needle through a mask of wax in the same way that the painter-etcher today etches his copper plates. The earliest known examples of etched armor are by the Milanese. They were followed not long after by their rivals at Augsburg. At first etching was used with considerable restraint, but in the sixteenth century armor was sometimes etched all over, and was further enhanced with gilding

(above) Italian helmet (sixteenth century); Museo Poldi-Pezzoli, Milan, Italy. In this example of a burgonet, with incised lines following the curve of the crown, the hinged cheek pieces are made to fasten under the chin.

(below) Lombard helmet and collar (sixteenth century), with the motto of the Borromeo family; Museo Poldi-Pezzoli, Milan, Italy. The technique of etching, considered to have had its origin in the work of the armorer, is used here to provide a rich, decorative effect.

and bluing of the metal to provide a colorful background for the designs.

Another process used by the armorer to decorate his products was that of embossing. This throwing of surfaces into low relief had been understood and practiced in classical times, when the metal was bronze. It was now applied to armor of steel. The artist-craftsmen of Milan, such as the Negroli brothers and Piccinino, and later the armorers of Germany (the Helmschmieds of Augsburg, Lochner and the Siebenburgers of Nuremberg, and the Seusenhofers of Innsbruck), began in the sixteenth century to produce armor which was in fact more decorative than useful,

because the embossing inevitably impaired the advantage of a smooth, glancing surface. The embossing was further enhanced with designs damascened, or inlaid, in gold or silver. This process was effected by engraving lines on the surface of the metal and hammering gold or silver wire into the grooves to make ornamental patterns, which were often set off upon a blue or purple background.

The armor of the Renaissance can hold its own with any other branch of applied art of its time. Many of the greatest pictorial artists lent their talents. Albrecht Dürer produced a series of designs for etching the silver armor

(left) Armor of Prince Emmanuel Filiberto (early sixteenth century); Armeria Reale, Turin, Italy. This damascened *cap-à-pie* suit of armor, with plumes crowning the helmet, was designed particularly for tournament use; a support for the lance was provided on the right of the breastplate.

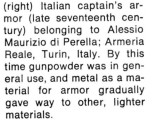

(right) Italian captain's armor (late seventeenth century) belonging to Alessio Maurizio di Perella; Armeria Reale, Turin, Italy. By this time gunpowder was in general use, and metal as a material for armor gradually gave way to other, lighter materials.

which the Seusenhofers undertook to make for the Emperor Maximilian I. Although this armor was never completed, Dürer's drawings have survived. Hans Holbein the Younger has given his name to a type of dagger, for which his drawings of the *Dance of Death* provided the design for the sheath. The armorers and artists of the day lived close together and intermarried. Daniel Hopfer, the engraver, married the daughter of Coloman Helmschmied, armorer, and the painter and engraver Hans Burgkmair the Younger lived in the house of Matthias Frauenpreiss, an Augsburg armorer. A painted shield, or pavise, in the British Museum depicts in colors a knight in armor kneeling before his lady, while the figure of Death hovers in the background. It is the work of a fifteenth-century French artist of the first rank. The Negrolis of Milan, who succeeded the Missaglias, were ennobled for their services, and Anton Peffenhauser, one of the great armorers, of Augsburg, was in his later years burgomaster, or mayor, of that city.

In Germany at the turn of the century (*c.* 1500) the pointed Gothic forms were succeeded by a rounded and blunter style. Toes of sabatons were made square, the cuffs of gauntlets were similarly modified, and the ripples of Gothic fluting were hardened into straight parallel lines. This style is commonly named after the Emperor Maximilian I, although it only came into fashion at the end of his life and lasted for a few years more. He was a great and discerning patron of the craft, encouraging the Seusenhofers to come from Augsburg and settle in his capital of Innsbruck. Maximilian's descendants inherited his liking for fine armor, and his son, Philip I "the Fair" of Castile, is represented by most interesting armor in the Real Armería in Madrid. His grandson, the Emperor Charles V, was one of the greatest patrons the craft has ever known. When he abdicated and retired to live near the monastery of San Yuste in Spain, he took with him six of his suits of armor to keep him company. Charles V is richly represented today in the Real Armería in Madrid, and also in the other Habsburg armory in Vienna; so also, in his turn, is his son, King Philip II of Spain.

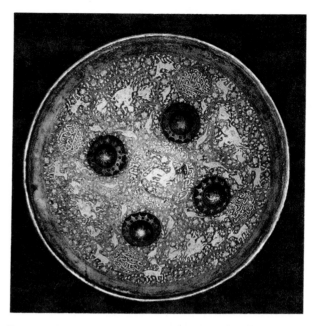

Persian ratchet, or circular shield (seventeenth century); Museo Poldi-Pezzoli, Milan, Italy. Gold is inlaid here to produce a design which combines figurative, abstract, and calligraphic elements. This damascening, or *koftgari,* included the use of precious stones.

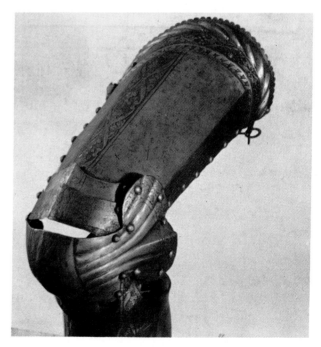

North Italian *cuisse,* or thigh plate (seventeenth century); Museo Poldi-Pezzoli, Milan, Italy. Hinged to the poleyn and the greave that cover the knee and the lower leg, this cuisse is decorated with both embossed and etched designs.

(above) Italian helmet (seventeenth century); Museo Poldi-Pezzoli, Milan, Italy. The so-called "lobster tail" on this burgonet protects the back of the neck with an extension of riveted plates. (below) Italian morion helmet (seventeenth century); Museo Poldi-Pezzoli, Milan, Italy. This etched and gilt example is typical of helmets worn throughout Europe in the seventeenth century.

Charles' dominions included some of the greatest centers of the craft in South Germany, but he was equally ready to patronize the armorers of Milan as well. His contemporaries, François I of France and Henry VIII of England, were also lavish patrons. Henry VIII set up his own workshop at Greenwich, with the armorers mostly drawn from Germany and Flanders, and François I followed suit, founding what has

come to be known as the "Louvre School." The work of the latter shows clearly the influence of the Franco-Italian School of Fontainebleau and of Giulio Romano, a pupil of Raphael, in its attenuated figure subjects. The Flemish armorers freely adopted the strapwork style of ornament propagated by Frans Floris. Their work is as typical of its time and of its country as any building, tapestry, or piece of carved furniture.

Early in the sixteenth century the use of gunpowder, whose explosive power was first adopted in Europe as a propellant for missiles in the fourteenth century, had become a very serious influence in war. Armor was found to be powerless against cannon and smaller firearms, unless it was made so thick as to be intolerably heavy. At the same time the value of strategy in war was recognized, and tactical movements had replaced the old set battles for which the commanders of opposing forces met at an agreed time and place. Centralized monarchies enabled armies to be properly organized and drilled. These changes resulted in the use of more mobile forces, such as light horsemen. But fine armor had such prestige that it took 150 years for it to disappear altogether. In the seventeenth century a heavily armed horseman was called a *cuirassier*. He replaced the lancer of the sixteenth century and the man-at-arms of the Middle Ages. He still had his uses in shock tactics; he could be trusted to charge home without flinching, and was employed freely in the Thirty Years' War in Germany. In the course of the Civil War in England (1642-1649) *cuirassiers* were dropped, and the last armor worn in battle was confined to the pikeman, who wore a helmet and a breast- and backplate, and tassets on his thighs. A coat of thick buff leather was found useful as a substitute for the heavier armor of steel. The breastplate continued in use for cavalry to a limited extent, and there was a sudden and unforeseen return to defensive armor in 1916, when steel helmets were issued to the troops of all combatant nations, and armored tanks were brought in to break the deadlock of trench warfare. The tank had the advantage over body armor in that it protected two or three men at once, and was propelled by its own machinery.

The mock battles of a purely military society were the foundation of the tournament, which became fashionable in Europe in the twelfth century. It became a highly regulated affair with strong social implications. Only gentlemen "of coat-armor" could take part in tournaments, and armor was modified to meet their special requirements, which were distinct from the requirements of the field of battle. As armor was worn at tournaments for only a limited time and for certain clearly defined events, such as jousting, it was as a rule made heavier than armor for the field, and was built up on the left side of the body, the side on which the combatants passed each other at the tilt. A jousting armor often weighed as much as 90 lbs. Various special forms of joust, such as the *Renzeug*, the *Stechzeug*, and fighting on foot at the barriers, had their own particular type of armor. Much of the best armor of the sixteenth century was that made for the tournament.

The last cap-à-pie (head to foot) armor was the one made for King Louis XIV by the Italian armorer Garbagnaus; it is now in the Musée de l'Armée, Paris. This is a *cuirassier* armor, complete from head to foot, and the whole surface is covered with engraved designs. A curious postscript to the history of defensive armor is that its representation persisted in portrait painting for the formal apparel of military sitters well into the eighteenth century.

Outside Europe, armor was freely worn until comparatively modern times. Its forms were governed by the exigencies of climate and by the materials at hand and the skill to use them. It is somewhat of a paradox that armor was last worn in places where the sun is extremely hot. Many of the horsemen of the Kalifa's army at the battle of Omdurman in the Sudan in 1898 wore long mail shirts and helmets and padded *jibbas* (shirt-like garment). It has often been said that the invention of mail of interlinked links took place in Asia, but F. M. Kelly showed that in many contemporary representations of the Christians and Saracens fighting in the Crusades, the former are shown wearing more mail than their opponents. Saracenic armor, as it is called, that is to say armor made and worn in the west of Asia, consisted very largely of mail in which plate was incorporated. There are even horse armors made in this way, covering the whole of the head and body of the animal. The Turks

produced a large and impressive helmet, around which the turban was wound. Their cuirasses consisted of circular plates like dish covers, fore and back, linked to each other by mail. The shields were of steel, circular in shape with four knobs on the front covering the fastenings of the handle on the inside. There was an extensive armor-making industry in Persia and India, but no country outside Europe produced the completely integrated steel covering of plates from

(above) Persian helmet (seventeenth century); Museo Poldi-Pezzoli, Milan, Italy. A covering of mail drops from the shallow skull cap to protect the sides and back of the wearer's head. (below) Japanese helmet of the Edo period (eighteenth century); Museo Orientale, Venice, Italy. After two hundred and fifty years without war, such Japanese armor as this was intended not only for defense, but also as parade dress. It was a symbol of the military class.

Benedetto Alfiere: Galleria Beaumont; Palazzo Reale, Turin, Italy. This collection of arms and armor was brought together and installed by order of King Carlo Alberto of Italy in 1833, at a time when many of the great European arms collections were being started.

head to foot. In Indo-Persian armor much use was made of damascening helmets and plates with gold and silver inlay (*koftgari*) work, and armor was inlaid with precious stones. There was a preponderance of mail, which was often reinforced with a cuirass called the "Four Mirrors," to denote the four larger plates (front, back, and two sides), and there was the "Coat of a Thousand Nails," a thick, highly decorative garment covered with velvet and studded with nails, which also served to some extent as a defense. The shield was like the Saracenic shield, small and circular and carried in one hand.

In the Far East armor developed in an entirely different manner. Japanese armor is unique. To the Western eye it is clumsy and grotesque, but Japanese smiths achieved a high reputation for their products, and their names are revered.

Japanese armor consisted of a *top* or helmet, generally with a curtain of large plates attached by silk ribbons to protect the neck. The face was often covered with a terrifying mask. Mail and brigandine work in the Western sense were used as adjuncts to the body armor of lacquered plates, and the large rectangular plates overlapping the shoulders and thighs. The whole subject of Japanese arms and armor is wrapped up with the convention of a strict military caste. It was swept away by the decision of the Emperor in 1868 to adopt Western practices. Southwest of Japan one finds among the Indonesian islanders a very elaborate armor made of rope, and, among simple peoples who do not work in metals, armor of wickerwork.

The principal public collections of European armor are the three great royal armories of the Habsburgs in Vienna and the Real Armería in Madrid, and the Royal House of Saxony in Dresden. Paris has an extensive and important collection in the Musée de l'Armée in Les Invalides, incorporating the old armory at Sedan and the private collection of the Emperor Napoleon III. In Turin there is the Armeria Reale, largely collected by King Carlo Alberto of Savoy, and in the Hermitage, Leningrad, are the collections of Tsar Nicholas I. The Metropolitan Museum of Art, New York, has a rich and representative collection formed in modern times. In England the Royal Armories of the Tower of London and the private bequest of the Wallace Collection combine to provide a valuable display, including the armors of Henry VIII.

For Eastern armor, the Metropolitan Museum of Art, New York, has the G. C. Stone Collection, and the Moser Collection is in the Historical Museum, Berne, Switzerland; this type of armor is also displayed in the Museo Stibbert, Florence, Italy. The Military Museum, Istanbul, has a representative collection of Saracenic armor, and collections of Indian armor are housed in the palaces of the Maharajah of Jaipur and the Prince of Alwar. Japanese armor is represented in the National Museum, Tokyo; the Tokugawa Museum, Nogoya City, and various shrines and temples in Japan; the Victoria and Albert Museum, London; and the Royal Ontario Museum, Toronto.

Armory Show

America's first comprehensive international exhibition of modern art, held at the 69th Regiment Armory, New York City, in the spring of 1913.

Known as the Armory Show, the exhibition included about 1,600 paintings, drawings, prints and pieces of sculpture. Although it included a large American section, assembled by William Glackens and occupying about three-quarters of the show, it also embraced works by most of the celebrated "modernists" of Europe, including Pablo Picasso, Henri Matisse, Constantin Brancusi, Wassily Kandinsky, Francis Picabia, Fernand Léger, Georges Braque, Georges Rouault, Aristide Maillol, and Wilhelm Lehmbruck. Also included were works by the great forerunners of twentieth-century art: Paul Cézanne, Vincent van Gogh, Paul Gauguin, and Henri Toulouse-Lautrec. One painting, *Nude Descending a Staircase* by Marcel Duchamp, now in the Philadelphia Museum of Art, became known to a whole generation as the popular image of all that was "modernistic" and "incomprehensible" in contemporary art.

The exhibition provoked a great deal of controversy. It was violently attacked in the press and caused near-riots in some places, but it gained valuable publicity for contemporary art in the United States. The Armory Show subsequently traveled to Chicago and Boston, altogether attracting a total attendance of about 250,000. During the course of the exhibition some 300 works were sold.

A 50th Anniversary Exhibition of the Armory Show, composed of nearly 400 of the original paintings, drawings, and sculptures, was held in 1963, again at the 69th Regiment Armory in New York. In addition to the works of art, the exhibition displayed historic documents relating to the original show, including contemporary photographs, cartoons, and newspaper clippings. *see:* United States Art and Architecture

Arnolfo di Cambio (c. 1240-c. 1302)

Italian sculptor and architect, first heard of in 1265, working as chief assistant to Nicola Pisano on the Cathedral pulpit in Siena. More is known about his sculpture than his architecture, but his

work as an architect is nevertheless of considerable importance. He began the construction of the Cathedral in Florence in 1296, and in 1300 he was recorded as the Capomastro (master builder). Evidence of his work remains in two front bays of the Cathedral. His name is also connected with two other churches in Florence: Santa Croce, begun in 1294/95, and probably carried out largely according to his design, and the Badia, built between 1278 and 1310 but extensively restored later.

The strong individuality of Arnolfo's sculptural style can be recognized in one of his first works, the Shrine of St. Dominic, church of San Domenico, Bologna, which was commissioned from Nicola Pisano in 1264 but executed by his assistants. Among the most important of his later works as a sculptor is the tomb of Cardinal de Braye in the church of San Domenico, Orvieto (completed in 1282). Unfortunately, this elaborate monument is no longer intact, and no proper reconstruction is possible. Another tomb of

◄ (left) Marcel Duchamp (born 1887): *Nude Descending a Staircase No. II* (1912), oil; Philadelphia Museum of Art: The Louise and Walter Arensberg Collection. Duchamp's Futurist-Cubist treatment of moving form caused public indignation at the Armory Show of 1913, which was organized by a group of American painters to exhibit progressive developments on both sides of the Atlantic. The show was seen in New York, Chicago, and Boston.

(right) Arnolfo di Cambio: Design for the façade of the Cathedral, Florence (1296–1462); Museo dell'Opera del Duomo, Florence, Italy. Arnolfo did not live to carry out all of his design for the Cathedral; Giotto, in 1334, was the first of several successors to direct the work. The marble facing remained incomplete, as in this drawing, until the reconstruction between 1875 and 1887.

Arnolfo di Cambio: *L'Assetata* (The Thirsty One), sculptured fragment from a marble fountain executed at Perugia; Galleria Nazionale dell'Umbria, Perugia, Italy. In contrast to the linear style of contemporary Gothic sculpture, Arnolfo's figures appear to be classical in their emphasis on simplicity and solidity of form. The figures are also notable for their expressive intensity.

similar complexity and originality, comparing very closely to that of Cardinal de Braye and therefore convincingly ascribed to Arnolfo, is that of Cardinal Annibaldi, church of San Giovanni in Laterano, Rome (completed 1276). This tomb is no longer intact, but the sophistication and originality of both works must have been remarkable and influential in their era.

Before Arnolfo, monumental architecture in this part of Italy had been the monopoly of the Cosmati family, noted for the inlaid tesserae (mosaic) work which was the dominant feature of their style. Arnolfo took over this form of decoration, but introduced many new designs, such as Gothic architectural features. Above all, he subordinated the whole design to individual figure sculpture, an approach that represented a radical departure from previous monumental styles. The central figure was the effigy. It was ministered to by angels or deacons, and set in a tabernacle surmounted by images of the Madonna and appropriate saints. The short squarish figures of the two deacons drawing back a curtain to reveal Cardinal de Braye's effigy are typical of his work.

Arnolfo's masterly classical style, with its emphasis on plane and volume, provides an astonishing contrast to the linear Gothic move-ment of the sculpture of his contemporary, Giovanni Pisano. The balanced and complementary poses of the two deacons in the Cardinal de Braye monument are truly classical in feeling, and the frieze from the Annibaldi tomb, depicting six deacons carrying the vessels of the Last Sacrament, has a grace and a measured rhythm that is even more purely classical in its harmony. Arnolfo's sculpture, with its feeling for plane, volume, and structure can be justly compared to Giotto's painting. However, his style was a strongly personal one, and no succeeding sculptor was able to imitate it.

Other notable sculptural works by Arnolfo include the tomb of Adrian V, church of San Francesco, Viterbo (1276), and two ciboria in the churches of San Paolo fuori le mura, Rome (1285) and Santa Cecilia in Trastevere, Rome (1293). As Capomastro in Florence he undertook the decoration of the façade of the Cathedral, which he completed up to the main tympanum before his death. The eight figures which survive are among the finest works of the period. Some of them, including the majestic and imposing seated *Madonna* and the very moving *St. John Lamenting the Dead Virgin*, are preserved in the Museo dell'Opera del Duomo, Florence.

see: Florence; Gothic Art and Architecture

Arp, Jean (Hans) (born 1887)

French sculptor, painter, graphic artist, and poet, born in Strasbourg. Arp attended the School of Applied Arts, Strasbourg, in 1904, and studied at Weimar Art School in 1905-1907. In 1908 he went to Paris, where he studied at the Académie Julian. He met Paul Klee in Weggis, Switzerland, the following year and Wassily Kandinsky in 1911. In 1912 he participated in the second *Blaue Reiter* exhibition, and met Robert Delaunay. He became acquainted with Max Ernst, Amadeo Modigliani, and Pablo Picasso in 1914, and was a co-founder of the Zurich Dada movement in 1916-1919. During 1919-1920 he was active in the Cologne Dada movement, met Kurt Schwitters and El Lissitzky, and made contact with the Berlin Dadaists. Arp helped to organize the first Surrealist exhibition in 1925, was a member of Michel Seuphor's *Cercle et Carré* group in 1930, and of the *Abstraction-Création* group in 1932-1934. Since World War II he has made several visits to the United States. Large retrospective exhibitions of his work have been held at the Museum of Modern Art, New York, in 1958, and the Tate Gallery, London, in 1962.

Arp was inspired in his early writing by Novalis and the German Romantics, and has continued to believe that art should express a spiritual, "mystical" reality. During his early development he was quick to recognize the implications both of the *Blaue Reiter* movement's closeness to pure abstraction, and of Cubism. He executed his first abstract reliefs in wood in 1917, and in 1919-1920, with Ernst, executed a series of "Fatagaga" paintings. The Surrealist movement allowed him to develop "the poetic, associational side of [his] work."

In the 1930's Arp's forms, always inherently sculptural, achieved three-dimensional expression. He produced torsos and "concretions," introducing the theme of growth and change which has been the dominant characteristic of his work. The first of his torn paper collages (*papiers déchirés*) also belong to this time. His biomorphic, "vegetable" forms are resolutely plastic and organic: Arp himself has written "art is a fruit growing out of man like the child out of the mother."

Arp is the author, with Lissitzky, of *Les Ismes de L'Art* (The Isms of Art), 1925, and of a short novel *L'Homme qui a perdu son squelette* (The Man who Lost his Skeleton), 1937-1939, produced in conjunction with Marcel Duchamp, Ernst, G. Huguet, G. Prassinos, and the writers Paul Éluard and D. Carrington. He collaborated with Sonia Delaunay-Terk and Alberto Magnelli

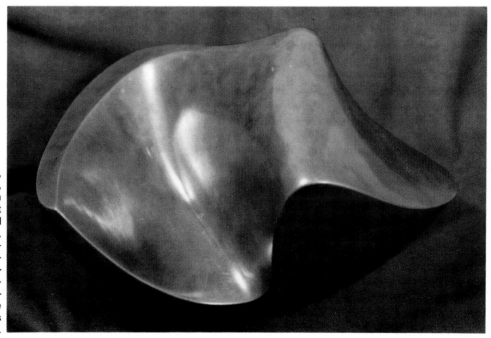

Jean Arp: *Ganymede* (1959), bronze; Private Collection, London. Arp has given an organic quality of movement to this highly abstracted form. Influenced by Cubism, the sculptor sought a harmonious balance of geometrical patterns in three-dimensional form. The form is further enhanced by the attention the artist gave to the surface texture as it creates a play of light and shadow.

on the publication of *Les Nourritures Terrestres* (1950). His monumental sculptures include a bronze, *Shepherd of the Clouds*, for the Ciudad Universidad, Caracas, Venezuela, 1953, and a bronze relief for the UNESCO Building, Paris, 1957. Typical of his works in sculpture are *Hybrid Fruit called Pagoda*, 1934, Tate Gallery, London, and *Growth*, 1938, Solomon R. Guggenheim Museum, New York. The Museum of Modern Art, New York, contains examples of his collages, painted wood-reliefs, and sculpture. *see:* Abstract Art; Blaue Reiter, der; Dadaism

Arpino, Cavaliere d' (c. 1568-1640)

Italian Mannerist painter, born in Rome. Arpino's real name was Giuseppe Cesari. He studied under his father, a native of Arpino, and continued to work in the Mannerist style during the period when the great innovations of the Carracci family, Caravaggio, and Gianlorenzo Bernini were revitalizing Italian art.

During his career, Arpino obtained numerous commissions and made a considerable reputation under papal patronage. Between 1589 and 1591 he painted frescoes in the church of San

Martino, Naples, and in 1598 he received the commission from Clement VIII for the Confessio in St. Peter's, Rome. From 1591 to 1636, when his popularity declined, he was periodically engaged at the Palazzo dei Conservatori, Rome, painting large historical scenes in a style which shows, in the forced grimaces and strained attitudes of the figures, the elements of a dying Mannerism. Under the patronage of Paul V, Arpino also painted the pendentives of the dome in the Cappella Paolina in the church of Santa Maria Maggiore, Rome, and the large lunette above the altar; the rest of the decoration was executed by Guido Reni and Ludovico Cigoli.

From 1603 to 1612, on commission from Pope Clement VIII, Arpino designed the mosaics in the dome of St. Peter's in Rome. The large picture of the *Ascension* in the church of San Giovanni in Laterano, Rome, is also attributed to him. Other works by Arpino include *Perseus and Andromeda*, Metropolitan Museum of Art, New York, and paintings in the Vatican.

(right) Cavaliere d'Arpino: *Perseus and Andromeda,* oil; Pinacoteca, Palermo, Italy. As a mannerist painter Arpino borrows various features of Renaissance and early Baroque style, and uses them with facility to portray Andromeda being rescued from the dragon by Perseus. The resulting painting is picturesque, but lacks true originality.

◄(left) Cavaliere d'Arpino: Interior of the cupola of St. Peter's, Rome; mosaic. Arpino decorated the interior of the dome (from 1603 to 1612) with representations of Christ, the Apostles, popes, saints, and angels. The top of the lantern, at the center, rises 452 feet above the cathedral pavement, creating one of the most impressive domes in the world.

Arretine cup with relief decoration (first century A.D.); Museum, Arezzo, Italy. Characteristic of Arretine ware, whose manufacture spread from Arezzo to other parts of the Roman Empire, is the bright red clay, the relief molding, the small size, and the lustrous glaze.

Arretine ware was usually made of red clay and consisted of small bowls, cups, or shallow dishes, usually without handles. The ware was of a rich color and often finished with a fine gloss. It was often decorated with molded reliefs copied from embossed silverware, with such motifs as flowers, masks, and mythological scenes.
see: Ceramics

Ars Moriendi (Latin: The Art of Dying)

One of the most famous block books, printed in Germany *c.* 1465, a devotional work, derived either from a Netherlands block book of *c.* 1450, British Museum, London, or from a set of engravings by the anonymous Master E. S. in the Ashmolean Museum, Oxford.
see: Block Books

Arras Tapestry

The French city of Arras became a center of tapestry production in the fourteenth century, under the patronage of the Dukes of Burgundy. The industry prospered throughout the fourteenth and fifteenth centuries, until the depopulation of the city by Louis XI in 1477.

The only surviving piece to bear the name of Arras is a hanging signed by Pierre Feré and dated 1402, but it is possible that a few *mille fleurs*, small panels with a floral design, now in the Musée des Arts Décoratifs, Paris, are products of the town.

Arrasene, a delicate wool or silk chenille thread, was used mainly for mantle and curtain borders. It was worked on a variety of materials, such as serge, silk, velvet, or canvas, and usually executed in tent, stem, crewel stitch, or couching.
see: Tapestry and Carpets

Arretine Ware

A red or, occasionally, black pottery, also called Samian ware or *terra sigillata*. The finest of these wares were produced in Arrentium (Arezzo), now Italy, from about 200 B.C. to A.D. 100. The term Arretine, however, is also applied to pottery of a similar type produced in other areas of the Roman Empire after the decline of the Arrentium potters.

Page from block book entitled *Ars Moriendi* (The Art of Dying), *c.* 1465; British Museum, London. Pages of this kind were first printed from single wood blocks by rubbing paper against the inked surface. Block books were popular in the fifteenth century, particularly in Germany.

Music room at the Palace of Sanssouci (seventeenth century); Potsdam, Germany. The Prussian royal palace in Potsdam was considerably enlarged in the mid-eighteenth century by Frederick the Great. Through the merchant Johann Gotzkowsky, and others, he collected masterpieces of art and furniture with which he decorated the re-done palace in the rococo style of the period.

National Gallery of Art, Washington, D.C.

Leonardo da Vinci (1452-1519): *Ginevra de' Benci.* In 1967 the portrait of *Ginevra de' Benci* was purchased by the National Gallery, Washington, D.C., for a record price estimated to be between $5,000,000 and $6,000,000. The details of the negotiations and sale were kept secret, but on February 6, 1967 the sale was announced, and on March 17 the first public exhibition in the United States was held. The portrait, painted *c.* 1480 and long in the collection of the Princes of Liechtenstein, was originally somewhat larger that its present 15⅛ inches by 14½ inches; prior to 1780 a strip was cut from the bottom and a new piece, 1¾ inches high, was added. This later addition is now masked off by the sixteenth-century Italian frame.

Art Dealing

Works of art have been bought and sold from the earliest times, and the art market was a favorite subject of speculation and investment in the days of Imperial Rome. Roman sales of art objects of all kinds were as well organized as those of today, and Suetonius records one at which the property of Caligula was dispersed, during which the Emperor directed the auctioneer to take bids from the nodding head of a sleepy spectator. The unfortunate man awoke to find himself the owner of a large part of the Imperial collection at inflated prices. It is evident from this that even methods of bidding were much the same as they are at the great auctions today. Dealers clustered in the vicinity of the Via Publica, just as they do in Bond Street in London or East Fifty-Seventh Street in New York. The *Satyricon* of Petronius describes the acquisition of works of art at the banqueting table.

Since the Middle Ages the art market has nearly always been divisible into two fairly clear-cut trends, represented on the one hand by the scholarly collector, and on the other by the rich man who buys for prestige and display. Although recently the use of art as a symbol of status has been called into question, this has always been one of its main functions. Churches vied with each other in acquisition of rich decoration for their interiors, while kings and princes surrounded themselves with art objects as an outward and visible sign of power.

During medieval times the art market barely existed. Kings and powerful nobles were patrons of the arts. They bought from each other, or sent works of art as gifts. Art objects were also desirable acquisitions among the spoils of war. Many of the works of the time, especially illuminated manuscripts, were executed in monasteries, and the Church commissioned works of art in all kinds of materials. The art market as the Romans understood it, and as we know it today, did not begin to flourish afresh until the beginning of the Renaissance. The Medici family of Florence, merchants and entrepreneurs, were buyers of works of art on a large scale, and other rising merchant princes followed their example. Popes and cardinals, also, did not hesitate to purchase old works and to commission new ones.

Very frequently an artist will not sell his paintings if he feels that they are particularly successful or are pivotal pieces, with the result that works in the private collection of the artist are often among his most important output. For example, Marc Chagall painted *The Green Violinist* in 1918, and it remained in his personal collection for eighteen years. It was finally purchased from the artist in 1936 and given by Solomon R. Guggenheim to the Guggenheim Museum in 1937. This painting, with its floating figures and animals, the village scenes in the distance, and the general dream-like atmosphere, is typical of much of Chagall's work.

François Boucher (1703-1770): *Aminta Returned to Life in the Arms of Silvia*, oil; Musée, Tours, France. Following the French Revolution the market for such paintings as this, created for the *ancien régime*, was radically reduced. Many works of Boucher and Watteau were shipped to England by such art dealers as Daguerre in the hope they would bring better prices there.

The princes of the Habsburg family bought from the markets of Antwerp, Florence, and Augsburg, where many of the principal dealers were located, from the beginning of the sixteenth century onward. The Emperor Maximilian I ordered tapestries from Brussels and became the patron of Albrecht Dürer. To finance his purchases he borrowed heavily from the bankers of Augsburg, Jakob Fugger II and his associates. Jakob Fugger II invested heavily in the mining industry of Augsburg and the surrounding area and made a fortune from organizing it. It is said that his resources were such that he could, if necessary, deliver three tons of gold in a single hour. Jakob collected paintings; his nephew, Raimund Fugger, made the first collection of classical antiquities in Germany; and Johann Fugger, Raimund's son, started to buy on a large scale in 1566.

It is essential to remember that at this time painting was not the most valued of art forms. Tapestries, richly decorated gold and silver work, and fine furniture were all usually more expensive and in greater demand. Such things were designed, and often made, by painters and sculptors as part of their craft. The painted chests (*cassoni*) of Italy are an excellent illustration of this essential unity of the arts.

The art market grew in importance during the next 50 years. By the seventeenth century such notable collections as those of Charles I of England and Louis XIV of France were being formed. Charles I was a scholar and a man of taste, whose remarkable collection was dispersed by the Puritans under Cromwell. It consisted of nearly 1400 paintings and 400 sculptures, many of the greatest importance.

In France both Cardinal Richelieu and Cardinal Mazarin, as well as making purchases for their royal masters, were themselves avid collectors. Richelieu brought classical marbles from Rome and bought paintings and tapestries.

Mazarin's taste was similar, but he added to the numerous paintings, tapestries, oriental rugs, and fine furniture a taste for Chinese porcelain, silks, and lacquer. These were comparatively new arrivals in Northern Europe. They came from Holland, where the Dutch had been bringing in Oriental cargoes taken from Spanish and Portuguese ships as prizes of war.

The acquisitions of art treasures made by Louis XIV were, for the most part, destined for the Palace of Versailles, and his agent was the Finance Minister, Jean Baptiste Colbert. When he received his appointment the King possessed 200 paintings; at the time of Colbert's death the total had risen to 2,000, many of which had been bought from the Mazarin collection.

Colbert at first wanted to refurnish the Louvre, and he succeeded in employing the architect Claude Perrault to make extensive additions to it. The King preferred to reconstruct his hunting lodge at Versailles, and this was extensively rebuilt and the gardens were greatly enlarged and replanned. Versailles became Europe's largest and most richly furnished palace. The interior decoration was supervised and planned by Charles Lebrun, who was director of the Académie Royale de Peinture et de Sculpture, which had been founded by Colbert. The latter also founded the *Manufacture Royale des Meubles de la Couronne*, in the Gobelins factory, Paris, which supplied furniture, tapestries, paintings, and other *objets d'art* to the Court.

Louis XIV lost his taste for buying works of art after his marriage to Mme. de Maintenon, who caused Leonardo da Vinci's *Leda* to be burned because it offended her sense of propriety. Philippe, Duc d'Orléans, the Regent for Louis XV, had a collection of pictures which was the finest in private hands in France and contained some from the collection of Charles I. It was sold in England during the 1790's. Philippe's son, Louis, who was morbid and neurotic, destroyed some of the paintings in a fit of religious mania, damaging the *Leda* and *Io* by Antonio Correggio, which were rescued and restored by Charles Coypel.

Louis XV became an extensive buyer of works of art when he took Mme. Le Normant d'Étioles as his mistress, making her the Marquise de Pompadour and buying for her the Château de Bellevue. Earlier in the eighteenth century the art dealer Edmé-François Gersaint had played a notable part in making Chinese works of art fashionable by selling them at his shop, *à la Pagode*. During the period of the Marquise de Pompadour's influence the art dealer Lazare Duvaux supplied works of art of all kinds to

the Court. His account books still survive. Soon after this came the foundation in London of the famous auction rooms by James Christie, now Christie, Manson & Woods, Ltd. Priced catalogues have been preserved since 1766, removing much of the element of conjecture.

In the last decade of the seventeenth century Augustus the Strong, Elector of Saxony and King of Poland, began to add to the already existing family collections on a large scale. In the first year of his reign he is reputed to have spent 100,000 thalers (about $70,000 at the cur-

(above) Shop of the Casa Pirota: Enameled plate (1525); Victoria and Albert Museum, London. (below) School of Bernard Palissy: Ceramic pitcher (sixteenth century). These Italian and French *objets d'art*, respectively, were typical of the specialized mid-nineteenth-century taste of the English collector Ralph Bernal.

(above) J. George: Snuff box decorated in enamel and gold (1755-1756); Louvre, Paris. Snuff boxes have long been favorite collectors' items. (below) Pair of Meissen *monkey groups* with Louis XV ormolu mounts. (bottom) Water buffalo, Ming jade. Both the Rococo Meissen porcelain and the gray-colored jade were sold at high prices during recent years at Sotheby and Co., London, the latter item bringing a price of nearly $30,000.

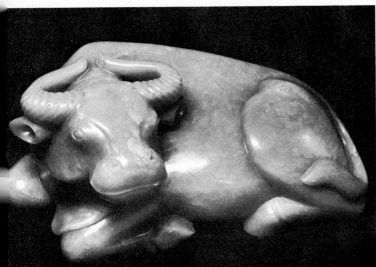

rent rate of exchange) on porcelain alone. He built the Zwinger, Dresden, for his art collection, and later acquired the Hollandische Palais for his porcelain collection, renaming it the Japanische Palais. He founded the Dresden picture gallery in 1694, principally with Dutch and Flemish paintings. His son, Augustus III, who was an even more prolific spender on paintings, sent an agent, Count Algarotti, to Italy. His minister, Count von Brühl, was also an ambitious collector. The two Electors bought more than 1,000 paintings for the Dresden collections.

Frederick the Great of Prussia was a man of taste who spent enormous sums on his acquisitions, especially those destined for the Palace of Sanssouci in Potsdam. By 1755 he had acquired more than 100 paintings, many of considerable importance, through the merchant and financier Johann Ernst Gotzkowsky, who not only had a large collection of his own from which he sold at intervals, but who was later entrusted by Frederick with the foundation of the Berlin porcelain factory. A record exists of one payment for pictures by Frederick to Gotzkowsky amounting to 115,520 Reichsthalers (about $78,000). Unlike Augustus, Frederick refused to impose taxes to pay for his acquisitions and several times rejected offers on this account.

Catherine the Great of Russia bought works of art, especially pictures, on a large scale. In 1769, six years after the death of von Brühl, she bought his entire picture collection, from which the Hermitage, Leningrad, has derived many of its finest paintings. She bought heavily at the notable Gaignat sale in Paris in 1768, and in 1772 she acquired about 400 pictures from the Crozat family, a collection formed by the banker and art patron Pierre Crozat. For these she paid 400,000 livres (roughly $140,000).

In England a number of collections were being formed in the middle of the eighteenth century and soon afterwards, which were later to become the subject of notable sales. Collecting in England received particular impetus from events on the Continent at the end of the eighteenth century. The French Revolution and the looting of Italy by Napoleon's troops considerably affected the subsequent course of art collecting. These two factors resulted in the removal of works of art from their owners on an unprecedented scale. Some were sold, some were destroyed, and some

Attributed to André Charles Boulle (1642-1732): Cabinet with marquetry of tin, brass, tortoise-shell, and decorated with ormolu mounts; Louvre, Paris. This elaborate piece of furniture in the Louis XIV style shows the richness of ornamentation favored by French connoisseurs of the late seventeenth and early eighteenth centuries.

André Charles Boulle: The so-called *Mazarine* chest. This was acquired by Louis XIV in 1708 for the Grand Trianon at Versailles. The inner legs were needed as additional support to the outer cabriole legs.

were later returned. Many were lost, and fortuitous discoveries in unlikely places today, when the object is not a forgery, are likely to be the result of this massive dispersal. The value of those works of decorative art which had been fashionable during the reigns of Louis XV and Louis XVI fell catastrophically. No one wanted paintings by Antoine Watteau and François Boucher, for example, for they reminded the Parisian buyer of the *ancien régime*. As a result many art objects were exported to England by the dealer Daguerre, who later followed them to London.

During the invasion of Italy, Napoleon's troops not only looted the collections of kings, the aristocracy, and the princes of the Church, but this kind of theft became a duty reinforced by

an army order. Later, removals to Paris were organized and supervised by the Baron Vivant-Denon, appointed by the director of the Fine Arts, Jacques-Louis David, for this purpose. English buyers in Italy were able to acquire pictures cheaply; it was more profitable to sell paintings at a low price than to lose them to marauding troops. In this way the two famous Claudes belonging to Prince Altieri were smuggled through the French lines in a small boat. Among the English collectors buying at the time was the eccentric William Beckford of Fonthill Abbey. His sale in 1823 was probably the largest and most important dispersal of works of art to be held in England up to that year. At this time the specialist collector did not exist. The taste of such buyers as Beckford was eclectic, and greater specialization of the kind to be seen in the Schreiber Collection, now in the Victoria and Albert Museum, London, began with the collection of Ralph Bernal, dispersed in 1855, which much influenced the future course of collecting. Bernal had concentrated on Sèvres porcelain and Italian maiolica, and prices for the latter in particular were high. They recovered from a fall owing to uncertainty caused by convincing fakes, and reached new and unforeseen levels before the end of the century. At this time, too, Bernard Palissy's sixteenth-century pottery was at the height of its popularity, a nineteenth-century fashion which has not been repeated. A dish brought £230 (£2,000: $5,600 by modern valuation—other prices in parentheses will indicate modern price equivalents) at the Bernal sale.

French furniture and porcelain, in many cases made little more than fifty years earlier, regained popularity after the Duke of Wellington's victory at Waterloo. George IV was a prominent buyer. The market for furniture was not governed by antique value; fine-quality reproductions, then completely new, were also realizing high prices. The King was followed by the 4th Marquess of Hertford, the principal creator of the Wallace Collection, and Sir Richard Wallace, although the prices they paid were small in comparison with those given by the House of Rothschild. Baron Edmond de Rothschild is reputed to have paid £30,000 ($504,000) for a *commode* once the property of Mme. du Barry—a price which exceeds anything paid before or since.

The picture market around mid-century can best be illustrated by a few examples. The National Gallery, London, had to pay £630 ($16,800) for the well-known *Giovanni Arnolfini and his Wife* by Jan van Eyck in 1842. A year or two before, Sir Edwin Landseer had sold the *Monarch of the Glen* for £350 ($8,400), and by 1874, when it was bought by a private collector, it had risen to £8,000 ($134,400). Andrea Mantegna's *Agony in the Garden* remained unsold in 1849 at £420 ($11,200), while Holman Hunt received £11,000 ($184,800) in 1874 for the *Shadow of the Cross*. Until the National Gallery paid £70,000 ($1,176,000) for Raphael's *Ansidei*

Madonna, in 1885, however, important *objets d'art* were generally more expensive than Old Master paintings. although disproportionately high prices were paid for the work of such living painters as William Powell Frith, whose *Railway Station* sold for £5,000 ($84,000) and Edwin Long, now forgotten, who received £7,350 ($126,000) for the *Babylonian Marriage Market*. It is impossible in the long history of the art market to find any tastes more paradoxical than those of the mid-Victorians in painting.

In the United States art dealing was dominated, up to the time of World War II at least, by the competitively acquisitive ambitions of a

An auction sale taking place at Sotheby and Co., Bond Street, London. The procedure at a few such galleries as this in London, Paris, and New York includes the advertising of each sale, the placing of a "reserve," or minimum price, on each item by the seller, and then the holding of the auction itself. In Paris the auctioneer is an independent expert who takes responsibility for the attributions of objects sold; in New York and London he is employed by the gallery and simply works for high bidding and an active turnover of property. London galleries are especially busy; Sotheby's in a recent year reported a turnover of about $20,000,000.

small group of millionaires. The pattern had been set by J. Pierpont Morgan at the turn of the century and was continued by collectors such as Andrew Mellon, Henry Huntington, Jules Bache, and Samuel H. Kress, often with the aid of dealers, notably Duveen's, but also including Wildenstein's and Knoedler's. This was the era of very large private fortunes and also the last time in which works of the highest quality were relatively plentiful, such as Thomas Gainsborough's painting *Blue Boy*, which sold for $875,000 in 1921.

Since World War II, the millionaire buyer has not disappeared (witness the activities of Charles Wrightsman and Paul Mellon), but the art market has nonetheless been obliged to operate on much lower levels. This was perhaps the natural result of a situation in which more and more people were becoming art conscious and had more money to spend. The idea of a work of art as security and as an investment has been with us since the earliest times, but the concept has been increasingly applied since World War II. In an unstable economic period many people

(right) French chest with decoration carved in high relief (sixteenth century); Musée des Arts Décoratifs, Paris The *cassone*, or chest, was one of the most sought-after pieces of furniture during the Renaissance, and major painters and wood carvers were commissioned to decorate chests for the wealthier families.

(left) Andrea Mantegna (1431-1506): *Agony in the Garden;* National Gallery; London. As an instance of the relatively low evaluation of old masters in mid-Victorian times, this painting by Mantegna remained unsold in 1849 at a price of $11,200 while *objets d'art* and the work of contemporary artists sold at prices greater than ◄ $100,000.

have seen works of art as a safe refuge for savings or spare capital.

The market has been dominated during this time by high taxation and inflation. The first has caused works of art to be bought, in those countries where the system operates, as gifts to museums against taxation rebates. This has led to the collector's buying not what appeals to him, but what the museum curator is prepared to take.

The American art market has also seen, since the war, an unparalleled interest in avant-garde art. As a result, art dealing at all levels has enjoyed a so far unbroken boom period, further helped by the scarcity of first-class works from before the 1850's and the tremendous prices realized by the productions of minor masters. There are over 300 galleries in New York City alone. The few really important pictures that come on to the market still tend to remain the prerogative of the big dealers or are sold by private negotiation. Increasingly high prices are now being paid for Old Master drawings and etchings as paintings come more rarely into the open market. The art market in the United States has never known a more generally prosperous period than in the years since World War II, and only a serious slump could show just how

inflationary and artificial postwar tendencies may have been.

Prices realized by the Impressionists and the immediate Post-Impressionists have been regarded as sensational, although they are lower in some cases than those paid for contemporary and recent work during the nineteenth century. Some of the Impressionists saw high prices being paid for their work during their lifetime. The *Danseuses à la Barre* of Edgar Degas, for instance, was bought for £21,000 ($336,000) in 1912, and Pierre August Renoir's *Mme. Charpentier* brought £3,500 ($58,800) in 1907. Any major Impressionist or Post-Impressionist work which came onto the market at present might be expected to fetch a minimum of $80,000. In 1958 Cézanne's *Boy in a Red Vest* sold at auction for $616,000, the highest price up to that time for an auction sale.

The taste of the 1890's for such objects as the *famille noire* and *famille jaune* vases of seventeenth-century China, and the less understandable demand for porcelain ginger jars decorated with the blue hawthorn pattern, gradually gave place in the 1920's to a fashion for early Sung wares. then to the more spectacular kinds of T'ang grave pottery, typified by the fighting

(above) Claes Oldenburg (born 1929): *Veal With Cream Sauce.* Artists have become, in the twentieth century, almost completely dependent upon art dealers for the promotion and sale of their work. The dealers can greatly contribute to the popularity of a style. A recent example of this is "Pop Art", which imitates as exactly as possible such commonplace items as food, or magnifies in a large painting a detail of a comic strip.

horses brought to England by George Eumorfopolous, and subsequently to a demand for Yuan and early Ming porcelain. This is now very much the scholar's preserve. In European porcelain there has been a movement away from excessive decoration toward the simpler, plainer objects of the early period. The Sèvres vases of Louis XV, which sold for very high prices in the nineteenth century, remain unaccountably low on the rare occasions on which they appear in the salesroom, despite the fashion for Rococo art and Louis XV furniture.

Almost a category by themselves, and certainly one of millionaire taste, are the small but expensive objects of *vertu* (curios) made by the Russian court goldsmith, Peter Carl Fabergé, (1896-1920), until about 1917. Chinese jades of the more ambitious kind, which have some relation to this aspect of the market, are also rising in price, and demand for the intricately decorated *cloisonné* enamels is increasing. German porcelain is now the most fashionable among collectors, and particularly high prices are being paid for the Rococo figures of Franz Anton Bustelli of Nymphenburg. Silver, too, has shared in the change of taste. The former high prices paid for Renaissance and seventeenth-century silver are no longer so noticeable, but there has been a marked appreciation in the plain silver of Queen Anne and the Rococo decorations of such silversmiths as Paul de Lamerie.

Generally, there are now two markets. On the one hand is the demand for fine craftsmanship implicit in the demand for French furniture,

finely carved jades. and Rococo silver. Prices paid for these have overtaken those for Old Masters of all but the finest quality and usually exceed those for medium-quality pictures. On the other hand, the market for painting and sculpture may be roughly divided into the ultra-fashionable, which is prepared to pay high prices for works which are the product of the latest movements, and that for the established masters, up to the early twentieth century. In this last category we have the example of Rembrandt's *Aristotle Contemplating the Bust of Homer*, which was bought by the Metropolitan Museum of Art, New York, in 1961, for $2,300,000, the highest price ever paid at a public sale for any painting. And in 1967 the National Gallery of Art, Washington, acquired Leonardo's *Ginevra de' Benci* for a price reputed to be between $5 and $6 million.

Arthois, Jacques d' (1613-c. 1686)

Flemish landscape painter, born in Brussels. Although he was well known in his day, little is now known of Arthois' life, and it is presumed that he worked in and around Brussels, often in collaboration with his brother, Nicholas.

Arthois was inspired by the countryside surrounding his birthplace. His large, naturalistic landscapes, usually sketched directly from nature

(top) Silver teapot, mark of the Bateman Family (1802-1803); Victoria and Albert Museum, London. At a high premium today are examples such as this from the Georgian period, admired for their classic simplicity.

and completed in his studio, are characterized by skillful contrasts of light and shade. Many of his paintings include figures or even religious scenes, but these are always subordinated to the grandeur of the landscapes. A large portion of his works are winter scenes.

Landscape with Figures, Kunsthistorisches Museum, Vienna, and *The Edge of the Wood*, Musées Royaux des Beaux-Arts, Brussels, are typical of his work. Other paintings by Arthois are in the Louvre, Paris, and the Glasgow Art Gallery, Scotland.

see: Flemish Art and Architecture

Three Chinese objects of art representing materials, styles, and craftsmanship for which high prices are paid. (far left) Jade carving of the summit of Huan Shan of Shensi (the Sacred Mountain of the West), with nine poems engraved on the thrones of the gods; Museo Poldi-Pezzoli, Milan, Italy. (left) Rice Cup from the Wan Li period (1573-1619), enameled porcelain; formerly Imperial Collection, Taipeh, Formosa. (right) Cloisonné enamel from the Ming Dynasty (fourteenth to seventeenth centuries); Museo Poldi-Pezzoli, Milan.

Peter Blume (born 1906): *The Rock* (1948), oil; Courtesy of Art Institute of Chicago, Illinois. Gift of Edgar Kaufmann, Jr. The enigmatic surrealism of this American painter is represented in the comprehensive collections of the Art Institute, which covers European, American, Oriental, and contemporary art.

Art Institute of Chicago

Founded in 1882, the Art Institute of Chicago replaced the Chicago Academy of Fine Arts. which had been established three years previously. It now includes a public museum of art; a junior museum for children; the Goodman Memorial Theater and School of Drama; a school of fine and applied arts which grants both bachelor's and master's degrees; and the Ryerson and Burnham libraries, which contain more than 70,000 books on art and architecture. The central building was opened in 1893 and has been expanded many times, most recently by the addition of a new gallery wing in 1962.

The collections of the Art Institute, the nucleus of which came from Chicago donors, are extensive and embrace many fields ranging from Far Eastern arts to contemporary American painting, sculpture, and graphic arts. Of extraordinary quality is the large group of works by late nine-

teenth-century French painters such as Édouard Manet, Paul Cézanne, and Georges Seurat, including Seurat's masterpiece *A Sunday Afternoon on the Island of the Grande Jatte* (1886). Of note also are the Clarence Buckingham collection of oriental art and the large and important collection of European and American prints and drawings. Among the many paintings of particular interest are El Greco's *Assumption of the Virgin* and Rembrandt's *Portrait of his Father*.

In addition to its program of special exhibitions, the Institute presents annually an exhibition of art from the Chicago area and an exhibition of contemporary American painting and sculpture. It maintains an active program of public education for school children and adults.

Art Nouveau

An international movement of "new art" which became current in Europe and the United States at the turn of the twentieth century. Art Nouveau is often characterized by certain recurrent stylistic elements, particularly by two-dimensional linear design and the use of sinuous, often plant-like arabesques. The movement took significantly varying forms in different countries, and it remains difficult to trace the passage of influences. In addition to its strictly stylistic aspects, Art Nouveau was important as a protest against nineteenth-century historicism; its readiness to use new materials, especially iron, and attempts to create and develop a universal style both for architecture, painting, and sculpture and for the applied arts give it a place as a precursor of modern art.

Called Art Nouveau in France, England and the United States, the equivalent movements received different names in each country. In France it was also called by such English names as "Modern Style" or "Yachting Style" as well as *Le Style 1900* or *Style Métro*. The Italian term was *Stile Liberty*, derived from Liberty's shop in the Strand, London, which specialized in orientalized fabrics; the more descriptive *Stile Floreale* was also used. In Germany it was called *Jugendstil*, after the magazine *Die Jugend*, started in Munich in 1896 by the German painter Georg Hirth. In Austria the new mode was known as *Sezessionstil*, after the exhibition which first publicized it. Belgium, one of the most important centers of the movement, gave it the name *Paling Stijl* (eel-style), after the curving line which was its most typical feature. The attempts of the artists concerned to popularize the movement resulted in a proliferation of new art magazines and exhibitions.

Although an antihistorical movement, Art Nouveau had many sources, depending often on national characteristics. Its English exponents drew on Celtic art, while the Spanish architect Antonio Gaudí formed his own unique interpretation through Moorish antecedents, among others. The influences of medieval manuscripts, Japanese prints, Gothic art, and of forms from the animal and vegetable kingdom were all variously utilized. Of nineteenth-century sources, French architectural metal constructions and the theories of Eugène Viollet-le-Duc were important, as well as the ideas of John Ruskin and the English Arts and Crafts Movement under William Morris.

The earliest known fully developed example of Art Nouveau is the design of Arthur H. Mackmurdo (1851-1942) for the cover of his book *Wren's City Churches*, which appeared in 1883. The work of William Morris in typography, together with the earlier achievements of William Blake in designing type and illustration as a unified whole, and some of Dante Gabriel Rossetti's designs for book covers, afforded rich antecedents to Mackmurdo, whose influence, with that of Aubrey Beardsley (1872-1898), was important throughout Europe. Beardsley's contribution to Art Nouveau lay in his unique line and sophisticated use of blank space on the page, reminiscent of the Japanese influence

Aubrey Beardsley (1872-1898): Illustration for Oscar Wilde's *Salome*. Beardsley's mannered use of black and white and his finely wrought line comprised a widely influential manifestation of the Art Nouveau movement. Both Wilde and his artist made of this narrative a revealing reflection of late Victorian decadence and artificiality.

which James McNeill Whistler helped to introduce in England. Like Gustav Klimt (1862-1918) on the Continent, Beardsley was fascinated by the theme of Salome, so associated with the *fin-de-siècle* "decadence" which was responsible for much that is mannered and artificial in the new style. Art Nouveau is inseparably connected with "art for art's sake"; the work of the writers Joris-Karl Huysmans and Oscar Wilde and of the French symbolist poets was greatly admired and appeared in many of the new magazines.

Probably the outstanding contribution of English Art Nouveau to the Continental movements was that of Charles Rennie Mackintosh (1868-1928), a Scots architect and designer whose work was highly praised at the Vienna *Sezession* exhibition. His most typically Art Nouveau works are the designs for Miss Cranston's

(right) Wardrobe decorated with hand painted floral designs; Villa Scalini, Carbonate, Italy. Simple and functional in design, compared to *fin-de-siècle* furniture in general, this Art Nouveau wardrobe is relieved of any latent severity by the colorful floral patterns. (far right) Victor Horta: Interior stairs of the Tassel House (1892); Brussels, Belgium. Art Nouveau style appears here at its boldest in the supporting iron column, foliating at the top into curved tendrils, and in the linear designs on the floor and in the balustrades. ▶

(left) Giuseppe Brega: Villino Ruggeri (1908); Pesaro, Italy. This example of the Art Nouveau style in Italian architecture shows the use of arabesque decoration in the form of trees and flowers, motifs which were more often used for interior decoration and furniture.

Buchanan Street Tearooms in Glasgow (1897). Mackintosh planned not only the layout for these, but also the mural decorations, in accordance with the prevalent notion that the architect or interior decorator should be responsible for every aspect of his project.

In Henri van de Velde (1863-1957) and Victor Horta (1861-1947), Belgium possessed one of Art Nouveau's most important theorists and designers, and one of its most productive architects. Van de Velde was active principally as a designer of interiors, furniture, and household equipment, but was also known as a graphic designer. In 1895 he built and furnished a house at Uccle, near Brussels, as a demonstration of his theories of

design. As was the case with Mackintosh in England, van de Velde's interpretation of the Art Nouveau concept of "organic" structure was abstract, as opposed to the "organic" forms imitated from natural life by the majority of his contemporaries.

Horta must be considered one of the few authentic Art Nouveau architects. The movement seldom achieved a successful large-scale three-dimensional interpretation of its successes in the design of smaller objects, such as glass, jewelry, and furniture, and in the decoration of flat surfaces. In Horta's Tassel House in Brussels (1892-1893) and the Maison du Peuple, also in Brussels (1895-1900), he created a valid personal style, with a very imaginative use of iron and, in the latter, glass. He also designed furniture, and the interiors of his houses show a profusion of intricate plantlike ironwork, of which the best-known example is the staircase of the Tassel House.

Among the Germans working in Munich may be mentioned Otto Eckmann (1865-1902), August Endell (1871-1925), Hermann Obrist (1863-1927), a Swiss who went to Munich in 1894, and Richard Riemerschmid (1868-1957). Eckmann was active as a type-designer and graphic artist in the rather florid German Art Nouveau style. Endell's Studio Elvira (1897-1898), now destroyed, incorporated an orientalized abstract relief on the flat façade, with an unusual asymmetrical disposition of door and windows. Obrist's distinctive work in embroidery used Art Nouveau abstracted plant motifs. Riemer-

schmid's designs emphasized to an unusual degree the importance of function; their simplicity is well illustrated by the chair in the Museum of Modern Art, New York.

Gustav Klimt's murals for Josef Hoffmann's Palais Stoclet in Brussels (1905-1911) unite two of the best-known members of the Viennese School. The architecture of Hoffmann (1870-1956) is calm and geometrical, contrasting with the sensuousness of Klimt's decoration. Klimt's paintings, often on literary themes, such as the *Salome* (1909) in the Galleria di Ca' Pesaro, Venice, were internationally famous, and constitute in their flowing line and delicately modulated color one of the rare examples of a painter completely at ease in a full Art Nouveau style. Other prominent members of the Viennese school were Josef Maria Olbrich (1867-1908), active as a designer and later as an avant-garde

(below) Victor Horta: Salon, Tassel House (1892); Brussels, Belgium. In Horta's work the curvilinear elegance of Art Nouveau expanded successfully into a full architectural scale, by use of glass and structural and decorative iron.

(below) Hermann Obrist: Wall hanging (1895); Stadtmuseum, Munich, Germany. The S-curves of Obrist's embroidered design work the essentials of this single plant—a whiplash, or cyclamen—into fluently yet flatly stylized decoration.

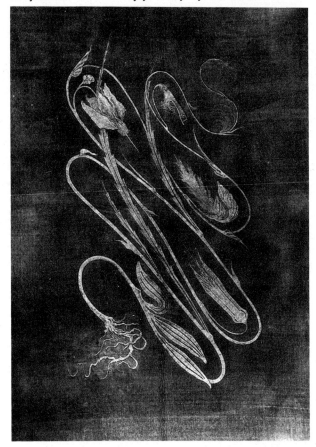

(above) Louis Comfort Tiffany (1848-1933): Favrile glass vase late nineteenth century; Cooper Union Museum, New York, given by Harry Harkness Flagler. Tiffany's organic use of line relates his work to the Art Nouveau movement; and his glassware, with its iridescent sheen, became popular again in the 1960's.

architect, and Otto Wagner (1871-1918), who taught both Hoffmann and Olbrich, and who utilized Art Nouveau motifs in his Majolika Haus (*c.* 1898) and the Stadtbahn stations he built between 1894 and 1901.

The French architect Hector Guimard (1867-1942) built the eccentric Métro entrances which gave Art Nouveau one of its names in France, with an imaginative use of glass and iron. The glassware of Émile Gallé (1846-1904), the jewelry of René Lalique (1860-1945), and the pottery of Auguste Delaherche (1857-1940) were other manifestations of French Art Nouveau, elegant and often luxurious, particularly in the applied arts. The same lushness is visible in the decoration of the Samaritaine Department Store (1905), Paris, by Franz Jourdain (1847-1935). Art Nou-

(left) Gustav Klimt (1862-1918): *Salome,* oil; Ca' Pesaro, Venice, Italy. Klimt developed the patterned, decorative terms of Art Nouveau into a vocabulary fully equipped to deal with such dramatic material as this.

veau was a very strong influence on painting and poster design in France. Toulouse-Lautrec's work in both media and that of Pierre Bonnard show the closest association with Art Nouveau, which had a strong effect on nearly all young European painters. These included Pablo Picasso, Wassily Kandinsky, Émile Bernard, Edvard Munch, Paul Gauguin, and Ferdinand Hodler, whose work also displays the influence of the English pre-Raphaelites on Art Nouveau.

The principal American artist working in a full Art Nouveau style was Louis Comfort Tiffany (1848-1933), whose glassware and stained glass windows had a considerable vogue in both the United States and Europe. Tiffany experimented with chemical and metallic substances to produce exotic glazes and iridescent sheens in his glassware, whose designs often derived from plant forms. The architect Louis Sullivan (1856-1924) used an elaborate form of ironwork decoration on some of his buildings of this

period, notably the Carson Pirie, Scott and Co. Building (1903-1904) in Chicago, whose complex convolutions are reminiscent of Gothic decorative elements.

Other important figures were the German architect and designer Peter Behrens (1868-1938), the Dutch textile designer Theodorus Colenbrander (1841-1930), and the Italian architects Giuseppe Sommaruga (1867-1917) and Raimondo d'Aronco (1857-1932), the latter of whom designed the buildings for the Turin Exhibition held in 1902.

Finally, mention must be made of the most extraordinary member of the whole movement, the Spanish architect Antonio Gaudí (1852-1926). His work in Barcelona will not fit closely into any category, but his use of plastic curving forms and unusual materials relates him to Art Nouveau. Gaudí's determination not to be bound either by conventional structure, materials, or techniques escapes being ludicrous because of

Louis Comfort Tiffany: Glass vases; Museum für Kunst und Gewerbe, Hamburg, Germany. These examles of Tiffany's glassware illustrate the highly personalized Art Nouveau combination of natural and artificial forms, of function and ornamentation. Favrile glass was the invention of Tiffany; in the process of making the glass, a variety of colors was used to create iridescent effects.

Antonio Gaudí (1852-1926): Church of the Sagrada Familia; Barcelona, Spain. This imaginative architect reflected in his nonconformist work, based to some extent on Gothic ideas, certain of the linear and organic characteristics of Art Nouveau. A deeply religious mystic, he conceived this church, begun in 1884 and never completed, as an enormous piece of sculpture rather than as conventional architecture.

the imagination and vigor of his designs, such as the fantastic spires of the unfinished Church of the Sagrada Familia (begun 1884) or the curves of the façade of the Casa Milá (1905-1907), an apartment building.

Gaudí's work illustrates the essential limitation of Art Nouveau, and that which made it only a transitional period in the development of most of its adherents. In the applied arts and in architecture, Art Nouveau was too individualistic to provide a viable new tradition in an age mov-

ing toward mass production and standardized components. Its aesthetic basis was often in direct contradiction to function, and apart from certain unique creations, such as those of Beardsley, Gaudí, or Klimt, its main importance may be said to be that it encouraged a profusion of new forms and ideas, some of which were to provide points of departure for later developments in the twentieth century.

see: entries for specific artists mentioned in this article

William Morris (1834-1896): Page from a handwritten manuscript of the Odes of Horace; Bodleian Library, Oxford, England. Morris, who guided the Arts and Crafts Movement during the latter half of the nineteenth century, derived many of his designs, as here, from natural forms. His practice of a modified medieval style of calligraphy and hand illumination provided the bases of his later production of fine books at the Kelmscott Press.

Arts and Crafts Movement

A movement that flourished in England during the latter half of the nineteenth century. Its goal was to bring art into the daily life of all social classes. There were a number of contributory factors, among them the teaching of John Ruskin and the work of the Pre-Raphaelite Brotherhood. However, the major figure and guiding force of the movement was William Morris (1834-1896)—architect, painter, interior decorator and designer, illustrator, poet, essayist, and Socialist.

Morris wished to break away from the traditional private and individual forms of art, existing, as he saw it, only for the rich and leisured classes, and to make art part of the life of the community. While accepting the great changes made by the Industrial Revolution, he hoped that, by a revival of the applied arts, based on the medieval ideals of craftsmanship and the

"hallowing of nature by art," the mass of society might be, in his own words, persuaded to: "Have nothing in your houses that you do not know to be useful, or believe to be beautiful."

To this end, the firm of Morris, Marshall, Faulkner & Co. was founded in 1861. Among the original partners with Morris were Dante Gabriel Rossetti, Ford Madox Brown, Edward Burne-Jones, and Philip Webb, the architect who had designed and built Morris' Red House at Bexley Heath. The firm, established on sound commercial lines in spite of its uncompromising idealism, had its first success at the International Exhibition of 1862. Showing stained glass designed by Rossetti, furniture and embroideries, it won two gold medals and took substantial orders. One of the pieces exhibited, the St. George Cabinet, designed by Webb and decorated by Morris, is now in the Victoria and Albert Museum, London. The firm remained in production until 1940.

The tendency of the Arts and Crafts Movement was always toward Socialism, since profound changes in the social structure were all that could put the work of the craftsman, with its emphasis on quality of material and execution, within the reach of the great majority of the wage-earning classes. Walter Crane, the painter and illustrator, wrote: "The decline of art corresponds with its conversion into portable forms of private property, or material or commercial speculation. . . . All really great works of art are public works . . . expressing the ideas of a race, a community, a united people; not the ideas of a class." Morris himself joined the Democratic Federation in 1883 and in 1885 founded the Socialist League, contributing in no small measure to the emergence of the Labour Party as a political power in the early years of the twentieth century.

In 1884 the Art Workers' Guild was formed, Morris being one of the earliest members. When a number of painters revolted ineffectively against the methods of the Hanging Committee of the Royal Academy Exhibition, the craftsmen and decorative artists who had supported them, under the leadership of Crane, combined in 1888 to form the Arts and Crafts Exhibition Society. At their exhibition in that year, woodcarving, metalwork, spinning, weaving, needlework, pottery, and basketwork were shown, in addition to painting and sculpture.

By this time the ideas of Morris and his associates, while not producing the desired social revolution, had had a profound influence on matters relating to architecture and the applied arts in general among the middle classes in Great Britain and on the Continent. Among the architects influenced by the movement were Norman Shaw, C. F. A. Voysey, Basil Champneys, W. R. Lethaby, and M. H. Bailie Scott. Their work had its major result in the town-planning movement of the twentieth century.

The greatest success of the movement was its revival of printing as an art form. This had begun in 1844 with the work of the Chiswick Press, but it was in the 1890's, with the work of Morris, Charles Ricketts, and Sir Emery Walker, that printing, combining legibility with aesthetic value, came into its own.

Morris had supervised the production of four books at the Chiswick Press, and in the years 1890-1891 he produced the first Kelmscott Press books, his own *Story of the Glittering Plain* and *Poems by the Way*. In all, 53 works were produced between 1891 and 1897, in types designed by Morris and inspired by the fifteenth-century printers, Jonson and Caxton, but with Gothic additions. The masterpiece of the Kelmscott Press is the *Works of Geoffrey Chaucer* (1896), decorated by Morris and with 86 illustrations by Burne-Jones. Ricketts' Vale Press productions owed a great deal to Morris, but were superbly illustrated by Ricketts himself and by Charles Shannon.

The English Arts and Crafts Movement of the nineteenth century had a profound effect on the development of popular taste, both then and in the present century, and it is to Morris and his associates that part of the credit is due for certain of the aesthetic standards of good twentieth-century furnishing and decoration.
see: Morris, William

Arundel, Thomas Howard, 14th Earl of (1585-1646)

English nobleman, renowned as a collector of works of art. Arundel was the first member of the English aristocracy to study, as an archaeologist, the antique European civilizations at first hand. During 1613 and 1614 he organized excavations in Italy with the young Inigo Jones, and with his findings he assembled the nucleus of

Burne-Jones, Sir Edward (1833-1898): First two pages of the Kelmscott Press edition of the Works of Geoffrey Chaucer (1896); British Museum, London. William Morris' friend Burne-Jones illustrated and ornamented this edition. Morris, who founded the press to revive printing as an art form, designed the so-called "Chaucer type". The overall weaving of the ornament evokes the medieval style.

Egid Quirin and Cosmas Damian Asam: Church of St. John Nepomuk (1733-1735); Munich, Germany (left) Interior view toward the altar. (above) Detail of ceiling and sculptured decoration. This tiny church, built adjoining the two brothers' own house and at their expense, is a masterpiece of the German Baroque. It intensifies the atmosphere of religious fervor through its illusionism, an effect produced by combined architectural and sculptural forms.

the first large English collection of Greek and Roman inscriptions, coins, and statues.

In addition to his passion for archaeological treasures, Arundel collected drawings and paintings. He admired Flemish and German painting of the sixteenth century, in particular the portraiture of Holbein the Younger, acquiring, among many others, portraits of *Edward VI,* National Gallery of Art, Washington, D.C., and *Christina of Denmark,* National Gallery, London. He also owned the magnificent collection of Leonardo da Vinci drawings now at Windsor Castle.

Arundel's interests were not, however, confined to the arts of the past. He was one of the first patrons of Daniel Mytens when the latter arrived in England *c.* 1618, and he sat for both Anthony Van Dyck (portrait in Kunsthistorisches Museum, Vienna) and Peter Paul Rubens (portraits in the Gardner Museum, Boston, and National Gallery, London). Evidence of the contemporary respect extended to Arundel is indicated in the dedication of Edward Norgate's *Miniatura or the Art of Limning.*

At the outbreak of the Civil War in 1642 Arundel left England. After his death in Padua four years later, his collections were gradually dispersed by the family over a long period. Much of the antique statuary found a final home in the Ashmolean Museum, Oxford, and his large libary was given to the Royal Society, the manuscript section passing to the British Museum, London, in 1831.

Asam Family
A family of Bavarian painters, best known for their frescoes in Bavarian churches. The first

important member of the family was Hans Georg Asam (*c.* 1649-1711), probably born near Wessobrunn. Among his principal works are the frescoes for the Church of Benediktbeuern (1688-1694), and the murals (*c.*1680/90) for the convent at Tegernsee, Germany.

The most notable artist of the family was the eldest son of Hans Georg, Cosmas Damian Asam (1686-1739), who was born in Benediktbeuern. With his brother, Egid Quirin (Aegidius; 1692-1750), Cosmas studied under Pierleone Ghezzi in Rome and he became a skillful painter in the Rococo style. He settled in Munich and decorated numerous churches in Bavaria and Switzerland, sometimes in collaboration with his brother, who was active as a sculptor. Their most notable joint work was at Freising Cathedral (1723-

1724). The brothers also worked in Munich, Innsbruck, Regensburg, and elsewhere. Cosmas also made prints from his own works, and was, for some time, court painter to the Elector of Bavaria.
see: German Art and Architecture

Ashbee, Charles Robert (1863-1942)

English architect, designer, writer, and art connoisseur, born in Isleworth, Middlesex. Ashbee was much influenced by the work and ideas of C. F. A. Voysey, Norman Shaw, Philip Webb, and other architects and designers associated with the Arts and Crafts movement under William Morris. In 1888 he founded the Guild of Handicrafts and, later, the London Survey Committee and The Essex House Press. He is also well known for his efforts to preserve old buildings, especially churches. Although closely connected with the Arts and Crafts movement,

George Bellows (1882-1925): *Dempsey and Firpo* (1924), oil on canvas 51 x 63¼"; Collection Whitney Museum of American Art, New York. Bellows was a leading member of the Ashcan School in New York City during the 1920's. This group of American painters depicted realistic scenes of life in the city, such as this championship boxing match.

Amico Aspertini: Detail from *Adoration of the Magi,* oil; Pinacoteca, Bologna, Italy. Aspertini based his compositions of soft forms and warm colors on the work of Francesco Francia and Lorenzo Costa. These two Renaissance painters ran a workshop in Bologna, in which Aspertini may have been a pupil in the late fifteenth century.

Ashbee was more far-sighted than Morris and his companions, who deplored machine-made objects. Ashbee recognized the permanence of the machine in modern life.

As an architect, Ashbee produced relatively few buildings of his own design, but examples of his silverwork can be seen in the Victoria and Albert Museum, London. Among his written works are *Craftsmanship in Competitive Industry*; *Modern Silverwork*; and *The Treasures of Benvenuto Cellini*.

see: Arts and Crafts Movement

Ashcan School

A school of American painters of city genre scenes. The Ashcan School was so called by its critics and the public, and the name superseded the original title "The Eight," under which it held its first exhibitions at the Macbeth Gallery, New York, in 1908. The original "Eight" were Robert Henri, William Glackens, George Luks, John Sloan, Everett Shinn, Maurice Prendergast, Ernest Lawson, and Arthur Davies. They shared no common style, but had an admiration for the philosophy and art of Franz Hals, Francisco

Goya, Édouard Manet and Honoré Daumier. The first five of the above painters studied under Thomas Eakins in Philadelphia. They were realists, concerned with social criticism and in opposition to the European Academic style. Technically there were considerable differences among the School's members. Many of them evolved a style reminiscent of magazine illustration, but the influence was reciprocal.

The center of the movement later shifted to New York, where in the early 1920's Gifford Beal and George Bellows were the leading members. There was a continuing emphasis on social and moral commentary. The Ashcan School was also instrumental in the organization and composition of the Armory Show in 1913.

see: Armory Show; Eight, The; United States Art and Architecture

Ashlar

see: Architectural Terms

Aspertini, Amico (c. 1475-1552)

Italian painter, draftsman, and sculptor, born in Bologna. Aspertini was probably a pupil of

(left) Jan Asselijn: *Fishing for Cuttlefish at Night,* oil; Royal Museum, Copenhagen, Denmark. This Italianate Dutch artist, influenced by the Arcadian landscapes of Claude Lorraine, was associated with the group known as "Bamboccianti," whose popular subject matter ran counter to the officially acceptable Baroque art.

(right) Basilica of San Francesco, Assisi, Italy, southern flank. Arches dominate the exterior from those crowning the powerful square campanile to those which support the buttressing along the side. This Gothic structure was begun almost immediately after the canonization of St. Francis, in 1228, and both the upper and lower churches are filled with frescoes showing scenes from his life. ▶

Ercole de' Roberti and also Lorenzo Costa. As a painter he shows a weak sense of composition, and his major work, the *History of the Crucifixion* (1506-1510), a fresco in the Chapel of Sant'Agostino in San Frediano, Lucca, suffers from the strained attitudes of the figures. His only known sculptural work is *The Dead Christ in the Arms of Nicodemus* (1526), on the façade of San Petronio, Bologna.

Aspertini's main importance lies in his drawings of scenes of Greek and Roman life. Three folios of these drawings exist; two sketchbooks in the British Museum, London, and the so-called Wolfegg Codex, Fürstliche Sammlungen, Wolfegg, Germany. In these he shows an interest in antiquity at its least ideal and intel-

lectual. The nervous line of the notebooks and their fantastic, often grotesque, imagination offer a bizarre contrast to the High Renaissance interpretation of antiquity in its more classical and formal aspects.

Asplund, Erik Gunnar (1885-1940)

Swedish architect, born in Stockholm. Asplund's early work combined classical forms and motifs with traditional Swedish forms. An example of his work of this period is the Skandia Cinema, Stockholm, designed in 1922-1923. During the following six years he was principally engaged on the design of the Central Library, Stockholm. Here, under the influence of Otto Wagner and of the international style, particularly the work of Walter Gropius, his style became progressively more simple and geometric. The building, completed in 1928, is a severe square edifice with a central drum tower and a minimum of external ornament.

Asplund was the architect in charge of the Stockholm Exhibition of 1930 and designed most of the buildings. His work on this exhibition was an important landmark in the development of both Swedish and European modern architecture. Using clean geometrical forms, with cantilevers and glass walls, the buildings' design and layout created a new environment, widely acclaimed at the time for its gaiety and imagination.

In his subsequent work Asplund attempted to interpret the international style in a more traditional way, while maintaining the ideals of Wagner, in a style which has been called "national functionalism." Examples of this are the Town Hall in Gothenburg (1933-1937), his department stores, such as the Bredenberg Store (1933-1935) in Stockholm, and the main achievement of his later years, the chapels of the crematorium in Skogskyrkogarden, outside Stockholm (1935-1940).
see: Scandinavian Art and Architecture

Asselijn (Asselyn), Jan (c. 1610-1652)

Dutch landscape painter, birthplace uncertain but is probably either Dieppe, France, or Diepen, Holland. Thought to be a pupil of Esaias van de Velde, Asselijn seems to have been in Italy between 1641 and 1645, and was in France in 1645-1646, before returning to Amsterdam in 1647. It was at this time that Rembrandt etched his portrait. In Italy, he became familiar with the work of Claude Lorraine, whose influence, together with that of Jan Both and Pieter van Laer, is discernible in Asselijn's work.

Among his better-known works is the *Angry Swan*, Rijksmuseum, Amsterdam. Other works are in the Los Angeles County Museum; the Fogg Art Museum, Cambridge, Massachusetts; the Uffizi, Florence; and the Louvre, Paris.

Assisi

A town in Umbria, central Italy, birthplace of St. Francis of Assisi (1182-1226), and the scene of his foundation of the Franciscan Order in 1209. The friary and basilica of St. Francis were built in the Gothic style between 1228 and 1253. The basilica consists of an upper and lower church, containing frescoes by the principal

thirteenth- and early fourteenth-century Italian masters and their pupils.

By far the most important of the painters employed at Assisi was Giotto. Due largely to the conflicting evidence of Giorgio Vasari's report and to varying stylistic indications in the frescoes, the actual extent of Giotto's work is now one of the most controversial problems of art history. However, the 28 large frescoes in the Upper Church depicting the *Life of St. Francis* are generally attributed to this Florentine master. Above these are works attributed to Pietro Cavallini, the School of Cimabue, and probably Giotto. In the vaults above the crossing are other works by him and his pupils; the *Crucifixion, Visions of the Apocalypse, Life of Mary*, and *Life of St. Peter*, are in the apse and transepts.

In the more austere Lower Church, the Chapel of St. Martin contains Simone Martini's *Scenes from the Life of St. Martin*. The *Scenes from the Life of St. Catherine* are probably the work of Andrea da Bologna. The walls of the nave of the Lower Church are decorated by early thirteenth-century frescoes, the oldest in the basilica attributed to the Master of St. Francis. Pietro Lorenzetti executed *The Madonna and Child with St. John and St. Francis* and the *Deposition* in the south transept. The Gothic ambo was decorated by a follower of Giotto.

(below) Giovanni da Gubbio: Church of San Ruffino (begun 1140); Assisi, Italy. The façade of this church, with its three rose windows, progresses harmoniously in style from the Romanesque of the bottom level to full Gothic at the top. (right) Detail of fresco portraying *The Appearance of St. Francis to Gregory IX*, Basilica Superiore, Assisi, Italy. This is one of twenty-eight scenes from the life of St. Francis; these frescoes have been attributed to Giotto, although present scholars question whether he executed them all.

Assyrian Art
see: Babylonian and Assyrian Art

Astbury Family
Family of Staffordshire potters. John Astbury 1686/1688-1743) is traditionally credited with the manufacture of red earthenware teapots and figures of soldiers and musicians in red and white. Through his collaboration with a Thomas Whieldon (1719-1795), the pieces that were decorated with a metallic oxide coloring were known as the Astbury-Whieldon Ware. John Astbury is also cited by a contemporary source as the first user of Devonshire white firing clays and calcined flints in the manufacture of earthenware, but it is more probable that this was the work of Whieldon. Although no authenticated pieces of his work are extant, since there are no identifying marks by either Astbury or Whieldon, signed examples by Astbury's son Thomas, who started business in 1725, and by his grandson, are preserved in the Art Institute of Chicago and the Metropolitan Museum of Art, New York.
see: Pottery and Porcelain

Atelier
French term for an artist's workshop or studio. One type is the *atelier libre,* or open studio, where for a specific fee any artist has the use of a studio and a model. In the nineteenth century Eugène Delacroix, Gustave Courbet, and several Impressionist painters frequented the studio of the model Suisse in Paris. Although there is no formal instruction in an *atelier libre,* it may also be called an *académie.* The Atelier Julian, opened in 1860 in Paris, did provide a teacher and would be referred to as a studio. Another well-known studio is the international Atelier Fernand Léger that reached its height in Paris during the 1920's.

Athenodorus of Teos
A name given to two unrelated Greek sculptors of whom little is known. The earlier is believed to have executed the statues of Apollo and Zeus which the Spartans dedicated at Delphi after the Battle of Aegospotami in 405 B.C.

The other Athenodorus, active *c.* 25 B.C., is believed to have been the son and assistant of Alexander of Rhodes, with whom he worked, together with Polydorus, on the marble group depicting *Laocoön and his Sons* found in Rome in 1506 and now in the Vatican Museum. This attribution depends on the identification of the piece with the one described by Pliny in his *Natural History.*

Stoa of Attalos II on the east side of the Agora; Athens, Greece. This is a modern reconstruction of the building of the second century B.C. Facing one side of Athens' most important public meeting place, the two-storeyed portico, with Ionic columns above the Doric, provided a walking area in front of a row of shops. The stoas of Zeus and Hermes, on the west and north sides respectively, were both built in the fifth century B.C.

Theseum, or Temple of Hephaestus (449-444 B.C.); Athens, Greece. Begun two years before the Parthenon, this best-preserved of Greek temples is a classic example of the Doric style. Its columns are slenderer than those on the Parthenon and its entablature, with a frieze of triglyphs and metopes, is heavier. The temple is called the Theseum because some of the relief sculpture illustrates the life of the hero Theseus.

Athens

From earliest times, the cultural, political, and economic center of Greece. The ancient city of Athens grew up around the rock of the Acropolis that, with its ideal defensive position, naturally attracted settlers. The remains of Neolithic settlements dating from the third millennium B.C. have been found on the Acropolis itself. The first man-made fortification, a wall of huge stone blocks built around the hill and called the Pelasgicum, dates from the late Bronze Age.

Plutarch, in his *Life of Pericles* (13-12 B.C.), wrote of the buildings on the Acropolis that " . . . they brought delight and adornment to Athens and the greatest amazement to the rest of mankind." The buildings to which he referred were erected under Pericles, after the earlier structures on the Acropolis had been destroyed by the Persians (480 B.C.). Although archaeological research and recorded descriptions have made it possible to reconstruct the plan of the Acropolis as it existed during the Age of Pericles, time, warfare, as well as the conversion of some buildings into churches and mosques

have destroyed many of them completely and left only remnants of others. The only extensive ruins still standing on the Acropolis are the Parthenon (built 447-438 B.C.), the Propylaea (begun 437 B.C. and never completed), the Erechtheum (built 421-405 B.C.), and the Temple of Athena Nike (built c. 426 B.C. and restored A.D. 1935-1940). Of these, the Parthenon, which remained intact until its interior was shattered by a gunpowder explosion in 1687, is the most impressive. In 1801-1803 Lord Elgin salvaged many pieces of sculpture and architectural fragments from the Parthenon; these are now in the Elgin Collection, British Museum, London.

On the southern slope of the Acropolis is the Theater of Dionysius, where plays were performed from the beginning of the fifth century B.C. Originally cut into the hillside, the theater was remodeled in the fourth century B.C. and again by the Roman Emperor Nero c. A.D. 60.

Theater of Dionysius (338 B.C.); Athens, Greece. The earliest Athenean dramas were probably given as part of Dionysiac festivals in the agora. According to tradition the first of three successive theaters of stone was built in this new location, on the south slope of the Acropolis, after the wooden benches of the agora theatre collapsed at a performance in about 500 B.C.

Connected to the theater by an arcade (the Stoa of Eumenes) is the Odeon (concert hall) of Herodes Atticus, built A.D. 161.

To the west of the Acropolis stands the hill known as the Pnyx, on the northeastern slope of which are the remains of a semicircular double-terraced structure, thought to have been the original meeting place of the Athenian assembly.

On this hill, and on nearby Hill of the Nymphs and Museum Hill, many remains of early settlements, which were cut into the rock, have been found. These include tombs, dwellings, steps and drainage systems. The rock of the Areopagus, where the council of elders met and where murder trials were held, stands midway between the Acropolis and the Pnyx.

The Agora, the commercial, political, and social center of ancient Athens, lay to the north of the Acropolis. Little or nothing remains of the many temples and public buildings that once stood there. The most important objects found

Roman times. Still standing in this area is the Aeolus, or Tower of the Winds, which dates from the first century B.C.

The largest structure in ancient Athens was the Temple of Zeus Olympus, erected southeast of the Acropolis between 174 B.C. and A.D. 132. Of its original 104 columns, 15 are still standing. On the Hill of Ardittos is the Stadium, built by Lycurgus in 330 B.C. and reconstructed A.D. 140 and again in 1894.

An excellent collection of Greek art from Neolithic times to the Roman period is housed in the National Archaeological Museum. Collections of art objects from later periods are found in the Byzantine and Benaki museums, and there are also a number of interesting Byzantine churches in the city.

see: Greek Art and Architecture

Atlan, Jean (1913-1960)

Algerian abstract painter, draftsman, illustrator, and lithographer, born in Constantine, Algeria, of Judeo-Berber parentage. Atlan studied philosophy at the Sorbonne, Paris, but later became interested in painting.

After his first one-man show in 1944, Atlan exhibited, in the Salon des Surindépendants, several compositions that are now in the Gertrude Stein Collection. This was followed by another show at the Galerie Denise René and, after 1946, by several European exhibitions. In 1945 he executed black-and-white lithographs for Franz Kafka's *Description of a Battle.*

Atlan has been compared to Marc Chagall for his use of color, and to Chaim Soutine for the distortions and violence apparent in his line, but he was, in fact, a highly original painter, not tied down to any formula and deriving his inspirations from his private view of events around him. His work is represented in several French and European collections.

Atlantes
see: Architectural Terms

Atrium
see: Architectural Terms

Attic
see: Architectural Terms

by archaeologists on the site of the Agora are now housed in the Stoa of Attalos II, a modern reconstruction of the original building that was erected between 159 and 138 B.C.

On the Colonus Agoraeus, a hill that overlooks the Agora from the west, stands the Theseum, the best-preserved Greek temple in the world. Built between 449 and 444 B.C., it is believed to have been a temple to the god Hephaestus; the name Theseum comes from the fact that some of its relief sculptures depict the exploits of the Greek hero Theseus. East of the Greek Agora a second commercial center was built during

Jean Baptiste Audebert: Engraved illustration from *Natural History of Monkeys* (1800); Bibliothèque Nationale, Paris. Audebert gave most of his attention as an artist to nature subjects, illustrating books on insects, monkeys, and birds, as well as painting miniature portraits.

Atwood, Charles B. (1849-1895)

American architect, born in Charlestown, Massachusetts. Atwood was trained at the Lawrence Scientific School of Harvard University and worked for a number of years for the architects Ware and Van Brunt, in Boston. In 1872 he set up his own firm. Two of his early works, executed during this period, are the Merchants Fire Insurance Building in Worcester, and the Five Cent Savings Bank in Lowell, both Massachusetts.

In 1875 Atwood became a designer with the New York firm of Herter Brothers, interior decorators, and his chief design at that time was the house of W. H. Vanderbilt on Fifth Avenue. In 1891-1893 he was employed by D. H. Burnham as designer-in-chief of the Chicago World's Fair, for which he designed some sixty buildings. Of these, the most important were the Music Hall, Peristyle, and Casino, designed as one unit, and the Art Building, a long, harmonious building with a classical façade of Corinthian columns and a central dome; the latter was his major achievement. His last work was the Ellicott Building in Buffalo, New York, on which he again worked as Burnham's designer.

Aubusson Tapestries and Carpets

The products of Aubusson, a minor center of tapestry production in the department of Creuse, France. Examples of Aubusson tapestry dating from before the eighteenth century are extremely rare. Since 1742, however, the Aubusson factory has produced knotted-pile carpets in addition to tapestry or smooth-faced carpets. Particularly in the eighteenth century, these were very popular, owing to their high quality, low price, and also their designs, produced by court painters such as Jean Baptiste Oudry. A national school of decorative arts, founded in 1869, maintains the high standard of work in the modern manufacture of Aubusson carpets.
see: Tapestry and Carpets

Audebert, Jean Baptiste (1759-1800)

French painter and etcher, born in Rochefort. Audebert studied in Paris and traveled to Holland and England. He chiefly excelled in drawings and engravings of animals and objects of natural history. He engraved the plates for *Natural History of Monkeys* (1800) and the *History of Hummingbirds* (1802), and also painted several miniature portaits and small genre pictures.

Auditorium

see: Architectural Terms

Audran Family

A family of French artists. Charles Audran (1594-1674), born in Paris, painted in the manner of Abraham Bloemaert. His brother Claude (1597-1674), also born in Paris, made an important contribution to the ornamental style of the eighteenth century, but none of his works survive.

Gérard Audran (1640-1703), the third son of Claude, was born in Lyons. His style was developed while doing engraving in Rome (1667-1670), and he was appointed engraver to Louis XIV. His best works are thought to be his engravings of Charles Lebrun's historical paintings.

The most important member of the family was Claude Audran III (1658-1734), born in Lyons, nephew of Gérard. In his decorative works in the royal houses, he evolved a pure Rococo style. They included projects for ceilings at Anet, Sceaux, Chantilly, and Versailles, drawings of which are preserved in the National Museum, Stockholm.

The fantastic lightness and brilliance of Claude Audran's arabesques can be studied in these drawings, although most of his finished works have disappeared. His influence, however, was considerable. His pupils included Claude Gillot, and above all, Antoine Watteau, whose decora-

tions at La Muette, now destroyed, were entirely in the spirit of his master. It was also Claude Audran, in his capacity as *concierge,* or caretaker, of Luxembourg Palace, who introduced Watteau to Peter Paul Rubens' *Marie de' Medici* series, which is now in the Louvre but at that time hung in the palace. This gave Watteau an opportunity to study the artist who was to be the major influence on his mature style.

The Grapes (1946), tapestry from the Berthaud studio at the Aubusson factory; Mobilier National, Paris. Many of the Aubusson designs have been provided by such artists as Picasso, Braque, Rouault, and Lurçat. The result has been to stimulate anew interest in tapestry weaving as a contemporary art.

(left) Gérard Audran: *Christ Carrying the Cross*, engraving and etching; Civica Raccolta Stampe Bertarelli, Milan, Italy. Engravings by this member of the gifted Audran family were valued in the seventeenth century for their refined taste and precise workmanship.

(below) John James Audubon: Plate No. 354 from *Birds of America* (published 1827-1838), aquatint; Victoria and Albert Museum, London. This is one of 435 plates—printed life-size in the first edition—which were engraved and hand colored by the English firm of Robert Havell, Jr., after the naturalistic watercolors painted by Audubon on his many American expeditions.

Jean Audran (1667-1756), born in Lyons, the brother of Claude III, is noted for his etchings. *The Rape of the Sabines*, after Nicolas Poussin, is considered the best of his numerous works.

Audubon, John James (1785-1851)

American illustrator and naturalist, born in Haiti and brought up in France. Audubon arrived in the United States in 1803 and revisited France during 1805-1806. On his return to America he settled in Louisiana and explored the still little-traveled hinterland of the Mississippi and Missouri rivers, pursuing the study of wildlife.

In 1820 Audubon decided to concentrate on the work of illustrating all known North American birds. Between 1826 and 1842 he traveled extensively in the United States and Canada, gathering material and preparing illustrations, and in England and Europe raising money. His works include *The Birds of America* (1827-1838) and his *Ornithological Biography* (1839). A later work, *The Viviparous Quadrupeds of North America* (1846-1854), was prepared in collaboration with his sons John and Victor and with John Bachman, the naturalist.

For the first edition of *The Birds of America*, Audubon placed his detailed studies of birds against illustrations of their natural habitats.

These studies are classic examples of their kind, distinguished by fine draftsmanship and decorative sense, and by the standard of the engravings, done by the English firm of Robert Havell, Jr.

Australian Art

Australian art in the Western tradition dates from the colonization of the subcontinent by the British in the latter half of the eighteenth century. However, before this, art forms dating back to prehistoric times had been created by the Aborigines, an Australoid race believed to have numbered some 150,000 before European settlement. The present Aboriginal population is about half this number.

Aboriginal Art. In the west and north of Australia, paintings on the walls of caves or rock shelters were discovered by Sir George Grey in 1838. These works, depicting strange human and animal shapes, are known as "Wonjina" figures and date back to a mythical period known as the "dreaming time." The "dreaming time" is interpreted differently by various tribes, but in general they all refer to the time before creation, when men lived in heroic shape in a world above the earth. Apart from these figures, rock engravings, depicting animals, are to be found in widely distributed areas. The "Mimi" figures, found in Arnhem Land, Northern Territory, are worth noting. They represent supernatural beings, often minutely depicted, sometimes in motion: hunting, running, and dancing.

The Aborigines also practice a kind of painting, principally secular and representational. This is done on squares of bark, using colors made from earths, charcoal, fat, and the juices of orchids. The color range is necessarily limited, consisting principally of reds, ochres, black, and white. The usual subjects are scenes of everyday life, including hunting, fishing, dancing, and the like, and sometimes illustrations of legendary happenings. A remarkable feature of this kind

Australian rock painting of mythical figure; Calder River region. This Aboriginal cult figure, painted in Northwest Australia, was most likely designed to ward off drought. The facial characteristics, together with the strong outlining of the head, suggest the rigidly conventional *Wonjina* type of figure. Unlike the prehistoric cave paintings of Europe, Australian examples of primitive art have always been found on rock surfaces at least partly accessible to daylight.

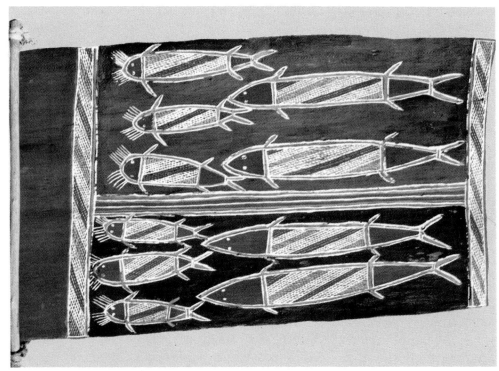

(above) Australian primitive painting of marine animals on bark; Aborigine Reservation, Arnhem Land, Northern Territory. The flat stylization in these fish forms is characteristic of much Aboriginal painting and carving.

(below) Australian rock painting of fish; Obiri, Arnhem Land, Northern Territory. In this part of Australia the so-called "X-ray" style evolved.

(right) Elizabeth Durack (born 1916): Sea-Reft (1961), oil and dammer on board; Collection of Dr. Darcy Williams, Sydney, New South Wales, Australia. Miss Durack has spent most of her life in the Australian outback, and her flat forms and somewhat bark-like textures reflect the style of the Aborigines.

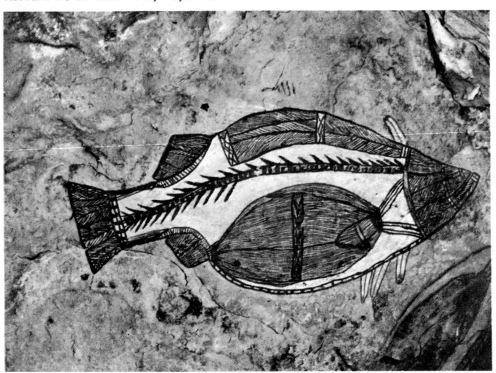

of work is the attempt to show the internal structure of animals and fish; this has been designated as X-ray painting.

Other art forms practiced by the Aborigines include the carving of figures representing legendary male and female beings, found mainly in Arnhem Land; the elaborately carved grave posts of Melville Island, Northern Territory; and the decoration of weapons used as spears, boomerangs, and woomeras, or spear throwers. The Aborigines paint their bodies elaborately for their corroborees, or secular and ritual dances.

Sand drawings, done with the fingers, are often very elaborate. They may be up to 10 feet across, and are used in sacred ceremonies.

Aboriginal art aroused little curiosity among the white settlers until the twentieth century, when the growth of interest in primitive art in Europe led Australian artists to look to this field for new forms. The visit of Rex Batterbee (born 1893), an established watercolorist, to Central Australia in 1934 had a curious effect on Aboriginal art. Albert Namatjira (1902-1959) of the Arunta tribe, who watched Batterbee at work,

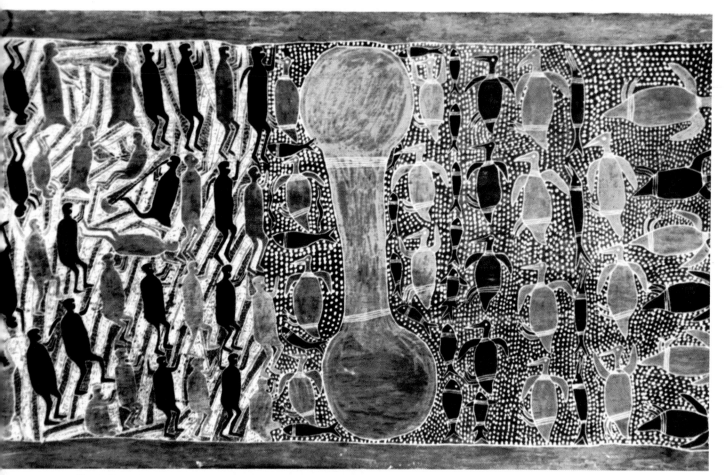

Detail from *Dance of the Seabirds*, an Aboriginal bark painting from the Gulf of Carpentaria, Northern Territory, Australia. The painting on bark of such symbolic figures as these, which has been practiced by the Aborigines of northern Australia for hundreds of years, generally serves to record totemic rites and historic events. Bark paintings are also thought by the Aborigines to possess magic powers which aid in hunting and fishing.

began to paint the scenes around him in the precise watercolor style of the Western artist. This style he taught to his sons and to other members of the tribe. Thus there exists a "school" of artists in the desert near Alice Springs, painting in a manner very different from the traditional style of their culture. Their paintings are represented in the principal Australian galleries and are often reproduced.

Among the artists influenced by the Aborigines is Elizabeth Durack (born 1916), who has spent most of her life in the interior. Her paintings are inclined to romanticize the Aborigine, depicting the rather pathetic condition of those who work around the homesteads of Central Australia.

Helen Lemprière (born 1907), who lives and exhibits mostly in Europe, has drawn on the palette of the Aboriginal artist, sometimes using only the materials employed by him, and on his legends of the "dreaming time," to produce large abstract and semifigurative compositions. Her work is represented in the Art Gallery of New South Wales, the Queensland National Gallery, and the Museum of Modern Art, Miami, Florida. Many other artists have used Aboriginal motifs in textile designs, pottery, and decorative work in general, but these applications lack much of the spontaneity of the original work.

The Pioneer Period (1788-1863). Western art in Australia may be said to have begun with the topographic artists who visited the new colony at the end of the eighteenth century with the expeditionary fleets and the convict transports. These men, military and naval officers and some civilians, were trained observers, but their ideas of painting were conditioned by the academic forms prevalent in England at that time.

Some of the early artists, convicts transported from England, often for minor crimes, achieved considerable success as painters. Among them were Thomas Watling (1762-?), who arrived in Sydney in 1792; Joseph Lycett (act. 1810-1825). who arrived in Sydney in 1810; and Thomas Griffiths Wainewright (1794-1852). Wainewright. the subject of Oscar Wilde's essay *Pen, Pencil and Poison,* had been an art critic in England and had exhibited at the Royal Academy. He was transported to Hobart, Tasmania, in 1837, for forgery. While in the penal settlement he painted a series of delicate portraits. His portrait of *Dr. Wilson,* in pencil and watercolor, is in the Tasmanian Museum and Art Gallery, and his work is also represented in the British Museum and the Royal Academy, London.

Among other convict colonists was Francis Howard Greenway (1777-1837), a pupil of John Nash, who was already known as an architect in England. Greenway gained a considerable reputa-tion as an architect in Sydney, under the patron-age of Governor Lachlan Macquarie, who eman-cipated him. He designed St. James Church (1836), which stands in the center of the city.

John Glover (1767-1849), described as the first resident Australian artist, arrived in Tas-mania in 1831, having gained some reputation in England as a watercolorist, sometimes being compared with J. M. W. Turner. His work is careful, full of detailed drawing of natural forms, but catches something of the spirit of the Austra-lian landscape.

The Romantic and Academic Period (1835-1885). In 1835 Conrad Martens (1801-1878) arrived in Sydney. He had studied in England and was much influenced by the innovations of John Constable and J. M. W. Turner, as may be seen in his watercolors of Sydney Harbor

Thomas Watling (1762-?): Detail of *Sydney Cove* (1794), oil on canvas mounted on board; Dixson Collection, Sydney, Australia. Watling, one of the convict artists of the late eighteenth and early nineteenth centuries, imposed on the conventional landscape style of his time a keen attention to the details of architecture and of human activity.

and his New South Wales landscapes. His *Sydney from Lavender Bay* (c. 1866) is in the Dixson Gallery, Sydney. Martens was popular among the wealthy landowners and painted many views of their country houses. Together with John Skinner Prout (1806-1876), who first visited Australia in 1840, Martens laid the foundations of academic art in Australia. Prout, born in Plymouth, England, was an accomplished water-colorist and attracted large audiences to his lectures in Hobart in 1844. In 1845 he helped to organize the first large exhibition of paintings there. Together with Nicholas Chevalier (1828-1902) and J. C. Armytage (active c. 1850), he contributed to E. C. Booth's comprehensive portfolio, *Australia*, published in London in 1873-1876.

Chevalier was a Swiss artist, who lived in Australia from 1855 to 1867. He became an artist on the *Illustrated Australian News*, the first cartoonist of the Melbourne *Punch*, and acted as official artist to the Duke of Edinburgh's expedition to New Zealand in 1867. He is remembered chiefly for his oils of the landscape of Victoria. His work is to be found in many Australian galleries. Two landscapes, *Sunrise on the River Yarra* and *River at Richmond* both dated 1861, are in Australia House, London.

One of the major figures of this period was Abram Louis Buvelot (1814-1888), who settled in Victoria in 1865. He had studied in Lausanne and Paris and had spent some time in Brazil. Buvelot was the first painter to make a serious

John Glover (1767-1849): *Glover's House and Garden* (c. 1831), oil on canvas; National Gallery of South Australia, Adelaide. The artist describes his subject in close and affectionate detail, combining the meticulous precision of the primitive with a degree of academic sophistication which appears in the atmospheric rendering of the background.

Sir Thomas Livingstone Mitchell (1793-1855): Detail of *The Lodden River* (1836), drawing; Australia House, London. This many-sided man sketched the countryside he discovered on one of his four expeditions as an explorer and soldier.

attempt to tackle the problems of rendering the brilliant landscape of the Australian bush on canvas. In 1869, three of his paintings were purchased by the National Gallery of Victoria. namely, *Summer Evening at Templestowe, Winter Morning at Heidelberg,* and *Waterpool at Coleraine.* The result of this early success was a series of excellent landscapes, in the tradition of John Constable and Jean Baptiste Corot, which did much to encourage the *plein-air* painters of the Heidelberg school. One of his watercolors, *The Pool* (1878), is in the Tate Gallery, London.

The Impressionist Period (1885-1918). The so-called Heidelberg school was actually a group of painters under the leadership of Tom Roberts (1856-1931), who returned from Europe in 1885. after four years of study, full of enthusiasm for the work of Jules Bastien-Lepage and the Barbizon painters. He painted scenes of Australian life with great vigor and mastery of color, depicting scenes ranging from sheep-shearing to city genre subjects. *Bailed Up* (1898), showing a mail coach held up by bushrangers, is in the Art Gallery of New South Wales.

The painters who gathered about Roberts worked mainly near Melbourne, at Eaglemont, and along the River Yarra. Among them was Charles Conder (1868-1909), a sensitive painter. whose delicate paintings on white silk fans were unique, and his *Departure of S.S. "Orient,"* in the Sydney Art Gallery, is the masterpiece which anticipated Australian Impressionism. Another of the group was Frederick McCubbin (1855-1917), who painted large bushland genre subjects, often romantic and sentimental but always technically excellent. Typical of McCub-

bin's work is *Down on His Luck* (1889) in the National Art Gallery, Perth, Western Australia, which depicts a "swaggie" or itinerant Australian laborer preparing for nightfall in the bush.

An exhibition held in Melbourne in 1889 was the manifesto of this group and exerted considerable influence on the development of Impressionist technique in Australia. This was the *Exhibition of 9" x 5" Impressions*, consisting of paintings executed on the lids of cigar boxes, which caused a great sensation at the time.

Perhaps the most important figure to emerge from the Heidelberg school was Sir Arthur Streeton (1867-1943), born in Victoria, who taught in Sydney before his first visit to Europe in 1897. Streeton's individual vision of the Australian scene, expressed in such paintings as *Still Glides the Stream* and *Purple Noon's Transparent Light*, in the National Gallery of Victoria, made him a major influence on the school of Australian landscape painting and a dominant figure at the Royal Academy Australian Exhibition in 1923.

Hans Heysen (born 1877) was much influenced

(left) Nicolas Chevalier (1828-1902): Detail of *Sunrise on the River Yarba*, oil; Australia House, London. The versatility of this Swiss artist, who lived for twelve years in Australia, ranged from his work as cartoonist for the Melbourne *Punch* to his portrayal, as here, of a particularly idyllic mood of nature. His treatment of landscape painting might be compared with that of the mid-nineteenth-century American Hudson River School.

(below) Tom Roberts (1856-1931): Detail of *Bailed Up* (1895), oil on canvas; Art Gallery of New South Wales, Sydney, Australia. Roberts, impressed with the *plein-air* style of the Barbizon painters while studying in France during the early 1880's, returned to Australia to portray genre subjects in a similar style, and so established the important Impressionist style of his own country. The coachman, Bill Bates, gave the artist full details from which to reconstruct this actual holdup of a mail coach by bushrangers, against the bright light of an Australian summer.

by the Paris Barbizon School. He has lived most of his life in and around Adelaide, the capital of South Australia, and his oils and watercolors of the gum trees and hills of the desert interior of Central Australia have a romantic grandeur equaled by none. Examples of his work are to be found in all the major Australian galleries and in galleries in Europe and America.

Another important influence was that of Julian Ashton (1851-1941), born in Penzance, England, who was educated at the West London School of Arts and the Académie Julian, Paris. In 1883 he opened an art school in Sydney, later founding the Sydney Royal Art Society. Among his most notable pupils were Jesse Jewhurst Hilder (1881-1916), a Sydney artist whose watercolors became very popular after his death, and George Washington Lambert (1873-1930). Lambert studied in Sydney and first won recognition with a landscape entitled *Across the Black Soil Plains* (1899), now in the Art Gallery of New South Wales, Sydney. He was a brilliant draftsman, believing in pure lines as the basis of all art; his figure paintings are all carefully composed and slightly mannered in style, as may be seen in *The White Glove*, and *Portrait of Sir Baldwyn Spencer*, Art Gallery of New South

Wales, Sydney. He was made an Associate of the Royal Academy in 1922.

A number of Australian painters at this time achieved success in Europe, notably John Russell (1858-1931), a friend of Vincent van Gogh, Pierre Auguste Renoir, and Henri Toulouse-Lautrec. His portrait of *Van Gogh* is now in the Stedelijk Museum, Amsterdam. He is little known in Australia and died in comparative obscurity. Others were Phillips Fox (1864-1915), who exhibited frequently in Paris and in 1908 was elected an associate of the New Salon before returning to teach at the Melbourne National Gallery School; and Rupert Bunny (1864-1947). Bunny studied at the Melbourne National Gallery School and went abroad on a scholarship. Like Fox, he exhibited in Paris at the Old Salon continuously from 1886 to 1900 and was a member of both the New and the Autumn Salons. Two large and elegant conversation pieces, *A Summer Morning* (1911) and *Endormies* (1911), hang in the Art Gallery of New South Wales, Sydney, and the National Gallery of Victoria, Melbourne, respectively. Shortly before his death, Bunny was given a retrospective exhibition in

(above) Rupert Bunny (1864-1947): Detail from *The Shrimp Fishers* (c. 1890), oil; National Gallery of Melbourne, Australia. This Australian artist lived and painted in France for nearly 40 years. He fully assimilated the techniques of French Impressionism, and exhibited with Monet and Renoir in the Paris Salons of the 1890's. This painting is typical of his Impressionist style; the woman with the parasol in the background, for instance, seems almost to merge with the bright sunlight.

(right) Frederick McCubbin (1855-1917): Detail from *Afterglow* (1912), oil on canvas; Collection of Miss Strella Wilson, O.B.E., Australia House, London. Most Australian artists developed Impressionism not so much as a revolutionary technique but as a means through which they could effectively communicate their ardent feeling for the life and landscape of their country. McCubbin painted these bathers, in a scene of late afternoon, after a painting of the same subject by the French Impressionist Pierre Auguste Renoir.

Melbourne. He is represented in the **Palais du Luxembourg**, Paris, and in the Wilsbach Gallery, Philadelphia, Pennsylvania.

One of the most individual figures of Australian art is Norman Lindsay, born in Creswick, Victoria, in 1879. He began drawing for a Melbourne newspaper in 1895 and in 1901 became a cartoonist for the Sydney *Bulletin*. He is best known for his erotic illustrations of works by such authors as Boccaccio, Casanova, and Petro-

nius; some of these, in translations by his son, the writer Jack Lindsay, were circulated privately in limited editions. The power and originality of his line can also be seen in his etchings and watercolors. The best of Lindsay's drawings were collected as *The Pen Drawings of Norman Lindsay* (1918). Lindsay's brothers, Sir Lionel Lindsay (1874-1961) and Sir Daryl Lindsay (born 1890), also achieved some prominence in painting.

Prominent among landscape painters during

Norman Lindsay (born 1879): *Captain Gondimar Funkle and Radolphus Jiblet* (1925), etching; Australia House, London. His ten years' work as cartoonist on the Sydney *Bulletin*, and his controversial illustrations for books and poems, proved this Australian artist capable not only of amusing, stimulating, and shocking his contemporaries but of doing so, as in this etching, through highly sensitive line and the adroit massing of black and white areas.

this period were Sir Will Ashton (1881-1963), an English-born painter who lived and worked around Adelaide, and Eliot Gruner (1882-1939), who further developed the traditional Australian landscape style.

The Post-Impressionist Period (1918-1939). Between the two World Wars a reaction against Impressionism took place, inspired by Post-Impressionism, Cubism, and other European movements.

In Melbourne, George Bell (born 1878), whose

Lulworth Cove is in the National Gallery of Victoria, and Arnold Shore (1897-1963) founded the Contemporary Art Society in the 1930's. In Sydney the Macquarie Gallery fostered a group of painters including Roi de Maistre (born 1894), who now lives in London and specializes in religious subjects and portraits, Roland Wakelin (born 1887), and Rah Fizelle (born 1891). These artists owed much to the influence of an Italian artist, Antony Dattilo Rubbo (1871-1955), who arrived in Sydney in 1897. After teaching at the Sydney Royal Art Society, he opened his own art school.

The Non-Figurative and Abstract Expressionist Period (1939-   ). Surrounding the Contemporary Art Society in Melbourne and similar groups in Sydney were many artists who had turned away from Post-Impressionist techniques in search of new departures. Among them were some who sought to apply the theories of Surrealism to the myths of early Australia, hoping in this manner to create an art form truly native to the country. Foremost among these are Albert Tucker (born 1914), Arthur Boyd (born 1920), and Sidney Nolan (born 1917).

Tucker was born in Melbourne and became president of the Contemporary Art Society. Just after World War II he served as an official artist with the Australian army in Japan, where he met and became friendly with the Franco-Japanese painter, Tsugouharu Foujita. He lived in Europe and America from 1948, returning to Australia in 1959 for a series of highly successful exhibitions. Examples of his work are in the Museum of Modern Art and the Solomon R. Guggenheim Museum, both New York.

Boyd, also born in Melbourne, comes from a family which has had artists for three generations. He is the most typically Australian of the modern painters, specializing in genre scenes of the Wimmera District, depicted in muted color with incisive line. He has exhibited a series of

(right) Albert Tucker (born 1914): *Tough Guy*, (1957), oil on canvas; collection of the artist. Tucker served as artist-reporter with the Australian army in Japan in 1947, and since World War II he has assimilated a number of contemporary trends. This study of character and environment is intensified psychologically through elements of abstraction, expressionism, and surrealism. ▶

◄(left) George Russell Drysdale (born 1912): *Snake Bay at Night* (1954), oil; Trustees of the Tasmanian Museum and Art Gallery, Hobart, Tasmania. Through strong expressionistic color the artist appears to be merging the forms of the human figures and the totem-like columns. He thus heightens the sense of identification between these Aborigines and the mystery of their religion.

large paintings in Australia and London, developing the theme of the half-caste bride of an Aborigine as a folk epic. His work is represented in all the main Australian galleries, and a retrospective exhibition of his work was held at the Whitechapel Gallery, London, in 1961. His brother, David Boyd (born 1924), now works in London and produces large figurative-expressionist canvases.

Perhaps the best known of the modern Australian painters is Nolan, who achieved fame with his series of pictures based on the life of Ned Kelly, the famous outlaw and Australian folk hero. Mythological figures play a great part in Nolan's work; apart from the folk heroes of Australia, he has drawn on the Greek Leda myth and has worked on African subjects.

These themes are treated with deliberate simplicity in bold colors, mostly on hardboard, with use of household enamels. *Inland Australia, Glen Rowan,* and *Woman and a Billabong* are in the Tate Gallery, London; and the Museum of Modern Art, New York, has one of his paintings. He was awarded a C.B.E. (Companion of the Order of the British Empire) in 1963.

William Dobell (born 1899), who was trained in London, owes much of his style to Renoir, as may be seen in *South Kensington Woman* and *Margaret Olley,* both in the Art Gallery of New South Wales. After his return to Australia in 1939, Dobell painted many excellent portraits, including the Prime Minister of Australia, Sir Robert G. Menzies. His work also includes landscapes and seascapes, full of movement.

George Russell Drysdale (born 1912) is a leading Australian regional painter. He was born in England, but arrived in Australia as a child. After studying under George Bell in Melbourne and visiting Europe, he traveled about Australia, painting the scenes and people of the outback or remote bush country. During World War II he had been influenced by Paul Nash and Graham Sutherland, but his work

owes more to his observance of the natives and areas of the Northern Territory, as can be seen in his spare figures in desolate landscapes, painted in hot, glowing colors. *Moody's Pub* (1941) is in the National Gallery of Victoria, and there are works in the Solomon R. Guggenheim Museum, New York, and the Tate Gallery, London.

Prominent among other contemporary painters in Australia are Godfrey Miller (1893-1964), Ian Fairweather (born 1890), John Passmore (born 1904), Jon Molvig (born 1923), John Olsen (born 1928), and Brett Whiteley (born 1939). Charles Blackman (born 1928) and Robert Dickerson (born 1929) may be described as figurative expressionists, whereas Ralph Balson (born 1890),

William Dobell (born 1899): Detail of *Portrait of Joshua Smith* (1944), oil on canvas; destroyed by fire. Combining a sumptuous brush technique with a flair for satire, Dobell has been one of Australia's most controversial artists (this portrait, for instance, led to a law suit). While the glowing surface of this work testifies to the early influence of Renoir, it also suggests something of the macabre manner of Francis Bacon.

(above) Charles Blackman (born 1928): *Double Image* (detail), oil; collection of the artist. The expressionistic device here is to juxtapose almost complementary modes of treatment on his horizontally divided canvas. Blackman represented Australia at the Biennale de Jeune, Paris, in 1962.

(right) Jon Molvig (born 1923): *Ballad of a Dead Stockman No. 11* (1959), oil on masonite; Art Gallery of New South Wales, Sydney, Australia. Molvig creates in this painting a mysterious and impressive atmosphere, the standing figures echoing the more intense presence of the prostrate one. ▶

Louis James (born 1920), and Lawrence Daws (born 1927) are abstract expressionists. All these painters are represented in the Museum of Modern Art and Design of Australia, Melbourne, and in state galleries. Leonard French (born 1928), whose style has affinities to that of Fernard Léger and Jean Lurçat, has specialized in murals, notably his huge monumental project for the Beaurepaire Physical Education Centre, Melbourne University.

Sculpture in Australia. Toward the end of the nineteenth century, the building boom in Australia resulted in commissions for large monumental works being given to several sculptors. This attracted sculptors from England and Europe and did much to encourage sculpture in Australia. Among early Australian sculptors of distinction were Charles Summers (1825-1878), who worked in Melbourne between 1853 and 1866 on the monument to the explorers Robert O'Hara Burke and William John Wills, and Thomas Woolner (1825-1892). Woolner had been a member of the Pre-Raphaelite Brotherhood and went to Australia, to the goldfields, in 1854. His first success came with a bust of *Alfred, Lord Tennyson* in 1857; thereafter he made many portrait busts and medallions. He executed the large statue of *Captain Cook* which now stands in Hyde Park, Sydney.

The most distinguished Australian sculptors of the early twentieth century were Charles Web Gilbert (1869-1925) and Sir Bertram Mackennal (1863-1931). Gilbert studied and worked in Australia, afterwards going to England where he gained recognition with his marble head entitled *The Critic* (1916), now in the Tate Gallery, London. His life-size bronze of the explorer *Matthew Flinders* stands near St. Paul's Cathedral, Melbourne. Mackennal studied at the National Gallery School, Melbourne, and went to England in 1885, where he quickly became well known for his monumental groups. He was elected a Royal Academician in 1922. Among his works are *Circe*, in the National Gallery, Melbourne; *The Earth and the Elements* and *Diana*, in the Tate Gallery, London; and several groups in London, including *Phoebus*, which surmounts Australia House, the equestrian statue of *Edward VII*, in Trafalgar Square, and a war memorial at Islington.

Another prominent sculptor before World War II was Harold Parker (1873-1962), whose symbolic stone groups of heroic proportions, completed in 1918, flank the entrance to Australia House,

London. His marble *Ariadne* is in the Tate Gallery, London. Two sculptors who worked on large monumental groups in Melbourne were Margaret Baskerville (1861-1930), and Theo Cowan (act. *c.* 1920), born in Sydney, who was the first native-born sculptress.

In recent years many sculptors have been commissioned to execute works in connection with new building projects, designed to replace the unambitious Victorian structures dating from the gold-rush era. Among these have been Daphne

(right) Lawrence Daws (born 1927): *Mandala IV*, oil on masonite; Mertz Collection, U.S.A. Daws, adhering to the style of Abstract Expressionism, places here against a violent red and black background a centralized form with esoteric and primitive connotations. ▶

Mayo (active *c.* 1930), who executed a large figure group for the City Hall, Brisbane, and the painter Arthur Boyd, whose fine totemic obelisk, one of his few essays in plastic form, stands in the forecourt of the Melbourne Olympic Pool. Tom Bass, born in 1916 in Lithgow, New South Wales, has achieved considerable success with his figurative, symbolic sculpture. He has strong views on the use of sculpture in civic development, and many of his works are to be seen in important architectural projects. These include

John Passmore (born 1904): *Jumping Horse-Mackerel* (1959), oil on masonite; Art Gallery of New South Wales, Sydney, Australia. Working as an abstract expressionist to create form through color, the artist here communicates through a vivid interaction of line and mass.

Lyndon Dadswell (born 1908): *Man and Horse,* bronze sculpture; Felton Bequest, National Gallery of Victoria, Melbourne, Australia. Dadswell, through his lecturing at the Sydney National Art School, has been active in encouraging younger Australian sculptors. His modeling of these sturdily balanced forms reflects the texture and malleability of clay as the original material, before being cast in bronze.

his *Trial of Socrates*, in the University of Melbourne; his work for the I.C.I. Building in Sydney; and, most recently, his *Ethos* for Civic Square, Canberra. He works mainly in metals and particularly with electrolytic copper deposits.

Since World War II many Australian sculptors have made England their home, and some have attracted considerable attention. Oliffe Richmond (born 1919), who studied with Henry Moore, has recently had a work bought by the Kröller-Müller Museum, Otterlo, Holland, and has had works commissioned by the British Arts Council and the London County Council. Neil Stocker (born 1925), who attracted the attention of critics in London with his large, abstract, molded forms, exhibited in London in 1961-1962.

Automatism

Automatism, in art, is the production of a work at the direction of the unconscious, and of pure chance. Its importance in twentieth-century art may be illustrated by the words of Jean Arp and André Breton.

Arp: "The law of chance which embraces all laws and is unfathomable, like the first cause from which all life rises, can only be experienced through complete devotion to the unconscious."

Breton makes automatism basic to his definition of surrealism: "Psychical automatism through which it is proposed to express in words, writing, or by any other means, the actual functioning of thought. It is dictated by thought, in the absence of any control exercised by reason, and apart from any aesthetic or moral preoccupation."

see: Surrealism

Autun

Town in east-central France, in the department of Saone-et-Loire. It was called Augustodunum by the Romans, under whom it flourished in the first century B.C.

Autun's former importance is attested by many Roman remains, chief of which are two well-preserved stone gateways, the Porte d'Arroux and the Porte St. André, both pierced by four archways and surmounted by arcades. There are also Roman ruins of ramparts, aqueducts, a theater, and a square temple of a local type, the Temple of Janus.

Tom Bass (born 1916): Decorative relief in metal provided for the New South Wales University of Technology project. This Australian artist reflects in modern terms something of the medieval propensity for architectural sculpture which is at the same time decorative, symbolic, and idiomatic.

(above) Sculptured capital showing the three kings being awakened by an angel (twelfth century); Cathedral of St. Lazare, Autun, France. The scene on this capital is part of a sequence of scenes of the birth and youth of Christ. These figures, from the Romanesque period, may have been executed by Gislebertus, who worked on the cathedral.

(below) Gislebertus: Detail from the tympanum over the main portal (twelfth century); Cathedral of St. Lazare, Autun, France. The distorted elongation of form and stylized curvilinear texture suggests Byzantine influence.

In the Middle Ages, Autun was ruled by the Dukes of Burgundy, who used the twelfth-century cathedral of St. Lazare as a chapel. The cathedral contains some of the most significant examples of Burgundian Romanesque sculpture, such as the capitals in the nave, and the *Last Judgment* on the tympanum of the west portal, executed largely by Gislebertus *c.* 1140. Also attributed to Gislebertus, one of the few Romanesque sculptors known by name, is a wooden statue of the Virgin and Child originally from Autun and now in The Cloisters, New York City.

Gothic additions to the St. Lazare cathedral in the fifteenth century include a central tower and chapels by Nicolas Rolin. Also found in the cathedral is the commemorative painting of *The Martyrdom of St. Symphorien* (which took place at Autun A.D. 179) by Jean Ingres (1780-1867). In the cathedral square is a Renaissance fountain. *see:* Romanesque Art and Architecture

Avebury Ring

Prehistoric ceremonial site, 9 miles from Devizes, Wiltshire, England. Encircled by a chalk bank some 20 ft. high and 1400 ft. in diameter, the Avebury site may be one of the largest of its kind in the world. Immediately within the circle, which can be entered at three points, is a ditch 40 ft. wide, and on the inner edge of this stands a circle of about 100 stones. Two smaller stone-marked rings, each 350 ft. in diameter, still exist within the site, and remnants of what may have been a third have been traced.
see: Stonehenge

Aved, Jacques (1702-1766)

French painter, born in Douai. Aved trained in Amsterdam under Bernard Picart (1673-1733). He is best known for his portraits. In 1721 he went to Paris, where he entered the studio of Alexis Simon Belle (1674-1734), and later, during the 1730's, he came under the influence of Jean François de Troy and Jean Baptiste Chardin. Aved was a regular exhibitor at the Salon between 1737 and 1759.

The influence of Aved's early contact with Dutch painting, particularly Rembrandt, some of whose drawings and paintings he possessed, is evident in the *Portrait of Madame Crozat* (1741), Musée Fabre, Montpellier, and in the *Portrait of His Wife*, shown in the Salon of 1740, now in the Courtauld Institute Galleries, London. The latter also enhanced his reputation as a fashionable portrait painter. A later portrait, *Madame Brion at Tea*, which was first exhibited in the Salon of 1750, was influenced by Chardin.

With less success Aved also produced a number of elaborate formal portraits, notably, *William IV* (1751), Mauritshuis, The Hague. His work is also represented in the Louvre, Paris.

Aventurine Glass

Type of glass that may be translucent, semiopaque, or opaque and of various colors, containing "gold" specks which are usually due to fine filings of brass or minute crystals of copper introduced into the batch during the melting process. The name indicates that the discovery of this technique, made on the island of Murano, Venice, Italy, was accidental.

Articles of aventurine glass were especially popular from the mid- to the late nineteenth century and were produced by English, Continental, and American glass factories. The best aventurine, or "goldstone," is still made on the island of Murano.
see: Glass

Avercamp, Hendrik (1585-1634)

Dutch landscape painter, born in Amsterdam or Kampen. Avercamp studied under Pieter Isaacsz (1569-1625) in Amsterdam, but was back in Kampen in 1613. His early style was influenced by the Flemish followers of Pieter Bruegel the Elder, and by David Vinckboons. Later the sharp silhouetting of the figures is softened, under the influence of the more atmospheric style that was Avercamp's most important contribution to Dutch landscape painting. He specialized in winter landscapes.

Jacques Aved: Portrait of Madame Crozat (1741), oil; Musée Fabre, Montpellier, France. In this painting Aved, taking Rembrandt as his guide, is endeavoring through the composition and the play of light to portray his subject's dignity without recourse to the customary eighteenth-century formalities of pose and expression.

Hendrik Avercamp: *Winter,* oil; Mauritshuis, The Hague. A group of Dutch painters in the sixteenth and seventeenth centuries was dedicated to painting popular genre scenes at different seasons of the year. Avercamp's work recalls the compositions of Arent Arentsz, Willem Buytewech, and Pieter Bruegel the Elder; his late work is distinguished by a soft silveriness of atmosphere.

Avercamp's paintings include *Scene on the Ice,* Rijksmuseum, Amsterdam; *Winter Scene with Skaters near a Castle,* National Gallery, London, and *Winter Landscape,* City Art Museum, St. Louis, Missouri.

Avignon

French city on the east bank of the Rhone, which prospered under the Romans. It changed hands many times, was the papal seat from 1309 to 1377, and remained in the possession of the Papacy until its annexation by the Republicans in 1791.

The Gothic fortress palace of the Popes was built between 1316 and 1370 by Popes Clement VI and Innocent VI. In the *tour de la garderobe* of the cloistered fortress are frescoes, thought to be by an artist called Robin de Romans, depicting the joys of the hunt and other pleasant pursuits. Standing on the same hill as the palace of the Popes is the Romanesque cathedral of Notre Dame de Doms (thirteenth century), which contains the splendid fourteenth-century Gothic mausoleum of Pope John XXII. Other notable Gothic churches are those of St. Didier, St. Pierre, and St. Agricol.

The current of the Rhone River is so strong at Avignon that it was not until 1178-c.1185 that it was bridged by St. Bénézet. This bridge was repaired many times and was finally abandoned in 1680. Four arches still remain, bearing the original Romanesque chapel dedicated to St. Nicholas, and with sixteenth-century additions.

The museum contains many examples of the medieval Avignon school of painting, which flourished during the fourteenth and early fifteenth centuries.

Ávila

A city of Old Castile, between Salamanca and Madrid, the birthplace of Santa Teresa of Ávila (1515-1582).

The medieval part of the town is enclosed by well-preserved walls (1088-1091), into which the apse of the fortified Romanesque cathedral was

(right) The papal palace in Avignon, France. One of the most extensive fortresses of the Gothic age, this palace with its high crenelated walls and its eight towers was built during the so-called "Babylonian captivity" of 1307-1377, when the Popes resided at Avignon under the domination of the French.

(below) The Rhone at Avignon, France. The city, rising up from the far shore, is dominated by the papal palace. The twelfth-century bridge in the foreground has not reached all the way across the river, which is particularly turbulent here, since 1680. The Romanesque chapel of St. Nicholas stands on the first of four surviving spans.

Ávila, Spain. Surrounding the medieval section of the city of Ávila are well-preserved walls, built between 1088 and 1091, when the Romanesque style flourished throughout Europe.

built. The present structure is Gothic, begun in the late twelfth century, and contains a *Pietà* (*c.* 1560) by Juan Bautista Vázquez (*d.* 1589). There are also excellent woodcarvings in the choir by Juan Rodriguez and Lucas Giraldo, executed between 1531 and 1636. The panels for the main altar are by Juan de Borgoña (*c.* 1470-*c.* 1536), and there are excellent examples of work in stained glass.

The basilica of San Vicente was begun *c.* 1109 and work continued into the Gothic period. The western portal, in Burgundian-Poitevin style, dates from *c.* 1150. The churches of San Andres, and San Pedro are both Romanesque.

The church of Santo Tomás (1482-1493) contains an altar panel by Pedro Berruguete (*c.* 1450-1503), executed *c.* 1494-1499, and the tomb of Prince Juan (1511) by Domenico Alessandro Fancelli (1469-1518). The façade of the church of San José dates from 1608 and is by Francisco de Mora (*c.* 1546-1610). The Portería chapel (1731) in San Antonio is by Pedro de Ribera (*c.* 1683-1742). In the church of San Segundo is a statue of the saint by Juan de Juni (*d.* 1577), executed *c.* 1571-1573.

Other noteworthy buildings include the baroque church of Santa Teresa, which stands on the site of the saint's birthplace; the fifteenth-sixteenth century Audienca; and the sixteenth-century Diputacion Provincial.

see: Romanesque Art and Architecture

Axminster Carpets

The manufacture of carpets in Axminster was begun in the eighteenth century by Thomas Whitty. At first Whitty based his designs on Turkish hand-knotted pile carpets. Later he was influenced by Peter Parisot, a former Capuchin monk from Lorraine who had a carpet factory in Fulham, London (1750-1755), and whose methods were based on those of the Savonnerie carpet manufactory in Paris.

Whitty won three awards from the Royal Society of Art between 1757 and 1759. His carpets were excellent in quality and cheaper than those of his competitors. His industry thrived, and to him must go much of the credit for bringing floor carpets to the English home. On his death, the business was continued by his son, but in 1835 the Axminster factory closed down, and the looms were taken over by Wilton. The factory was reopened in 1937.

see: Tapestry and Carpets

Ayrton, Michael (born 1921)

Painter, sculptor, theater designer, book illustrator, author, and lecturer, born in London. Ayrton was educated in London, Paris, Vienna, and Italy and has had exhibitions in many European capitals and in New York. Ayrton's sculpture *Icarus Transformed No. 1* is in the Tate Gallery, London. There are other examples of his work in the United States in the Boston Museum of Fine Arts and in the Philadelphia Museum of Art.

Baalbek

Once an ancient temple-city, Baalbek is situated 3,850 feet above sea level on the watershed separating the Leontes and Orontes Rivers in Lebanon.

The city owed an early economic prosperity to its central position on the main caravan trading routes, but was more famous as a religious center. Egyptian and Assyrian inscriptions refer to the city as Baalbeki, probably because the god Baal was worshipped there. Baalbek suffered greatly from both invasion and natural disasters, until it had declined, in the nineteenth century, to an insignificant township under Turkish rule. Today it is an agricutural and tourist center.

Although appreciation of Baalbek's ruins began in Europe during the sixteenth century, when Martin von Baumgarten (1507) and Pierre Belon du Mans (1553) drew attention to the town, the first official expedition to the site was made by a German team under Professor Otto Puchstein in 1895-1905. This group in the succeeding decade found three temples of archaeological interest; two situated within the acropolis, the third some 300 yards away in the center of the town. Built between the first and third centuries A.D., these important temples were dedicated to Jupiter, Bacchus, and Venus.

The largest of the temples was the one dedicated to Jupiter; it stood on the acropolis and was approached by way of an imposing stairway. Six of the fifty-eight Corinthian columns that once surrounded the temple's shrine are still standing. Each is 62 feet high and $7\frac{1}{2}$ feet in diameter and is composed of three blocks bound together with bronze cramp pins.

The smaller Temple of Bacchus is south of the Temple of Jupiter on the acropolis. Also Corinthian, the Temple of Bacchus is better preserved and is regarded as Lebanon's most beautiful monument of the Roman era. The inner enclosed space of the temple, with a width of 75 feet and a length of 87 feet, is accessible through a beautifully ornamented portal; the interior is also lavishly decorated.

The Temple of Venus is a circular structure which originally had a dome made of stone. Its preservation is due to its having been transformed into a Byzantine chapel dedicated to St. Barbara.

Baburen, Dirck van (c. 1595-1624)

Dutch painter, born in Utrecht, Netherlands; one of the leading members of the Utrecht school. Baburen was a pupil of Paulus Moreelse and spent several years between 1612 and 1621 in Rome, where he was strongly influenced by Caravaggio. *The Deposition* (1617), church of San Pietro in Montorio, Rome, is based on Caravaggio's *Deposition* (c. 1603) in the Vatican. Following his return to Holland, Baburen became one of the leading masters of the Tenebristi, a group of painters who worked in the manner of Caravaggio, exploring the dramatic effects of contrasting light and color.

During his short lifetime Baburen enjoyed a considerable reputation, being at one time employed by the Prince of Orange; yet few of his works survive. One of the most important is *The Procuress* (1622), Museum of Fine Arts, Boston, Massachusetts.

see: Dutch Art and Architecture; Tenebrism; Utrecht School

Babylonian and Assyrian Art

The Babylonians were a Semitic race who had appeared in central Mesopotamia by around 2500 B.C., while the Assyrians, another Semitic people, occupied the northern part of the same river-land, farther from the Persian Gulf. However, Babylonians and Assyrians were not the first peoples to dominate Mesopotamia; the brilliant civilization of the Sumerians preceded theirs

Capitals of the Temple of Bacchus (first to third centuries A.D.); Baalbek, Lebanon. This well-preserved temple was built during Roman times in the Corinthian style, as seen in the capitals decorated with acanthus leaves, a typical feature of this architectural style.

Stele showing the triumph of Naramsin; Louvre, Paris. The geometrical rigidity of this Sumerian sculpture is enlivened by the naturalistic modeling of the victorious king and soldiers. The Sumerian civilization, which preceded that of the Babylonians and Assyrians, had a great influence on the later art of Mesopotamia.

by many hundreds of years, and both of the newer cultures inherited the technological skill and artistic traditions of the older one.

Unfortunately, the Babylonians and Assyrians remained in greater or lesser conflict throughout their history. The Assyrians destroyed Babylon in the seventh century B.C., and because of this and the city's later despoilation by the Persian Emperor Xerxes and by Alexander the Great, the art and history of the Babylonians are very imperfectly known. It is chiefly the Babylon of the Neo-Babylonian period (612-539 B.C.), which arose after Assyria had fallen, that the German archaeologist Robert Koldewey discovered between 1899 and 1914.

Early Babylonian Art. The Sumerians were not a Semitic race. The emergence of Semitic elements in the midst of the Sumerian civilization began about 2370 B.C., when a Semitic leader named Sargon (Sharru-Kinu) seized the throne of Akkad and rapidly extended his control over all of Mesopotamia, even making expeditions as far as Asia Minor. A noble bronze portrait head, perhaps of this monarch, was found in excavations at Nineveh in 1932. Its elegance is combined with an earthy realism which reflects the energy of the newcomers.

During Sargon's reign stelae were erected to commemorate victories on the field of battle, and his grandson Naramsin continued this tradition with a remarkable victory stele (now in the Louvre, Paris), in which landscape, space, and narrative are skillfully harmonized. Similar technical skill is shown on fine cylinder seals of the period, cut for the wealthy.

A Sumerian revival set in about 2150 B.C., and it was only at the beginning of the eighteenth century B.C. that the Semitic-speaking element regained supremacy in Mesopotamia. This occurred under the leadership of Hammurabi, King of Babylon, who by his conquests made his city the capital of the region.

It is now possible to discern the flowering of an art which can be specifically called Babylonian. Perhaps the best example of the period is the stele containing the code of Hammurabi, which is now in the Louvre, Paris. The King is shown receiving the laws from the hands of the sun god. Other examples of the artistic activity

(above) Male head, diorite; Louvre, Paris. This portrait, presumably of Hammurabi, King of Babylon, was found at Susa, an ancient capital of Elam, now Iran. (below) Head of an Akkadian ruler, bronze; (Courtesy, Directorate General of Antiquities) Baghdad, Iraq. This bronze came from Kuyunijk on the Tigris River in Iraq, the ancient site of Nineveh.

of this period have been found at Mari (the modern Tell el Hariri), a city on the middle Euphrates which was conquered by Hammurabi. These include fine frescoes and sculptures found in the palace, and large and small terra-cotta reliefs and cylinder seals, which show the Babylonians absorbed in their duties to their gods.

Shortly after Hammurabi's death Babylon was conquered by the Kassites, who are believed to have originated in Central Asia; their rule lasted until the thirteenth century B.C. Under the Kassites art declined, although these people continued the Babylonian practice of decorating palaces with frescoes and they seem to have introduced to Mesopotamia the decorating of building façades with sculptured and molded bricks. It was the custom of the Kassites to mark land boundaries with elaborately carved stones called *kudurru;* some of these stones bore relief portraits of Babylonian kings.

A relief found in a temple of the sun god at Abu Habbah (the ancient Sippar), north of Babylon, and a fine limestone lion's head from

the same site show that during the centuries after the fall of the Kassites, when Babylon was ruled by kings of a variety of origins, artistic levels remained high. Indeed, the Babylonians seem to have shown special skill in the rendering of animal subjects. But cruel wars with Assyria took their toll, and it was only after the fall of Assyria in 612 B.C. that Babylon emerged for a brief cultural and artistic triumph.

Assyrian Art. Whereas the art of Babylon is largely lost except for a handful of monuments, Assyrian art is exceedingly well known, particularly from the ninth to the seventh century B.C., when it was at its zenith. This is largely due to the discoveries of such mid-nineteenth-century archaeologists as Henry Layard and Paul-Émile Botta who set out to find the site of Nineveh, one of the Assyrian capitals, which they rightly guessed to be hidden in one of the innumerable mounds of Mesopotamia. Layard, an Englishman, began his excavations in 1845 at Nimrud (the ancient Kalakh), south of the town of Mosul, where he found three palaces of the ninth, eighth, and seventh centuries B.C. Botta, a Frenchman, worked to the north of Mosul at Khorsabad (the ancient Dur-Sharrukin), where he found another palace, this one of the late eighth century.

Neither of these palace sites was in fact Nineveh, which it fell to Layard to discover in 1849 at Quyunjiq, a vast site across the Tigris River from Mosul. Here he unearthed a splendid palace built by the Assyrian King Sennacherib around 700 B.C. Shortly afterwards, Layard abandoned archaeology for politics, but his work was carried on by Hormuzd Rassam and W. K. Loftus, who found at Quyunjiq the last and finest of the Assyrian palaces, that of Ashurbanipal, built about 650 B.C. Thus, Assyrian palaces were unearthed ranging in dates from the ninth to the mid-seventh century B.C. They were ornamented with magnificent gateway figures in the form of huge monsters, while friezes of low-relief sculptures decorated the stone dados (or orthostates),

Lion from Susa, Elam, terra cotta; Louvre, Paris. Susa was formerly the winter residence of the Achaemenian rulers in the Elamite kingdom, and this lion may have decorated a palatial entrance there. Terra-cotta animals appeared in the golden age of Elam art in the second millennium B.C.

Statue of Queen Napir-Asu, wife of King Untashgal, bronze; Louvre, Paris. King Untashgal, a Kassite, ruled Babylon from 1234 to 1227 B.C. Under the Kassites art declined; this rigid garment with the stiffly curved pleats and the heaviness of the figure is reminiscent of earlier Sumerian art.

the upright slabs facing the lower part of the walls of the palace rooms.

In addition, a host of individual monuments came to light, in the form of stelae, statues, inscriptions, fresco paintings, and other works of art. To this astounding series of Assyrian discoveries, subsequent exploration has succeeded in adding relatively little.

As a result of the nineteenth-century discoveries, the scholars of the Western world acquired large quantities of documents in cuneiform writing, from which they were able to decipher and extract, among other items, a detailed knowledge of Assyrian history from the earliest times to the fall of Assyria in 612 B.C. The kings' annals, compiled in regular form by their chroniclers, are now preserved with only a few breaks from the thirteenth to the seventh century, thus covering the period of Assyria's greatest imperialism. These are extremely important for the interpretation of the palace reliefs of the same period, the art of which expresses itself in the form of pictorial chronicles.

The palaces, with their wealth of reliefs and other decoration, reveal a great deal about the Assyrians' ideas and their devices for representing the world around them. The reliefs, in particular, also provide an enormous fund of information about the Assyrians' military campaigns and the physical appearance, costumes, and armaments of the peoples against whom they fought. In these relief sculptures the Assyrians revealed themselves as the supreme masters of the art of narrative in the Near East, with an interest in vivid self-description which is closely paralleled in their royal annals.

Many of their artistic devices were age-old and inherited from the Sumerians. The most important of these has been called "the culminating scene," in which a whole series of events is presupposed and represented at its peak moment. Often, it takes the form of a simple ritual act or a scene of submission by a defeated enemy; sometimes it is a tranquil dialogue between two or more characters. Generally, the scene is expressed in a well-knit, symmetrical composition.

Narrative expressed in terms of a continuous non-repeating frieze was foreign to the Sumerian world, however, and the Assyrians may have taken this idea from the Hittites of Asia Minor. In the palaces of Asia Minor the dado of the stone wall base was carved, and the idea of the stone facing of walls in architecture was basically alien to Mesopotamia, where stone is not normally found. Among the Hittites, however, such carved scenes were somewhat primitive.

The earliest Assyrian experiment in narrative which survives is on an obelisk, the so-called

Stele bearing the Code of Hammurabi, from Susa, Elam (*c.* 2000 B.C.), basalt; Louvre, Paris. Above the carved words of the Code of Hammurabi is a scene carved in relief of the Babylonian king receiving the laws from the sun-god Shamash.

White Obelisk of Ashurnasirpal I (eleventh century B.C.); the king was an earlier namesake of the builder of the northwest palace at Nimrud. This monument uses the method of a wound-around strip, proceeding from the bottom to the top—a device similar to that which is found in Rome in the scenes on Trajan's Column.

Strong evidence of the Assyrians' early interest in the problem of representing movement can be seen in the Altar of Tiglath-Pileser I, found at Ashur (the modern Qal'at Sharqat), which shows the monarch twice in the same scene in different attitudes. By the time of Ashurnasirpal II (ninth century B.C.), as can be seen from the sculptures from his palace at Nimrud, the narrative has been transferred to the dado-slabs of the palace rooms. The frieze from his throne room is carved in two horizontal registers separated from one another by a band of cuneiform inscription praising the King. With few exceptions, the subjects of the two registers run from left to right in a continuous pattern, though not always in a strictly continuous sequence of events; the sequence is sometimes from upper to lower register, as, for example, in the scenes where bulls and lions are hunted in the upper register and sacrificed to a diety in the lower.

An intermediate step in the evolution of these narratives in stone on the wall was probably carried out in fresco painting, but very little of early date survives. The sculptures were, in fact, once painted, and many traces of color still exist. In general, events are depicted practically without depth, and take place within an area parallel to the viewer's path. Sometimes events are simultaneous, and a fiction of distance is created by placing those farther off higher up in the field; there is, however, no real perspective. A number of other conventions were also employed, such as the presence of the King in each scene, and the depiction of the Assyrians as larger than their enemies and ever victorious.

Ashurnasirpal II's scenes of war, which form a single, continuous frieze with those of hunting, depict the crossing of a river by the army and vaguely allude to a geographical setting by means of small bushes in the background. If the river indicated is the Euphrates, then this frieze represents the King's western campaign (879 B.C.); but there is no certainty, for the scenes are unlabeled and the representation of the enemy is somewhat unspecific. Nevertheless, from the bronze gates of the same king at Balawat, it can be seen that the labeling of such scenes of war with a line of cuneiform to identify the conquered people was already being practiced. This tradition is continued on the bronze gates of Shalmaneser III, son of Ashurnasirpal II, at Balawat, and on this King's celebrated *Black Obelisk* from Nimrud (now in the British Museum, London). The obelisk shows the Israelite Jehu and other princes in a series of "culminating scenes," doing homage to their Assyrian conquerer.

For almost a century after the death of Shalmaneser III, Assyria was torn by internal dissentions and its art declined. A revival can be seen in the palace of Tiglath-Pileser III (745-727 B.C.) at Nimrud. The art of Tiglath-Pileser III's reign does not possess the grandeur and dignity of that of the ninth century, but it is important, for it shows, for the first time, a clearly

traceable continuity in narrative, expressed in the events described.

The compositions of Tiglath-Pileser III are similar in form to those of Ashurnasirpal II, with a double register of reliefs separated by a band of text but with the important difference that they are now a version of the royal annals. It is obvious that the carved scenes can represent only a few events, while words can describe many episodes in a few lines, but there is now no longer any doubt of the general connection between text and illustration.

The reliefs of Tiglath-Pileser III were found by Layard and Rassam at Nimrud, not in their original position but partly removed for incorporation in a palace of King Esarhaddon (seventh century B.C.), which was never finished. Layard's drawings of these slabs make it possible to reconstruct the original arrangement, though only a few of the sculptures now survive and they are dispersed over various parts of the world. Recently it has been possible to insert the key piece that proves that, though very broken, the upper series is meant to illustrate Tiglath-Pileser III's defeat of the Babylonians in 730 B.C.

The lower register, with scenes showing the pursuit of wild men on camels, clearly describes

One of a pair of bronze lions with eyes of white stone and shale; Louvre, Paris. The lions guarded the entrance to the Temple of Dagan, Mari, nineteenth to eighteenth centuries B.C. Mari, a city in northern Mesopotamia on the Euphrates River, was the seat of a powerful dynasty of Semitic peoples. Mari art appeared between that of Sumeria and Babylonia in the second millennium B.C.

a campaign against the Arabs. We know from the royal annals that one of Tiglath-Pileser III's campaigns was directed against a certain Shamshi. Queen of Arabia, who had "violated the oath by Shamash (the sun god)." Mention is also made of the "Masai. Tamai. Sabai. Hayapai. Badanai [peoples] on the border of the lands of the setting sun (to the Assyrians. Arabia was in the southwest) whom no one knew and whose home is far off. They heard of the glory of my majesty; camels. female camels, all kinds of herds, as their tribute they brought before me with one accord and kissed my feet . . . Idi-bi'ili

I set up as overseer of the Egyptian frontier." All this can be seen in the reliefs.

In these reliefs of Tiglath-Pileser III an occasional inscription indicates the name of a city; otherwise, it seems that the spectators were meant to make such identifications with the aid of the annals. Generally, these reliefs are simple in composition and basically symmetrical in arrangement, with two lines of figures flowing to a central point. The sculptures of Tiglath-Pileser III's successor. Sargon II, at Khorsabad, show the same arrangement of two friezes, separated by a horizontal band of annals. The subject of

(right) Mural painting ▶ showing a ritual scene (second millennium B.C.) from a palace at Mari, Mesopotamia; Louvre, Paris. The largest palace at Mari, and the best preserved, was built for the ruler Zimrilin in the eighteenth century B.C., and consisted of rooms arranged around several courtyards. The murals seen here decorated the walls of a courtyard which probably served as the temple for sacrificial rites. An adjacent courtyard, containing a podium and a mural painting of Zimrilim, was undoubtedly used as a throne-room. The art of Mari inherited and developed numerous features of Sumerian art, and later influenced Babylonian art.

(left) Mural paintings showing the sacrificial offering of fire and water (second millennium B.C.), from the Palace of Zimrilim, Mari, Mesopotamia.

the frieze is loosely related to the text, but the city or the people conquered is usually indicated by an epigraph. The sequence flows along horizontally, though simultaneous events are sometimes indicated, as in the Siege of Musasir. There is also something new: occasionally the system of the double register is discarded so that the whole slab is thrown together to make a single vast ground, thus producing a scene with some of the qualities of a landscape or seascape. An example is a fragment of a series showing Phoenicians in ships bringing cedar and other timber, probably past the island of Tyre (or perhaps Arvad), to build Sargon II's palace.

Under Sennacherib, the successor of Sargon II, this experiment was carried further. In his palace at Nineveh, which Sennacherib ambitiously called "the Palace without a Rival," the system of using the whole "canvas" is frequently employed. One scenic space is formed, with the center of interest spread over the whole through a series of figures or groups loosely related to a local setting; a reminiscence of the central horizontal band of text is sometimes afforded by a river which divides the picture into upper and lower halves. Scale-patterns conventionally indi-

cate rocky or mountainous ground, an undulating horizon line covered with such scale-patterns evokes a mountainside; and sometimes a row of trees at the top of the hills suggests an interest in receding space.

The reliefs depicting the Seige of Lachish are not mentioned in the surviving royal annals. The events of the fall of this city are referred to in passing in the Bible in the description of the troubled reign of King Hezekiah (II Kings, 18). Although the annals of Sennacherib do not mention the seige, it is identified by a caption above the figure of the King, who sits on his throne receiving the submission of the surrendering inhabitants. These are two types: men wearing short kilts and a peculiar headdress with a hanging end, and others with tight, curly hair and long robes. The former are evidently the natives of the city, while the latter are probably the Jews, the emissaries of Hezekiah, who were treated with merciless severity for having persuaded the city to resist.

The Siege of Lachish reliefs are also important in another way: they show the Assyrian artist wrestling with the problems of perspective. He attempts to give depth to his representation of

Ruins of the city of Mari, on the Euphrates River in northern Mesopotamia (now Syria). The excavation of Mari was conducted in 1934 and 1935 under the sponsorship of the Musée du Louvre, Paris. A complex of temples, palaces decorated with murals, sculptured monuments, and cuneiform tablets were unearthed, all of which testify to the existence of a civilization before the time of the Babylonian domination. Mari was an active center during the period of the ancient city-states of Sumeria, and its own independent dynasty flourished as early as 2800 B.C. In the eighteenth century B.C. the Babylonian King Hammurabi conquered the city and established Babylonian domination.

the siege mound, up which the siege engines are brought, by cutting the mound into a series of diagonal strips arranged in the form of a pyramid.

A good example of the style of Sennacherib's reliefs is seen in the series illustrating the moving of colossal figures of bull-men for the gateways of his palace. Here the actual building of the palace is depicted, in a more detailed manner than in the Sargon II building scenes, which showed only the floating of the cedar logs. These scenes can be related to the elaborate description of such work narrated in Sennacherib's annals, though the annals themselves are no longer inscribed on the walls.

Another relief from Sennacherib's palace can only be interpreted by reference to a passage in the King's annals. It shows Luli, the Phoenician King of Sidon, who had fled to the city of Tyre and was forced to escape by sea from the vengeance of Sennacherib. "Luli, fearing to fight me, fled to Iadnana (Cyprus) in the midst of the sea. My terrifying splendor overcame him. He fled to Iadnana and there he died." This important identification of the drawing of this sculpture (now lost) shows conclusively that the scene of warships depicts the Phoenician fleet, and that, in the background behind the escaping King, there is a representation of the harbor of Tyre. The harbor is dominated by the famous Temple of Melkarth, with its twin pillars, noted by the Greek historian Herodotus as a landmark which was visible at sea.

Half a century after the exploits of Sennacherib were recorded on the walls of his palace at Nineveh, the sculptures of the palace of Ashurbanipal, also at Nineveh, were created. These are in a class by themselves and form the high-water mark of ancient Near Eastern artistic achievement.

One scholar has suggested that these later artists refused to pursue any further the innovations of Sennacherib in the treatment of receding space because they considered them aesthetically barbarous; this is inferred because there are no further examples of this form of representation. The more probable explanation is that the artists of Ashurbanipal, as they created their war and hunt scenes, were interested in other things.

When they wished to express the wild melee of battle, as in the great battle scene at the Ulai River, in which the Elamites were crushingly defeated, they took the whole height of an enormous slab and filled it with a turmoil of madly struggling figures. After the capitulation of the city of Madaktu, when the artists wished to depict order, pacification, and discipline, they showed formal processions of prisoners, headed by a band of musicians, leaving the city.

Simultaneous action is frequently depicted, but usually merges into a sequence of events. Careful thought is needed to grasp the fact that sometimes the reliefs show a sequence of juxtaposed events in which the same characters repeatedly participate. In the lion hunt scenes, for example, Ashurbanipal often appears to be fighting a number of the beasts at the same time. Actually he faces them one by one, as they are released from cages; but whereas the King is depicted only once in a scene, several of the lions, which he kills in successive encounters, are shown, and sometimes a single lion is represented in more than one posture.

The lion hunt is set in an arena enclosed by rows of shield-bearing soldiers, and in the background is a landscape dominated by a wooded hill with a monument at its summit. Some citizens of nearby Nineveh, with their picnic bags slung over their shoulders, can be seen climbing the hill to get a better view.

In a smaller, yet equally magnificent series of

(above) *Kudurru,* or stele, of King Melishipak II (twelfth century B.C.); Louvre, Paris. This stele is decorated with mythological animals representing the heavens and the underworld. (below) *Kudurru* of King Melishipak II (twelfth century B.C.); Louvre, Paris. The *Kudurru,* a monument in stone, characterized Kassite art.

High relief showing Gilgamesh, the great Near Eastern folk hero, with a lion cub and a sword, from Khorsabad (eighth century B.C.); Louvre, Paris. This Assyrian work may have been part of a palace gateway at Khorsabad, and served to protect the household from evil spirits.

scenes, the King, either on foot or on horseback, shoots a lion, grapples with it, or transfixes it with his sword. In yet another register he shoots at a herd of gazelles from a concealed position in a pit, while farther on a roundup of wild asses is taking place.

The reign of Ashurbanipal was followed by a period of confusion during which art declined, and shortly afterwards by the collapse of Assyria itself (612 B.C.). There was to be no revival, but the influence of Assyrian art, particularly of the continuous narrative frieze, made itself felt later in Greece.

While the relief friezes constitute the chief and most notable form of Assyrian palace decora-tion, they are not the only ones. In fact, they are one element of a scheme, partly magical and partly political, whose purposes were to ward off evil influences from the royal person, to please the gods by recording the king's exploits in their honor, and to point and record a moral for the benefit of the king's hostages, allies, and other guests.

The main task of keeping out evil influence fell to the pairs of colossal gateway figures, called *sedu* or *lamassu* (creatures with bodies of lions or bulls, eagles' wings, and bearded human heads), who flanked the main doorways of the palaces. They faced outwards, sometimes with an attendant divinity standing behind, ready to spring at the evil spirits. There are good examples of these gateway figures from the palace of Ashurnasirpal II at Nimrud, and from that of Sargon II at Khorsabad. In the former examples, a curious feature is the provision of five legs, two seen from the front, three from the side; this is due to the impulse to fuse two separate views into one, to suggest movement and life.

Splendid Assyrian frescoes of hunting scenes and scenes of war from the period of Tiglath-Pileser III, which were found in the provincial governor's palace at Tel Barsip in north Syria in 1921, establish a close connection between relief friezes and fresco painting. Fresco painting in Mesopotamia and indeed, in the Near East in general, has a long history, going back as far as the early part of the second millennium B.C., or even to Sumerian times. In the Assyrian palaces it played an important role in the decoration. The predominant colors were black, red, blue, and green. The figures were outlined in black, and sometimes only patterns of rhomboids or religious symbols were shown, but the effect was always extremely vivid.

The Assyrians did not excel in statuary, though some dignified portraits in the round of kings, both standing and seated, have been pre-served from the ninth and eighth centuries B.C.

The best-known is that of Ashurbanipal, now in the British Museum, London. A unique nude female figure representing the goddess Ishtar, which was dedicated by King Ashurbelkara (eleventh century B.C.) as a cult statue, has also survived (British Museum, London), but is now headless. Many similar works of art, such as carved stone bowls, metal vases and furniture, superbly engraved cylinder seals, carved ivories, painted and glazed ware and glazed bricks were found in the Assyrian palaces, showing the wealth and luxury with which the occupants surrounded themselves.

Neo-Babylonian Art. While it is difficult to establish important differences between the arts of Assyria and Babylonia because knowledge of Babylonian art is so patchy, it certainly seems that the types of objects and even techniques popular in Assyria were absent or less usual in Babylonia, and vice versa. The terra-cotta plaque, the *kudurru*, and the fine jewelry at which Babylonian artists and craftsmen excelled seem un-

Relief showing the figure of King Sargon II holding an ibex, and the figure of an attendant, from the Palace of Sargon II, Khorsabad (eighth century B.C.); Louvre, Paris. While the figures are stylized, the ibex, a wild goat of the Near East, is rendered in a very realistic manner. Assyrian sculptural relief, largely found in the palaces of the rulers, served to protect the king from evil and to honor his exploits.

Reconstruction of a glazed brick relief from the Throne Room of the palace of King Nebuchadnezzar II (c. 570 B.C.); Staatliche Museen, Berlin. This example of Neo-Babylonian art is characterized by floral patterns, stylized trees, and a row of angry lions. Glazed colored tiles were the most popular interior decoration of this late Babylonian period.

Low relief showing a man using a net to catch deer; British Museum, London. Scenes of hunts and of wars were favorite subjects of Assyrian art, and were represented most often in frieze sculpture or mural paintings. In this example the details of the net apparatus are shown with such clarity that it is possible to use the relief to reconstruct Assyrian hunting techniques.

common in Assyria, and palaces with scenes sculptured in relief on their walls seem unknown in Babylonia. However, taken as a whole, the artistic tradition and the artifacts in the two countries were probably much alike.

Some types of celebrated Babylonian products —their famous weavings and tapestries—have disappeared forever, yet their appearance is probably preserved in another medium characteristic of the Neo-Babylonian renaissance. This consists of the decoration of entire walls of buildings, both inside and out, with glazed colored tiles, in rich green, yellow, brown, and blue. These tiles were often modeled in relief to form large figures, as on the famous Ishtar Gate, which once formed the entrance to the inner city of Babylon. A reconstruction of this gate, with its reliefs of bulls and dragons repeated in a regular pattern, is now in the Staatliche Museen, Berlin. Similar glazed-brick reliefs appeared on the walls of the Processional Way, the broad, elevated avenue which was Babylon's main thoroughfare. The reliefs from the throne room of King Nebuchadnezzar II's palace (c. 570 B.C.) consist of patterns of floral designs and graceful stylized trees, with a dado of snarling lions along the lower part of the walls.

This ceramic art was highly esteemed by the Achaemenid Persian kings who succeeded the Neo-Babylonians, and was continued in their palaces. It seems thereafter to have remained dormant for many centuries until it was magnificently revived in medieval Persian and Seljuk art to beautify mosques.

Babylonian and Assyrian Architecture. The earliest known buildings in Mesopotamia, which were erected by the Sumerians during the Jemdet Nasr period (c. 3100-2100 B.C.), were shrines in the form of reed huts, similar to those still built to a considerable size in southern Iraq. Such buildings are known only from ancient illustrations. Soon afterwards, the Sumerians began to build stronger structures of mud-brick, their façades varied skillfully by buttresses and half columns, and their surfaces decorated with thousands of small inlaid clay cones with dyed heads, arranged in patterns. The best-known surviving example of this technique is the White Temple at Warka (the ancient Uruk). At another site, Tell Uqair, were found considerable remains of a Jemdet Nasr temple, with fresco paintings of animals and rosettes in the interior.

These early Sumerian temples were built on a brick platform, sometimes encircled by an oval enclosure-wall, and the construction material was either sun-dried or kiln-baked brick. In the third

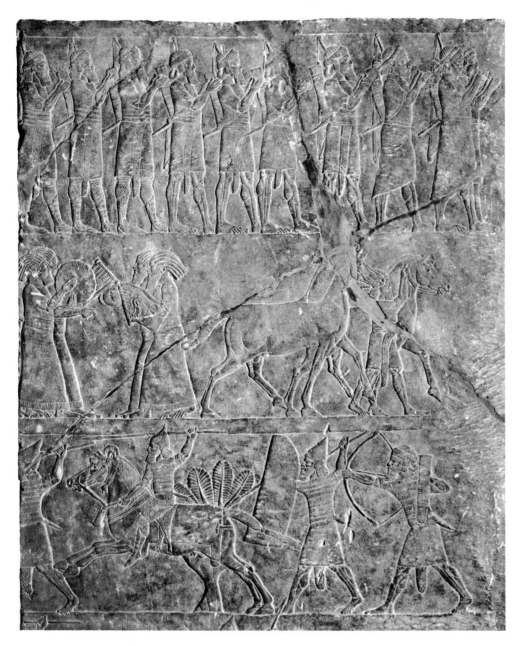

Low relief with scenes of war, from Nineveh (seventh century B.C.). The battles of the rulers Sennacherib and Ashurbanipal were recorded in continuous friezes on the walls of their palaces at Nineveh. This frieze shows the procession of captured warriors at the top, while fighting continues in the two relief bands below.

millennium B.C. the temples were sometimes adorned with columns covered with polychrome mosaic of stone inlays. The sanctuary (cella) of the temple was usually a long, narrow room, entered through one of its long sides.

The most characteristic feature of Mesopotamian religious architecture, surviving until late times, was the ziggurat, or temple-tower. The peoples of Mesopotamia believed that their gods dwelled in high places, and the ziggurats are thought to have been conceived as artificial mountains, the ascent of which might allow man to communicate with his dieties. Ziggurats rose

in tiers, at first rectangular and later square, and were surmounted by shrines. The early development of the ziggurat can be seen in the White Temple at Warka, which is built upon a large terrace. Gradually the number of stages increased, until in late Assyrian and Neo-Babylonian times there were seven tiers; in these later ziggurats the sides of the tiers were painted different colors.

Probably the most famous of the ziggurats was the seven-tired Etemenanki at Babylon, the biblical Tower of Babel. It was torn down by Alexander the Great when he conquered the city, and all that remains today is a 295 foot-square outline in the ground of the first tier. The best preserved ziggurat is the one at Ur (the modern Tell el Muqayyar), a three-tiered structure measuring 130 feet by 190 feet at its base.

The city of Babylon, as it existed during the time of Hammurabi, is now below the water level, and little is known about its architecture. However, at Mari the well-preserved ruins of a contemporary palace complex have been found. Although smaller and less regular, it is similar in plan to later Assyrian palaces.

Babylonian architecture of the Kassite period is not very well attested, but a fine ziggurat survives in ruins at Dur-Kurigalzu. The Kassite temple had a long cella with the entrance in one of the short walls, like a Greek temple. This plan later became standard in Assyrian temples. An innovation in Kassite architecture was façade decoration with large plastically modeled baked bricks; this style does not seem to have spread to Assyria, but it was revived and further developed during the Neo-Babylonian period.

The city of Babylon was destroyed by Sen-

Low relief depicting a naval expedition, from the Palace at Khorsabad; Louvre, Paris. In this scene the sculptor has depicted in realistic detail various types of marine life, while the water is rendered in stiffly curved, stylized patterns. Every element is shown from the most complete view; fish and boats in profile, turtle and crocodile from above.

nacherib in 689 B.C. and was rebult to its greatest splendor during the Neo-Babylonian period. Today, even the extent of the city's once-formidable fortified enclosing-walls is uncertain, and little remains of its numerous palaces, temples, and public buildings. Undoubtedly the largest building in the city was the palace complex of King Nebuchadnezzar II, built *c*. 570 B.C., which measured 600 feet by 900 feet. With the exception of the large throne room, the functions of its many chambers cannot be established.

Assyrian architecture followed a slightly different course from the Babylonian. Small palaces belonging to the late second millennium B.C. have been found at Ashur; some were ornamented with gaily colored frescoes in square panels, showing heraldic designs of goats and trees.

The great period of Assyrian palace-building lies between the ninth and seventh centuries B.C. The palace of Ashurnasirpal II at Nimrud (*c*. 850 B.C.) shows the typical palace plan already fully established. Basically the Assyrian palace consisted of a number of functional units (administrative offices, residential apartments, religious shrines, etc.) grouped around open courts, with the entire complex enclosed by fortified walls.

The two largest courts were the great court, surrounded by public offices, and the state court, surrounded by the chambers in which foreign dignitaries and other honored guests were received. Rooms were high-ceilinged and narrow; often they were entered through vaulted or arched doorways, flanked by great figures of human-headed bulls or lions. The walls were of brick, on a hewn stone base. A special type of building, the *bit-hilani,* was added to the palace complex by kings of the late eighth century B.C. It was a small pleasure kiosk with an entrance leading through columns, and was derived from north Syria
see: Sumerian Art

(left) King Ashurnasirpal II from Nimrud (ninth century B.C.); British Museum, London. This superb piece is one of the few known examples of Assyrian statuary. The figure is conventional in pose, yet the impression of the work is clearly one of kingly power and command. Although the statue has been carved in the round, it was meant to be viewed from the front.

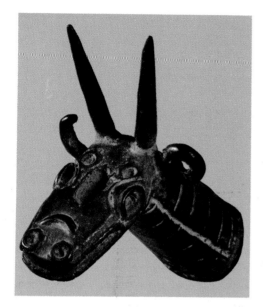

(above) Impression of a seal, from Mesopotamia; Louvre, Paris. This seal, perhaps of a royal house, is decorated with mythological figures. (below) Devotional figure, bronze; Louvre, Paris. In this Babylonian sculpture the figure is praying to the god Amurru to grant long life to the ruler Hammurabi.

(above) Dragon head, bronze (sixth century B.C.); Louvre, Paris. The dragon symbolized the god Marduk in Babylonian mythology. (below) Cylindrical vase from a tomb at Susa (second millennium B.C.); Archaeological Museum, Teheran, Iran. The handle of the vase is composed of a pair of figures in an attitude of prayer.

(below) Low relief of King Ashurbanipal hunting lions, from Nineveh (seventh century B.C.); British Museum, London. This frieze, in the form of a continuous narrative, shows the king killing a lion and several of the lions he will kill in successive encounters. Assyrian sculptors created the most naturalistic representations of animal life in the art of Mesopotamia.

(above) Il Bacchiacca: *Mary Magdalen;* Palazzo Pitti, Florence, Italy. The elongation of the fingers and neck and the sharply pointed facial features are characteristic of the Mannerist style, which was dominant in Florence and Rome during the second quarter of the sixteenth century.

(below) Il Bacchiacca: *Baptism of Christ,* scene from a predella panel of the altarpiece with scenes from the life of Sant'Acasio; Uffizi, Florence, Italy. Bacchiacca executed many mythological and biblical scenes, which he placed in landscape settings, and into which he crowded many figures in elegant dress. In this case the artist has treated the costumes with great attention to detail, but has made no attempt to reconstruct the dress of the original baptism.

Bacchiacca, Il (1494-1557)

Italian painter, born in Florence. Francesco d'Ubertino Verdi, called Il Bacchiacca, studied, according to Giorgio Vasari, under Perugino and Andrea del Sarto. Bacchiacca developed a fluent and polished style in which the influences of Del Sarto, Michelangelo, Perugino, Fra Bartolommeo, Bronzino, and Lucas van Leyden's prints are discernible. His work is extensive and includes the *Adam and Eve,* Johnson Collection, Philadelphia Museum of Art, which is based on Perugino's *Apollo and Marsyas* in the Louvre, Paris. Two panels with *Scenes from the Life of St. Joseph,* National Gallery, London, were originally part of the decoration of a room in the home of Pier Francesco Borgherini in Florence, together with panels by Del Sarto, Jacopo Pontormo, and Francesco Granacci. Other important works are the *Madonna and Child with the Infant St. John* and *The Legend of the Dead King,* Gemäldegalerie, Dresden, Germany, in which the artist's enthusiasm for Michelangelo is especially apparent, and the elaborate and decorative *Gathering of Manna*, National Gallery, Washington, D.C.

As well as scenes of mythology, allegory, and the Bible, Bacchiacca painted portraits. *The Old Man with a Skull,* Staatliche Kunstsammlungen, Kassel, Germany, and the *Portrait of a Woman,* Staatliche Museen, Berlin, betray the milieu in which he was trained, which was close in style to the work of Del Sarto and Franciabigio (Francesco di Cristofano Bigi). Four tapestries, after Bacchiacca's designs, and illustrating the *Months of the Year,* are in the Uffizi, Florence.

see: Florentine School

Baccio d'Agnolo: Façade of the Palazzo Bartolini-Salimbeni (1517-1520); Florence, Italy. Baccio worked primarily in Florence during the High Renaissance. Although his architectural innovations were severely criticized, notably by Michelangelo, this palace was frequently imitated in Florence as well as in other Italian cities, and is perhaps Baccio's finest work. The alternation of triangular and curved pediments both horizontally and vertically, and the horizontal alternation of large windows and small niches on the second and third levels create a sequence of rhythms that organize the façade.

Baccio d'Agnolo (1462-1543)

Italian architect and sculptor, born in Florence. Bartolommeo d'Agnolo Baglioni, called Baccio d'Agnolo, worked mainly in Florence and Rome in the High Renaissance style. He began his career as a woodcarver and between 1491 and 1495 worked on the decorative carving of the choir of the church of Santa Maria Novella, Florence.

Baccio studied architecture, probably in Rome, and after 1500 was engaged in Florence, with Il Cronaca (Simone del Pollaiuolo) and Antonio da Sangallo the Elder, on the construction of the Sala Grande in the Palazzo Vecchio. From 1507 to 1515 he was commissioned to complete the drum of the cupola of Santa Maria del Fiore, the Cathedral of Florence. This work was later interrupted after Michelangelo's severe criticism of the design.

Baccio designed a number of palaces and villas in Florence, including the Villa Borgherini and the Palazzo Bartolini-Salimbeni, 1517-1520, as well as the campanile (bell tower) of the church of Santo Spirito in 1511. In these works Baccio demonstrates the fusion and transformation of elements of Brunelleschi's architecture with the new expression of Tuscan High Renaissance architecture.

He was famous among his contemporaries for his personality as well as his work, and his studio in Florence was visited by celebrated artists and humanists, among them Michelangelo, Andrea Sansovino, and the young Raphael.

see: Florence; Renaissance Art and Architecture

Baciccia, Il (1639-1709)

Italian painter, born in Genoa. Known as Il Baciccia, Giovan Battista Gaulli was a student of Luciano Borzone in Genoa; he evolved a style involving the use of a rich palette and free brushstrokes, which was influenced by Peter Paul Rubens, Anthony Van Dyck, and Bernardo Strozzi, who had worked in Genoa a generation before Baciccia. Baciccia became a skillful fresco painter, able to adapt a richly colorful and decorative style to this medium, after copying the works of Perino del Vaga in Genoa and studying the illusionistic dome paintings of Correggio during a visit to Parma in 1661.

Baciccia went to Rome before 1660 and came under the influence of his great contemporaries Pietro da Cortona and Gianlorenzo Bernini. On canvas he executed the *Virgin and Saints* in the church of San Rocco, 1659, and the *Trinity* for the church of Santa Maria sopra Minerva. Although most of his portraits are lost, there remain the *Self-Portrait* in the Uffizi, Florence, and the intimate *Portrait of Pope Clement IX, c.* 1668, in the Accademia di San Luca, Rome.

Among Baciccia's frescoes in Rome is *The Glorification of the Franciscan Order,* 1707, in the church of the Santissimi Apostoli, Rome. Bernini secured for Baciccia the commission for the painting of the frescoes in the church of the Gesù, Rome, executed from 1668 to 1683. On the ceiling of the nave is *The Adoration of the Name of Jesus,* painted 1674-1679, which is Baciccia's greatest illusionistic fresco. In this work he epitomized Bernini's concept of painting: the unification of fresco, painted stucco, and

(left) Baccio d'Agnolo: Campanile of the church of Santo Spirito; Florence, Italy. This High-Renaissance bell tower shows a strong separation of levels which balances the vertical direction.

(right) Il Baciccia: Sketch for the ceiling fresco of the church of the Gesù, Rome (c. 1669); Galleria Spada, Rome. In this oil sketch Baciccia presented the final design for one of the finest examples of ceiling decoration of the High Baroque period. ▶

Jacob Adriaensz Backer: *The Gray Boy;* Mauritshuis, The Hague, The Netherlands. The soft, rich textures, the heavy cascade of drapery, and the gentle light of Backer's portrait reveal the influence of Rembrandt.

architecture on one surface, without any frames separating the painted parts from the architectural decoration. The illusionistic effect is further enhanced by the use of rich warm colors and the emphasis on areas of light and dark. Baciccia's work in the church of the Gesù, continuing in a style using the innovations of Bernini and Cortona, started a new approach to illusionistic ceiling painting in the period of the High Baroque style.
see: Baroque Art and Architecture; Bernini, Gianlorenzo; Illusionism; Pietro da Cortona

Backer, Jacob Adriaensz (1608-1651)
Dutch painter, born in Harlingen, Friesland and the pupil of Lambert Jacobsz in Leeuwarden. Backer settled in Amsterdam in 1633, where he painted portraits in the typical northern style, his subjects usually being wealthy burghers or bourgeois philanthropists. Rembrandt's influence is evident in Backer's early works, and his later works suggest the influence of Bartholomeus van der Helst.

A number of Backer's paintings are in the Rijksmuseum, Amsterdam, among them *Five Governors of the Nieuwe-Zijds-Huisziittenhuis* [Almshouse], *Amsterdam.*
see: Helst, Bartholomeus van der; Rembrandt van Rijn

Backhuysen, Ludolf the Elder (1631-1708)
Dutch marine painter, etcher, and portraitist, born in Emden. Backhuysen studied under Allart van Everdingen and Hendrick Dubbels in Amsterdam, where he spent most of his life. He specialized in paintings of turbulent seas, and is often compared to the marine painter Willem van de Velde the Younger.

Backhuysen achieved considerable success and was patronized by Peter the Great of Russia. The English painter J. M. W. Turner may have been influenced by his paintings, which include *Boats in a Storm,* Dulwich Gallery, London, and *Dutch Ships Wrecked on a Rocky Coast,* National Maritime Museum, Greenwich, London. Backhuysen is also well represented in the National Gallery, London, and his portrait of his wife, *Anna de Hooghe,* is in the Rijksmuseum, Amsterdam.
see: Everdingen, Allart van; Velde, Willem van de, the Younger

Baçó, Jaime (1409/17-1461)
One of the most important Valencian Spanish painters of the mid-fifteenth century. Jaime (Jacomart) Baçó is recorded as active in Naples from 1442 to 1447. In 1444 he painted an altarpiece for the church of Santa Maria della Pace, near Naples, lost in the destruction of the church in 1528. By 1447 he had entered the service of Alfonso V of Aragon, holding the office of court painter under both Alfonso and his successor, John II.

Attributions of paintings to Baçó are highly controversial. His style is basically Gothic in feeling, although his grasp of structure and eye for naturalistic detail suggest more modern Italian and Flemish influences. He is known to

Jaime Baçó: *Saint Ilde-fonso and Cardinal Alfon-so Borgia,* panel from the altarpiece in the Borgia Chapel (1444-1457); Collegiata of Játiva, Valencia, Spain. This altarpiece is attributed to Baço because of stylistic similarities with his known works, such as the altarpiece in the church at Cati, Spain. The rich, naturalistic details, notably in the robe of the saint, reflect Flemish influence.

have collaborated with Juan Rexach (died after 1484), and it is probable that a number of commissions accepted by Baçó were actually carried out by Rexach and others.

The most securely documented work attributed to Baçó is the polyptych of *St. Lawrence and St. Peter Martyr* (1460) in the church at Cati, near Tortosa, Spain. Further attributions, on stylistic grounds, include the altarpiece (1444-1457) in the Collegiata, Játiva, Spain; the retable of *Scenes from the Life of St. Martin* (1447-1457), Diocesan Museum, Segorbe, Spain; and the retable executed for the Carthusian monastery of Valdecristo, Spain, now in the Episcopal Palace, Segorbe, Spain.

see: Spanish Art and Architecture

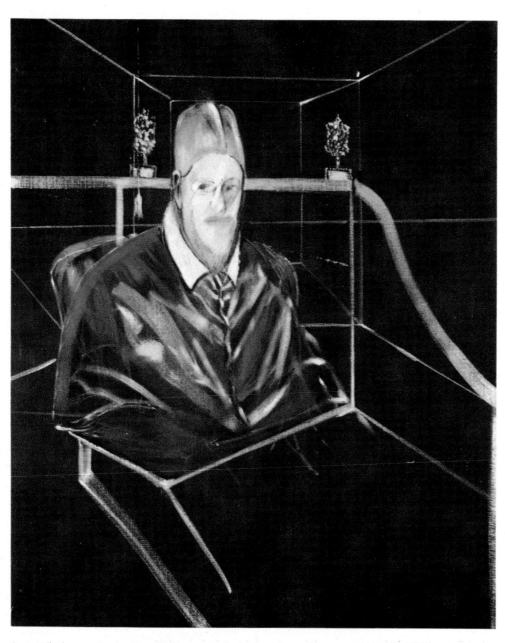

Francis Bacon: *Study After Velázquez's Portrait of Pope Innocent X* (1953); William A. Burden Collection, New York. Bacon has freely reinterpreted the original work to create a strange portrait. The sitter, whose features are blurred, is treated almost as an isolated sculptured portrait bust rather than as a person on a throne, which adds to the nightmare quality of the picture.

Bacon, Francis (born 1909)

British painter, born in Dublin. Bacon settled in London in the late 1920's and in the early 1930's was painting in a style reminiscent of Pablo Picasso. He subsequently destroyed most of these works and only resumed painting in 1944, when the *Three Studies for Figures at the Base of a Crucifixion*, Tate Gallery, London, initiated the figurative, expressionist canvases for which he is best known.

Bacon has always concentrated on the single figure in a position of physical and psychological isolation. He finds inspiration in newspaper photographs which show people unposed, and uses his highly synthetic idiom to convey a frightening mixture of horror, anguish, and bestiality. In his variations on Diego Velázquez's *Innocent X*, Galleria Doria-Pamphili, Rome, he transforms the pontiff into a series of images of terror and isolation. Typical of these variations is *Study after Velázquez's Portrait of Pope Innocent X* (1953), William A. Burden Collection, New York.

Until 1957 Bacon's palette tended to be somber and his textures flat, as in *Two Americans* (1955), Harold Weinstein Collection, Chicago. A series of imaginative portraits of Vincent van Gogh introduced a bolder, considerably brighter range of color, and fuller textures. These developments may be seen in *Study for Portrait of Van Gogh III* (1957), Joseph H. Hirschorn Foundation, Inc., New York, and in the later *Three Studies for a Crucifixion* (1962), property of the artist. In 1963 a retrospective exhibition of Bacon's work was held in the Solomon R. Guggenheim Museum, New York.

Bacon, John (1740-1799)

British sculptor, born in Southwark, London. Bacon began his career decorating and modeling delftware and porcelain figures. In 1763 he began to work in marble and in 1796 won the Royal Academy gold medal for sculpture with his bas-relief of the *Escape of Aeneas from Troy*. He was elected a Royal Academician in 1770.

Among the many busts executed by Bacon are those of *Dean Colet* (1798) for St. Paul's School, London; *Inigo Jones* (c. 1780), Carpenter's Hall, London; *George III*, Royal Collection; and the monument to *Lord Chatham* (1779), Westminster Abbey. His statue of *Dr. Johnson* (1796) is in St. Paul's Cathedral. Bacon's equestrian statue of *William III*, now in St. James's Square, London, was completed after his death by his two sons, John (1777-1859) and Thomas (1773-after 1800).

Bacon, Sir Nathaniel (c. 1585-1627)

English painter, active in Suffolk. An isolated figure in the history of English art. Bacon painted exclusively for his own family. He was the first English artist to show the influence of Caravaggio or to produce a landscape painting. From stylistic evidence it appears that he visited Utrecht, The Netherlands, and was familiar with the works of Hendrick Terbrugghen.

Of Bacon's six known works, four are self-portraits, the most distinctive of which is now in the collection of Lord Verulam, Gorhambury, Hertfordshire, England. Painted in about 1620, it is a full-length portrait of the artist in his study, surrounded by the objects of his varied interests. The interest in still-life painting suggested in this self-portrait is echoed in *The Cook-maid*, also at Gorhambury. Bacon's only extant landscape, now in the Ashmolean Museum, Oxford, is painted in miniature on copper. It derives from the tradition of Paul Bril and is interesting only as a curiosity.

Bada, José de (1691-1755)

Spanish architect, active in the district of Granada. Bada was in charge of work at Granada Cathedral from 1717, and in 1722 designed the Sagrario Portal for that building. In the same year he designed the façade of Málaga Cathedral, which was executed by his pupil Antonio Ramos.

Bada was an eclectic architect whose style fluctuated between weak academicism and extravagant Baroque. It was in the latter style that he designed the Old Town Hall of Granada between 1722 and 1728.

see: Granada; Spanish Art and Architecture

Badalocchio, Sisto (c. 1581-1647)

Italian painter and engraver, born in Parma. Badalocchio was probably a pupil of Agostino Carracci in Bologna, and after the latter's death in 1602 he went to Rome to act as an assistant to

Sisto Badalocchio: *The Holy Family;* Courtesy Wadsworth Atheneum, Hartford, Connecticut. The soft and delicate quality of this painting, and its subtle gradations of shadow, are characteristic of the north Italian painters of the sixteenth and seventeenth centuries from the area around Parma and Bologna.

Annibale Carracci. Between 1602 and 1607 Badalocchio and Giovanni Lanfranco, as assistants to Francesco Albani, executed Annibale's designs for the frescoes in the San Diego Chapel of the church of San Giacomo degli Spagnuoli. In 1607, again in collaboration with Lanfranco, he produced a series of watercolors based on Raphael's frescoes in the Vatican. In 1609, before returning to Bologna, Badalocchio executed four frescoes, after cartoons by Albani, in the Palazzo Verospi.

In the following years Badalocchio executed two frescoes in the Palazzo Bentivoglio in Gual-

tieri, painting in the style of the Carracci and in lively colors. These frescoes represent scenes from the *Life of Hercules* (1613), and an allegory, *Glory* (1613). He also made many engravings after Guido Reni.

Other works by Badalocchio include *St. Francis of Assisi*, Museo di Parma, Italy and *St. Jerome*, Musée du Puy-en-Velay, Le Puy, France.
see: Albani, Francesco; Lanfranco, Giovanni

Badger, Joseph (1708-1765)

American primitive painter, born in Charlestown, Massachusetts. Badger worked as a glazier and housepainter, teaching himself to draw and paint from about 1740 onward. He produced a number of portraits in which the charm of his simple and direct vision is thrown into relief by his attempt to imitate the current classical style. After the death of John Smibert (1688-1751), by whom he had been much influenced, Badger became the principal portrait painter in Boston.

Badger's works include the *Portrait of His Son*, Metropolitan Museum of Art, New York, and *Mrs. John Edwards* (c. 1750), Museum of Fine Arts, Boston.
see: United States Art and Architecture

Baerze, Jacques (active c. 1390)

Flemish woodcarver and sculptor. Little is known of Baerze's life, but it seems likely that he was born in Termonde, and it is possible that he executed an altar there, and another at Biloque, at some time before 1390. These altars, which are now lost, attracted the attention of Philip the Bold, Duke of Burgundy, who commissioned Baerze to make similar ones for the charterhouse of Champmol, Dijon.

One of these altars, completed in 1391, represents, in its pictorial quality, a departure from the traditional type of altar. It was made up of a number of small reliefs representing *The Adoration of the Magi*, *The Entombment*, and, in the central position, *The Crucifixion*, which included more than twenty finely carved figures, a number of horses, and simple scenery such as hills and buildings. On the outer wings of the altar were paintings by Melchior Broederlam, who probably also painted and gilded the figures which had been carved by Baerze.

Many of the reliefs from this altar, which were restored between 1841 and 1843, are now in the Musée des Beaux-Arts, Dijon. The Art Institute of Chicago owns the highly realistic *Crucifix* from *The Crucifixion* scene.

see: Broederlam, Melchoir

Baglione, Giovanni (c. 1573-1644)

Italian painter and biographer, born in Rome. Baglione belonged to the stylistic period of Late Mannerism, although he tried to assimilate the new trends of Baroque art. In the beginning of the seventeenth century he was influenced by Caravaggio's work in Rome, but later Baglione became strongly opposed to the *Caravaggisti* group of painters. He was in Naples from 1590 to 1592, and in Mantua from 1621 to 1623, where he studied the works of Domenico Fetti. Baglione also attempted to paint in the manner of the Bolognese Baroque masters.

Baglione was patronized by Pope Sixtus V; Clement VIII, who chose him, along with other artists, to execute large altarpieces for St. Peter's; and Urban VIII, for whom he worked on the decoration of St. Peter's. Among his other works are the fresco of *The Life of the Virgin* in the church of Santa Maria dell'Orto, Rome; *The Last Supper* in the church of San Nicola in Carcere, Rome; and paintings in the Cathedral of Perugia and the Cathedral of Loreto.

Baglione is principally remembered as an art historian and biographer. His most important books in this field are *The Nine Churches of Rome* (1639), and the *Lives of the Painters, Sculptors, and Architects in Rome from 1572 to 1642* (1642). The inclusion of Caravaggio, Gianlorenzo Bernini, and Peter Paul Rubens in the more than eighty biographies of the *Lives* illustrates Baglione's awareness of and admiration for Baroque art.

see: Baroque Art and Architecture; Mannerism

Joseph Badger: *Mrs. John Edwards* (*c.* 1750); Courtesy, Museum of Fine Arts, Boston (Gift of Dr. Charles Townsend). Badger, an early American painter who taught himself to draw and paint, rose to prominence as the principal portrait painter of Boston in the mid-eighteenth century. Like the work of many Americans of this period, the painting is crude in some aspects, but is at the same time rather strong and bold. The painter has succeeded in conveying a very powerful sense of personality.

Bagnacavallo (Bartolommeo Ramenghi) (1484-1542)

Bolognese painter, the pupil of Francesco Francia, Raphael, and Dosso Dossi. Bagnacavallo was one of Raphael's assistants in the decoration of the gallery of the Vatican, and he was also responsible for the decoration of the convent of San Michele in Bosco, Bologna, Italy.

Among Bagnacavallo's works are *The Circumcision*, Louvre, Paris and *Madonna and Child*, Pinacoteca Nazionale, Bologna, Italy.

Bailey

see: Architectural Terms

Baillairgé, François (1759-1830)

Canadian sculptor, architect, and painter, born in Quebec. Baillairgé was the most noted member of a family of sculptors active through four generations in Quebec from 1770 to 1850. He studied at the Académie Royale in Paris between 1779 and 1782 and from this time painted in a French classical style. Baillairgé's major work was done between 1787 and 1799 for the Basilica of Quebec.

Léon Nikolaevich Bakst: (above left) *Potiphar's Wife,* a costume design; Civica Raccolta Stampe Bertarelli, Milan, Italy. (above right) *The Blue God,* costume for Nijinsky, the lead dancer of the *Ballet Russe* of Sergei Diaghilev. (below) *Scheherazade* costume designs, watercolor. Bakst became famous for his designs for the *Ballet Russe* in Russia. Later his costumes and stage designs became popular in Western Europe and the United States.

Bakst, Léon Nikolaevich (Lev Samuilovitch Rosenberg) (1868-1924)

Russian painter and stage designer, born in St. Petersburg. Bakst studied at the Imperial Academy of Arts, St. Petersburg, and in Paris from 1895, where he became interested in the aestheticism of the classical theater. Subsequently Bakst became one of the artists associated with Sergei Diaghilev when he was publishing his famous and influential Russian art periodical, *Mir Iskusstva* (World of the Arts), 1898-1904.

Bakst had already toured Greece and designed sets for Greek tragedies produced at the Russian Imperial Theaters and the Hermitage Court Theater, when, in 1909, he began his great period of achievement with Sergei Diaghilev's *Ballet Russe*. His work during this association won him universal recognition and exerted a tremendous influence on stage design, stage costume, and contemporary Russian art in general. In Paris, the *Ballet Russe* and the splendor of Bakst's décor were received with great enthusiasm, and

Léon Nikolaevich Bakst: Poster design for Nijinsky in Claude Debussy's ballet *The Afternoon of a Faun,* for the *Ballet Russe.* Bakst first worked for the *Ballet Russe* in 1909 under Sergei Diaghilev, and designed costumes for such dancers as Nijinsky and Anna Pavlova. His accomplishments during this period gained him universal recognition and his work had a marked influence on European ballet and other theatrical décor of that time.

Jerónimo Balbás: Chapel of Kings (1718-1737); Cathedral, Mexico City, Mexico. The influence of Spanish architectural style on Mexico was very pronounced; this example shows the same lavish decoration that was the dominant characteristic of Spanish baroque style. The overwhelming complexity of the gilded details (particularly the rich foliated elements) almost seems to dissolve the solid forms, including the wooden figures, into a shimmer of gold.

Bakst's work had a marked influence on European ballet and other theatrical decoration during this period.

Shortly before the Bolshevik Revolution, Bakst returned to Russia and founded a school of painting. Later he returned to Paris and London and his primary interest—stage and costume designing. His work with Diaghilev's company took him on extensive tours of Europe, and in 1914 he visited the United States to design the set for Anna Pavlova's *Orientale* ballet.

Among Bakst's most notable achievements are his designs for the ballets *Scheherazade, The Specter of the Rose,* and *The Afternoon of a Faun,* and his costumes for the ballet *Firebird.*
see: Costume, Theatrical; Russian Art and Architecture; Stage Design

Balbás, Jerónimo (active 1706-1750)
Spanish sculptor, born in the region of Andalusia. Balbás executed a number of altars in Andalusia including the high altar of the Sagrario cathedral, Seville, made between 1707 and 1709 and destroyed in 1824. It was widely imitated throughout Seville. In 1714, Balbás designed the choir stalls for the church of San Juan, Marchena, with an exhuberant mixture of stylized Mannerist and theatrical Baroque elements. In this work he used *estípites,* shafts that thicken and then taper toward the top, for the first time in Spanish sculpture.

In 1717, Balbás traveled to Mexico where he was responsible for introducing the decorative Rococo forms, which replaced the prevalent more massive decorative elements found in the

Late Baroque style. Balbás' most influential work in Mexico was the semi-circular high altar for the chapel of Kings, Cathedral, Mexico City, executed between 1718 and 1737. In this work he again used *estípites*, and the altar served as a model for local artists.

see: Mexican Art and Architecture

Baldacchino
see: Architectural Terms

Baldassare d'Este (First half fifteenth century-c. 1502)

Italian painter, born in Ferrara. The natural son of Niccolò III d'Este, Baldassare was a por-

traitist at the Este and the Sforza courts.

From 1461 to 1469 he lived in Lombardy where he painted, in the castle of Pavia, the portraits of Galeazzo Maria Sforza and his wife. In addition to a number of portraits of the Este family and courtiers painted "from life," in 1472 Baldassare decorated a chapel in the church of San Domenico, Ferrara, with *Scenes from the Life of Saint Ambrosius*. In spite of many biographical references, his known works are few. With the exception of the *Portrait of Borso (d'Este)* in the Trivulzio Collection, Milan, and the signed *Portrait of a Man* in the Cook Collection, Richmond, England, the other works are all attributions.

Baldassare d'Este (attribution): *The Family of Uberto de' Sacrati;* Alte Pinakothek, Munich, Germany. The artist was a popular portraitist at the Este and the Sforza courts in Ferrara and Pavia, Italy, in the last half of the fifteenth century. Baldassare's style is noted for its composition, almost that of a miniaturist, and for its atmospheric light. Notable in this painting is the landscape on the left executed with great attention to detail almost as an independent miniature.

Baldinucci, Filippo (1624-1696)

Italian biographer, art historian, and collector, born in Florence. A scholar of painting and drawing, Baldinucci was artistic advisor to Cardinal Leopoldo de' Medici and helped in the selection of his art collection; for Cosimo III de' Medici he catalogued the family collection of drawings, now in the Uffizi, Florence. Baldinucci himself was an avid collector of drawings and his private collection of about one thousand drawings was acquired by the Louvre, Paris, in 1806.

The first results of his historical research were published in 1681 (the work was completed by his son in 1728) under the title of *An Account of the Masters of Drawing from Cimabue to the Present Time*. The biographies, in six volumes, were intended as a revision and an addition to Giorgio Vasari's *Lives* (published 1568), and covered the period from 1260 to 1670. Among his other literary works are *The Beginning and Development of Engraving in Copper* (1686), *The Life of Filippo Brunelleschi* (published 1812), and *The Life of Gianlorenzo Bernini* (1682). The last named work was commissioned by Christina, Queen of Sweden, who was a patron of the arts and a close friend of Bernini in Rome. It is still the most complete source for information on Bernini and reveals the thoroughness of Baldinucci's scholarship.

see: Bernini, Gianlorenzo, Medici Family

Baldovinetti, Alesso (c. 1425/26-1499)

Florentine painter and worker in stained glass and mosaic. Baldovinetti may have been a pupil of Domenico Veneziano, and his work also shows the influence of Fra Angelico and Antonio Pollaiuolo. During the earlier part of his life he may have worked with the goldsmith and engraver Maso Finiguerra.

The frescoes that Baldovinetti executed for the churches of Santissima Annunziata (1460-1462) and San Miniato (1466), both in Florence, are now in a poor state of preservation due to his experiments in the use of pigments and color and the subsequent deterioration of his materials. Three panels that he painted for the series on the doors of the silver cupboard of Santissima Annunziata, which had been begun by Fra Angelico, are now in the Museo di San Marco, Florence. His work in portraiture derives, as do other early profile portraits, from medallions.

(above and left) Alessio Baldovinetti: Two details of the *Annunciation* (1466); chapel of the Cardinal of Portugal, church of San Miniato, Florence, Italy. Evident here is Baldovinetti's use of luminous light (surrounding the figures of the Virgin and the Angel) and the excellent linear precision.

Alesso Baldovinetti: *The Nativity* (1460-1462), fresco; Chiostro dei Voti, church of Santissima Annunziata, Florence, Italy. This fresco dates from Baldovinetti's most active period. Here the major scene of the religious narrative is restricted to the near foreground. In the middleground can be seen the angels who are announcing the birth of Christ to the shepherds. The entire background is taken up by a landscape which is remarkable for the sense of sunlight.

Other works by Baldovinetti include *Portrait of a Lady*, National Gallery, London, and *Madonna Adoring the Child* (*c.* 1460), Louvre, Paris, in which his linear precision and interest in landscape may be seen.

Baldung-Grien, Hans (c. 1484/85-1545)

German painter, draftsman, and designer of woodcuts, tapestries, and stained glass. Baldung-Grien was probably born in Schwäbisch Gmünd and is believed to have worked under Albrecht Dürer in Nuremberg for a period before 1508. In 1509 he became a citizen of Strasbourg, where he worked for three years.

During this period of activity in Strasbourg, Baldung-Grien painted a number of small altarpieces and religious panels in a style much influenced by Dürer. This influence can be seen in the panel representing *The Mass of St. Gregory*, Museum of Art, Cleveland, Ohio. Between 1512 and 1516 he completed one of his major works, the high altar of the cathedral of Freiburg. Dur-

ing this period his palette acquired richer and more brilliant colors, as can be seen in such works as the *Mystic Pietà*, now in the National Gallery, London.

Baldung-Grien returned to Strasbourg in 1517. His art now entered a new phase, a change being particularly evident in his choice of subject matter. He began to paint idealized human figures in allegorical compositions with a moral message and to use soft, glowing colors. One of his favorite themes was an allegory of *Death and the Maiden*, on which he based a series of paintings. Lucas Cranach's influence is evident in some of Baldung-Grien's works; *Portrait of a Woman*, Thyssen Collection, Lugano, Switzerland, was probably a direct copy of a Cranach. Baldung-Grien's iconography was probably influenced by his early sympathy with the Reformation, expressed in a woodcut of 1521 showing Martin Luther protected by the symbol of the Holy Ghost.

Other works by Baldung-Grien include *Por-*

trait of a Man, National Gallery, London, and *Adam and Eve*, Thyssen Collection, Lugano. A complete sketchbook is preserved in the Karlsruhe Gallery, Karlsruhe, Germany, and many of his drawings are in German and Swiss museums. *see:* German Art and Architecture

Balen, Hendrick van (1573-1632)

Flemish Italianate painter, born in Antwerp. The pupil of Adam van Noort, Balen studied in Italy before returning to Antwerp in 1592. He usually collaborated with other painters, notably Joos de Momper, Jan Bruegel, and Frans Snyders, in the execution of small biblical and mythological scenes, and small pictures on wood and copper. The teacher of both Snyders and Anthony Van Dyck, Balen was himself influenced by Van Dyck as evidenced in late works. He is also indebted both to the Mannerists, in *The Marriage of Peleus and Thetis* (1608), Gemäldegalerie, Dresden, and to Peter Paul Rubens, in his *Holy Family* altarpiece in Antwerp cathedral. The

Hans Baldung-Grien: *Portrait of Christoph von Baden* (1515); Alte Pinakothek, Munich, Germany. Most of Baldung-Grien's portraits show the same three-quarter view as this example. Here the individuality of the sitter is portrayed through the careful attention given to the distinguishing facial characteristics such as the very thin lips and the distinctive shape of the eyes and nose. The artist has also carefully recorded such costume details as the decoration of the hat, the lacing of the shirt, and the fur collar.

Hans Baldung-Grien: *Vanitas* (1529), Alte Pinakothek, Munich, Germany. This is one of the many allegorical works by Baldung-Grien. Some of the elements in this painting are almost impossible to explain since Baldung-Grien devised a very personal symbology. The figure of Vanity, looking at herself in a mirror, is perhaps intended to remind the viewer of the temporary nature of human beauty. This figure is emphasized by the contrasting dark background and by its central placement in the composition.

cathedral contains other works by Balen, and he is also represented in Copenhagen and in Paris.

see: Antwerp Mannerists; Bruegel Family; Dyck, Anthony Van; Rubens, Peter Paul; Snyders, Frans

Balestra, Antonio (1666-1740)

Italian painter, born in Verona where he first studied under Giovanni Ceffis. In 1687 Balestra went to Venice where he entered the studio of Antonio Bellucci through whom he came under the influence of the work of Pietro Liberi and Luca Giordano. In 1690 he was in the school of Carlo Maratta in Rome, and in 1694 he received a prize from the Roman Accademia di San Luca. In this same year Balestra traveled to Naples to observe for himself the work of Luca Giordano, Giovanni Lanfranco, and Francesco Solimena. From 1697 to 1718 he made various trips to Bologna, Venice, Parma, Vicenza, and Milan, after which time he settled permanently in Verona where he directed a school. His pupils included Giambettino Cignaroli and Giuseppe Nogari.

An eclectic artist, Balestra reflected the influence of the soft colors of Antonio Correggio and the formal academic composition of Maratta. Until the time of Giorgio Anselmi, Balestra was the leader of painting in Verona, and, as such, influenced northern Italian artists of the area around Venice as well as indirectly influencing the development of baroque painting in Austria.

As an engraver Balestra designed the illustrations for Michele Sanmicheli's *Five Orders*, which included the portraits of the great architects Sanmicheli, Leone Battista Alberti, Andrea Palladio, Vincenzo Scamozzi, and Giacomo Vignola.

Examples of Balestra's work are to be found in Italy in religious and public buildings in

(right) Antonio Balestra: *Madonna and Saints Stanilaos Kotska, Luigi Gonzaga, and Francesco Borgia* (1704); church of the Gesuiti, Venice, Italy. The sweeping diagonal of figures from lower right to upper left and of the curving swirl of clouds and angels identify the painting as an early eighteenth-century Italian work. Balestra was an eclectic painter and as such drew on many varied sources for his canvases.

◄ (left) Hendrik van Balen: *Banquet of the Gods;* Musée des Beaux-Arts, Angers, France. Van Balen studied in Rome in the last decade of the sixteenth century, where he absorbed the taste for classical subject matter. He later worked in Flanders and he often collaborated on his mythological paintings with Jan Bruegel, who painted the landscape and still-life details for this scene.

Verona, Vicenza, Venice, Bergamo, Bologna, Brescia, Parma, and Padua. In the basilica of Santa Giustina in Padua, the large *Discovery of the Bodies of Saints Cosmas and Damian*, signed and dated 1718, is an example of Balestra's work at the end of his complex formative period and numerous trips. Here he reveals, in an intricate formal structure, the desire to give compositional order to elements taken from Roman academic painting, yet remaining dependent on Venetian color.

see: Giordano, Luca; Veronese School

Giacomo Balla: *Flags at the Monument to Victor Emmanuel II in Rome* (1915); private collection, Rome. In developing the Futurist ideas of representing dynamic movement on canvas Balla arrived at an abstract style. The Futurists, a group of painters in Italy in the second decade of the twentieth century, issued manifestos which were commitments to the age of technology. In this painting, broad areas of color describe form and movement. The word *Futurista* can be seen in the signature.

Balla, Giacomo (1871-1958)

Italian painter, born in Turin, but who worked and lived in Rome for most of his life. In 1910, Balla with his pupils Gino Severini and Umberto Boccioni, along with Carlo Carra and Luigi Russolo, signed the Futurist Manifesto originally published on February 20, 1909 by Filippo Tommaso Marinetti in the French newspaper *Le Figaro*. This manifesto was essentially a commitment to the age of machine technology.

Although Balla's basic orientation was realistic, his style manifested expressionist, impressionist, and divisionist elements. As well as proving himself a skillful designer, Balla also succeeded in his attempts to use light effects with non-objective matter and to express dynamic movement and sound on canvas. This is especially notable in his *Leash in Motion* (1912), Museum of Modern Art, New York. It is from this time that his style became clearly futuristic.

In 1917, Balla worked on the scenic design for Igor Stravinsky's ballet *Song of the Nightingale,* and *Fireworks,* performed by Sergei Diaghilev's *Ballet Russe.*

Among Balla's most important works, those of his Futurist period, are *Swifts: Paths of Movement Dynamic Sequences* (1913), and *Speeding Automobile* (1912), both Museum of Modern Art, New York, and *Automobile and Noise* (1912), Peggy Guggenheim Collection, Venice. *see:* Futurism

Balthus (born 1908)

French painter of Polish extraction, born in Paris. Balthasar Klossowsky, known as Balthus, was the son of a painter and art critic. He had no art school training but began to paint seriously at the age of sixteen and was influenced by Pierre Bonnard and, more strongly, by André Derain, who were both friends of his parents.

In 1933 Balthus attracted notice of the surrealists with a composition entitled *La Rue,* and his first exhibition was held at the Galerie Pierre, Paris, in the following year. His style is reminiscent of the German New Objectivity group, who offered angular, mechanistic interpretations of the objective world. Balthus' later works are realistic, but with a personal, mystic interpretation of reality, as in the *View of Commerce Saint-André* (1951-1954), private collection, where the figures, slightly blurred, give the painting a dream-like quality

Balthus has held exhibitions both in Europe and in the United States. His portraits *André Derain* (1936) and *Joan Miró and His Daughter Delores* (1938) are in the Museum of Modern Art, New York.

(above) Balthus: *Joan Miró and His Daughter Delores* (1937-1938); oil on canvas; Collection, The Museum of Modern Art, New York, Mrs. John D. Rockefeller, Jr. Fund. Balthus began to paint seriously at an early age, without instruction, and his work reflects in a somewhat primitive style a personal interpretation of reality. Here the portrait is of Miró, a surrealist painter.

(left) Balthus: Detail of *View of Commerce Saint-André* (1951-1954); private collection. In this painting the blurred images of the figures give a dream-like quality to the scene. Although the scene appears to be a random view of a street, the placement of the figures reveals a considerable amount of careful planning.

Balusters
see: Architectural Terms

Balustrade
see: Architectural Terms

Bamboccianti
A group of painters, primarily Dutch and Flemish, who worked in Rome during the second quarter of the seventeenth century. The name Bamboccianti seems to derive from their leader Pieter van Laer (*c.* 1592-1642), nicknamed "Il Bamboccio" (from the Italian meaning 'clumsy baby') because he was a hunchback. They specialized in genre paintings of low-life scenes set in the streets of Rome. These scenes, called derogatorily Bambocciate, were painted on a small scale based on the format of the Cabinet Pictures, which portrayed scenes of daily life, made by contemporary artists working in The Netherlands.

The members of the Bamboccianti group belonged to the Schildersbent guild in Rome (founded in 1623), which served to protect these artists from the rules set by the Accademia di San Luca, the powerful academy in Rome. The

Michelangelo Cerquozzi: *The Morra Players;* Meambrini Collection, Rome. Cerquozzi was considered the best painter of the Bamboccianti group. The majority of the paintings by the members of this group were works, such as this one, which showed Roman daily life, and made no pretense to elevated or noble subject matter. This type of work was rejected by a majority of the art theorists of the seventeenth century not simply because the subject matter was considered inappropriate for great art, but because the brush strokes, which were free and loose, were considered inferior to a very clear and carefully outlined style.

Faustino Bocchi (1659-c. 1742): *The Killjoy;* Tosio Martinengo Collection, Brescia, Italy. This party scene is typical of Bamb------ccianti subject matter with its portrayal of dwarfs and other deformed people in a grotesque narra------tive painted with bizarre fantasy, irony, and im------piety.

members of the Accademia thought that Bam------bocciate subjects were too vulgar to suit the current taste for classicizing, monumental baroque painting. The main patrons of the Bamboc{cianti were private collectors and in the 1630's the style enjoyed its greatest popularity.

The style of the group derived from the style and subject matter of Van Laer, who was in Rome from 1625 to 1639. The most important BambOccianti artist was Michelangelo Cerquozzi (1602-1660), a Roman by birth, whose work tended to be purely anecdotal, as in *The Bath,* Incisa della Rocchetta Collection, Rome, and *The Wool Carder,* Galleria Nazionale, Rome. Jan Miel (1599-1663) arrived in Rome in 1636 and, after a period as assistant to Andrea Sacchi, turned to painting Bambocciate subjects in works such as *Roulette Players,* Royal Collection, Eng------land, only to revert once more to the classical manner in 1650. Michael Sweerts (1624-1664) was in Rome by 1646 and remained there until 1654 or 1656. His paintings are characterized by a static, still-life quality, and a soft, subtle gray tone, as in *Feeding the Hungry,* Rijksmuseum, Amsterdam, and *Portrait of a Boy,* Wadsworth Atheneum, Hartford, Connecticut. Johannes Lin------

gelbach (1622-1674) was in Rome from 1645 to 1650. He specialized in genre scenes with em------phasis on the background and setting, which often contained antique ruins. Typical examples are the *View of the Forum Romanum,* Marquess of Bath Collection, England, and *The Piazza del Popolo,* Balella Collection, Rome.

The second generation of Dutch painters working in Rome and in northern Europe, who maintained the principles of the Bamboccianti even when the movement declined in Italy in the 1650's, included Jan (*c.* 1618-1652) and Andries (*c.* 1612-1641) Both, who may have collaborated on the *Capriccio with Figures in the Forum Romanum,* Rijksmuseum, Amsterdam. Nicolaes Berchem (1620-1683), Jan Asselyn (1610-1652), and Karel Dujardin (*c.* 1622-1678) were in Rome in the 1640's and produced genre and landscape scenes based on the Bamboccianti as well as on the French landscapist in Rome, Claude Lorraine.

see: Asselyn, Jan; Berchem, Nicholaes; Both, Jan and Andries; Cabinet Picture; Cerquozzi. Michelangelo; Dujardin, Karel; Dutch Art and Architecture; Laer, Pieter van; Lingel------bach, Johannes; Miel, Jan; Schildersbent (Bentname); Sweerts, Michael

Baccio Bandinelli: Marble relief panels from the choir screen; Cathedral, Florence, Italy. In this example can be seen the sculptural excellence for which Baccio is considered one of the finest sixteenth-century sculptors in Italy. He was one of the favorite sculptors of Cosimo I de' Medici, Duke of Florence.

Bamboccio, Il
see: Laer, Pieter van

Bandinelli, Baccio (1493-1560)

Florentine sculptor, the son of a goldsmith, who pursued a life-long rivalry with Michelangelo and Benvenuto Cellini. Contemporary accounts describe him as untalented, but examination of his work shows that, although never attaining the heights reached by Michelangelo or Cellini, he had considerable ability.

Bandinelli studied under Giovanni Francesco Rustici. His earliest important work is the copy of the *Laocoön*, commissioned by Pope Clement VII for Francis I of France, now in the Uffizi, Florence. When Michelangelo fled from Florence in 1530 on the return of the Medici family, Bandinelli gained favor. He was commissioned by Cosimo I de' Medici to execute the marble group of *Hercules and Cacus* (1534) for the exterior of the Palazzo Vecchio, Piazza della Signoria, Florence. This work shows the marked influence of Michelangelo's colossal statue *David*, which at that time stood opposite the *Hercules and Cacus* at the entrance to the Palazzo. He also executed the series of reliefs on the choir screen of the Cathedral, Florence, Italy.

Bandinelli was superseded at the court of the Medici by Cellini and Bartolommeo Ammanati but managed to secure a place for his own tomb in the church of Santissima Annunziata, Florence. There, with the assistance of his son Clemente, he executed his last work, *The Lamentation Over the Dead Christ*.

Bandinelli is also important for having founded two of the first academies of art, in The Vatican

(1531) and in Florence (*c.* 1550). The Florentine academy was to influence the founding of similar institutions both in Italy and in France.

see: Academies of Art; Florence; Michelangelo Buonarroti

Banks, Thomas (1735-1805)

English sculptor, educated at Ross-on-Wye, Herefordshire, and subsequently apprenticed to the sculptor William Barlow in 1750. Shortly afterward Banks was employed by the architect and landscape gardener William Kent. A frequent exhibitor at the Royal Academy, Banks was awarded a gold medal in 1770 for a bas-relief of *The Rape of Proserpine.*

In 1772 Banks won a Royal Academy traveling scholarship to Rome, where he carved a number of works in the current Neo-Classical style, including *Thetis,* Victoria and Albert Museum, London, and *Cupid Catching a Butterfly,* later sold to the Empress Catherine of Russia. Banks returned to London in 1779 and, in 1781, paid a short visit to Russia where he executed works for the Empress and for Prince Grigori Potemkin. Following his return to England, Banks executed a high-relief of *Shakespeare Between the Dramatic Muse and the Genius of Painting* (1789), now in the gardens of New Place, Stratford on Avon; and his most famous work, the monument commemorating *Miss Penelope Boothby* (1793), Ashbourne church, Derbyshire.

Banks was elected an Associate of the Royal Academy in 1784 and became a Royal Academician in 1786. Among his other more important works are the marble bas-relief of *Caractacus Before Claudius* (1780), Stowe House, Bucking-

Francesco Baratta: *Rio della Plata,* one of the four giant marble figures on Gianlorenzo Bernini's Fountain of the Four Rivers (1651); Rome. This monumental figure, with its complex twisted, reclining position and strongly emphasized anatomy is a good example of the powerful sculptural style of the period. See page 398.

hamshire, and *The Four Quarters of the Globe* (1783), since destroyed, for the north front of the Customs House, Dublin.
see: Neo-Classical Style

Baños, San Juan Bautista de
see: Carolingian Art and Architecture

Baptistery
see: Architectural Terms

Baratta, Francesco (c. 1590-1666)
Italian baroque sculptor, probably born in Carrara and active in Rome. Baratta settled in Rome in 1626 with Andrea Bolgi and he worked there under the direction of Gianlorenzo Bernini during the 1640's, executing the relief *The Ecstasy of Saint Francis* in the Raimondi Chapel in the church of San Pietro in Montorio, and assisting in the decoration of the pilasters and chapels of Saint Peter's.

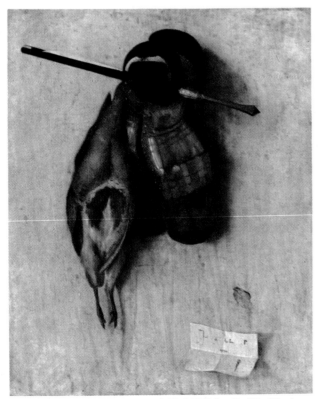

Jacopo de' Barbari: *The Dead Bird* (1504), oil; Alte Pinakothek, Munich, Germany. In this painting, one of the first still lifes ever painted, the artist worked the assorted elements on the wall into an interesting composition. His signature is written on a piece of paper stuck to the wall.

Other examples of Baratta's work in Rome can be seen in the church of San Nicola da Tolentino where he collaborated with other sculptors on the decoration of the Gavotti chapel and on the main altar, and in the Piazza Navona where he executed the *Rio della Plata,* one of the four giant figures on Bernini's Fountain of the Four Rivers.
see: Bernini, Gianlorenzo

Barbari, Jacopo de' (c. 1440-c. 1516)
Painter and engraver, possibly a Venetian, influenced by Alvise Vivarini and Antonello da Messina. Nothing is known of Barbari's activities before c. 1500, but after that date he is known to have worked in Nuremberg for Emperor Maximilian and later to have been in the employ of the Archduke Frederick III of Saxony and of Joachim I of Brandenburg. In 1510 he became court painter to Margaret of Austria, Regent of the Netherlands.

Barbari's early works show a mixture of Venetian and German influences. His studies in the proportions of the human body are known to have influenced the young Albrecht Dürer, although Barbari's later works were influenced by both Dürer and Lucas Cranach. He has been credited with having painted one of the first still lifes, *The Dead Bird* (1504), now in the Alte Pinakothek, Munich, but he is chiefly remembered for his engravings, some of which show the influence of Lucas van Leyden, and his woodcut *View of Venice* (1500).

Among Barbari's paintings are *Old Man Embracing a Young Woman,* Johnson Collection, Philadelphia Museum of Art; *The Sparrowhawk,* National Gallery, London; and works in Berlin, Paris, Dresden, Verona, and Munich.
see: Still-life Painting

Barber Institute, Birmingham, England
An integral part of the University of Birmingham, the Institute was founded in December 1932 by Dame Martha Constance Hattie Barber in memory of her husband, Sir William Barber, Bart. Dame Barber stipulated that the income from the trust funds that she set up should be used to purchase "works of art or beauty of exceptional and outstanding merit, comprising pictures painted not later than the end of the

Charles Daubigny: *The Reaping,* oil; Louvre, Paris. The artist, a leading member of the Barbizon School, has painted the landscape in a traditional manner based on direct observation in opposition to a more heroic, academic style that was then popular.

nineteenth century, furniture, tapestries, needlework, lace, medieval manuscripts, finely printed books and other works of such merit as aforesaid but not pottery or china."

The Institute galleries were opened in 1939 and now house one of the most varied and interesting English provincial collections. As well as many *objets d'art,* drawings, and miniatures, the Institute possesses paintings by Giovanni Bellini, Sandro Botticelli, Gustave Courbet, Edgar Degas, Thomas Gainsborough, Paul Gauguin, Frans Hals, Henri Toulouse-Lautrec, Edouard Manet, Claude Monet, Nicolas Poussin, Peter Paul Rubens, J. M. W. Turner, Anthony Van Dyck, and Jean Baptiste Camille Corot.

Barbican
see: Architectural Terms

Barbizon School
Name given to a group of painters who, from the early 1830's, lived and worked in the village of Barbizon on the edge of the forest of Fontainebleau, France. Their aim was to create a mode of landscape painting based on a direct observation of nature; in the words of their leader, Théodore Rousseau, "to keep in mind the virgin impression of nature." The school's ideas were influenced by John Constable and other English landscape painters, as well as by the Dutch masters of the seventeenth century. Although unwilling to sacrifice certain traditional aspects of

(left) Théodore Rousseau: *The Oak Tree,* oil; Louvre, Paris. Rousseau, the most prominent member of the Barbizon School, probably painted this subject in the area at the edge of the forest of Fountainebleau in France where the village of Barbizon was located.

(right) Henri Harpignies: *The River Loire at Nevers,* oil; The Elisabeth Severance Prentiss Collection, The Cleveland Museum of Art. Painters of the Barbizon School such as Harpignies generally sketched their painting *en plein air* (outdoors), although they often completed the work in the studio. ►

landscape painting, they were opposed to the kind of heroic and historical landscapes favored in academic circles.

The Barbizon painters followed the practice of sketching *en plein air* (outdoors), although they completed their works in the studio. Many Impressionists began by following this procedure but the Barbizon painters' unity of tone and avoidance of strong, bright color, and the serene and generalizing temper of their work sets them apart from Impressionism.

Among the most prominent members of the Barbizon school, in addition to Rousseau, were Charles Daubigny, Jules Dupré, and Narcisse Virgile Diaz de la Peña. Characteristic works include Rousseau's *The Edge of the Woods* (1853), Metropolitan Museum of Art, New York; Diaz de la Peña's *Forest Scene* (1867), City Art Museum, St. Louis; and Daubigny's *Evening,* Metropolitan Museum of Art, New York. Jean François Millet, a member of the school, differed from most of the others in his concentration on scenes of peasant life. A part of Jean Baptiste Camille Corot's career is associated with the Barbizon school.

By the middle of the nineteenth century Barbizon had become a much favored center for artists. Painters such as Constant Troyon, Henri Harpignies, Antoine Chintreuil, and Charles Jacques were closely connected with the school. Its strong influence appears in Harpignies' *Pasture near Honfleur* (1855), Musée du D. Jean Faure, Aix-les-Bains, and Chintreuil's *The River Loire at Nevers,* Cleveland Museum of Art. Many of the Impressionists display the influence of Barbizon in their early work, notably Claude Monet in his *A Ride in the Forest* (c. 1865), collection of Clifford Curzon, London, and Alfred Sisley in his *Fontainebleau Forest* (1865), Petit Palais, Paris. Ironically, the style of the Barbizon group, originally an attempt to escape from academic conservatism, became the basis for academic landscape painting in the second half of the nineteenth century.

see: Chintreuil, Antoine; Corot, Jean Baptiste Camille; Daubigny, Charles; Diaz de la Peña, Narcisse Virgile; Dupré, Jules; Harpignies, Henri; Impressionism; Landscape Painting; Millet, Jean François; Plein Air; Rousseau, Théodore

Barcelona

A city and seaport, the principal commercial center of eastern Spain since the twelfth century. Many of Barcelona's finest buildings date from the thirteenth to the fifteenth century. Foremost among these is the cathedral, which was erected on the site of an early Christian church between 1298 and 1448. Despite the addition of a façade designed by Juan Oriol Mestres in 1887, the cathedral remains the best preserved example of Catalonian Gothic architecture. The vaulted nave is divided into three aisles by soaring pillars which further enhance a feeling of great height. Subdued lighting is provided by the magnificent stained-glass windows. Many of the wood carvings on the end-panels of the choir stalls were executed by Bartolomé Ordonez in 1517-1519.

Other Gothic churches in Barcelona include Santa María del Mar (1328-1383), the columns and vaulting of which are similar to those of the cathedral; Santa María del Pino (1453), a more austere, pillarless construction with an aisleless nave and huge internal buttresses; and Santos Justo y Pastor, which was begun c. 1345. The most notable of Barcelona's Romanesque churches are San Pablo del Campo (914, restored 1117) the oldest parish church in the city, and San Pedro de las Puellas (945).

Much of the secular Gothic architecture has been rebuilt or renovated since its original construction. Of the Casa Consistorial, the Town Hall, only the north-east façade remains of the building of 1369-1378; the Universidad Literaria, the University founded in 1430, was restored in

1841 and enlarged in the 1950's. The fifteenth-century Casa de la Diputación, the meeting place of the Catalan parliament, was rebuilt, on an adaptation of Michelangelo's plan for the Palazzo dei Senatori, in 1569-1617. Little changed, however, are the Archivo de la Corona de Aragón, a Gothic structure built for Charles V in the sixteenth century which now houses a collection of medieval documents; and the Palacio Real Mayor, the palace of the Counts of Barcelona, which dates largely from the fourteenth century.

During the eighteenth century Ventura Rodríguez built the severe operating theater for the Royal College of Surgery (1761), and Manuel Amat designed the Palacio Virreina (begun 1722). Between 1716 and 1727 French engineers erected a number of military buildings in a modified version of the French academic manner of the time. The windows of the Arsenal first introduced to Spain the French segment-arched design.

By far the most important architectural developments in Barcelona in the twentieth century are the designs of Antonio Gaudí. Despite his completely individual style, Gaudí's use of vegetation-like forms and lines classify him as an important exponent of Art Nouveau. In Barcelona, he was responsible for the unfinished Templo Expiatorio de la Sagrada Familia (begun 1882), a number of private houses and apartment buildings, and the Muncipal Park (1900-1914). *see:* Art Nouveau; Gaudí, Antonio; Spanish Art and Architecture

(left) Interior; Cathedral, Barcelona, Spain. One of the best-preserved examples of Catalonian Gothic architecture, the Cathedral has a vaulted nave divided into three aisles by soaring piers. Around the apse are large radial chapels located between the buttresses.

(right) Luis Borassá: *Saint Peter Walking on the Water* (early fifteenth century); panel from the altar of Saint Peter, church of Santa Maria in Tarrasa, near Barcelona, Spain. Borassá was the leading artist of the second phase of Catalan painting, during which time contact with other Christian countries increased. He introduced a new concept of vitality in movement and facial expressions and in this example the composition of boats and figures in perspective is a bold departure from the conventions of the period, made dramatic by the fine simplicity of the drawing. ▶

Ernst Barlach: *The Avenger* (1914), wood; private collection. The artist, a German expressionist sculptor and designer of woodcuts, has conveyed a strong sense of action and power in this compact statue. The silhouette is very strong, composed of large, unbroken lines that increase the clarity of the outline. The long line from the right fist to the left foot imparts a great sense of thrust to the figure; this is augmented by the treatment of the slightly divergent upward curving lines created by the massive left arm and the drapery between the knees. The work has a feeling of tension, suggesting strong potential energy about to be released, and convincingly implies the idea of righteous retribution.

Barlach, Ernst (1870-1938)

German expressionist sculptor, illustrator, and poet, born in Wedel, Holstein. Barlach studied in Hamburg, Dresden, and Paris, and in 1906 traveled in Russia, where he was strongly impressed by peasant wood carvings. He worked in both wood and bronze, basing the style of his wood carvings on fourteenth-century German Gothic work and treating his subjects with a powerful sense of tragedy. His major works were the war memorials in Magdeburg (1929) and Hamburg (1929) and some religious carvings in Saint Catherine's Church, Lübeck (1930). He is also known for small wood carvings of individual figures, such as peasants and beggars.

Barlach gained considerable fame during the 1920's but lost favor under Hitler, when much of his work was either removed from Germany or destroyed. A partial revival of his popularity followed the end of World War II, with several exhibitions in Germany and elsewhere. There are many collections of his work in Germany; the most important is the small Barlach Museum near Lüneburg. His unconventional war memorial *Hovering Angel* (1927) is in Güstrow Cathedral, and a cast of the angel's head is in the Museum of Modern Art, New York. Examples of his work are also to be found in the Art Institute of Chicago; the Cleveland Museum of Art; the Art Museum, Seattle; and the Detroit Institute of Arts.

see: Expressionism

Barnaba da Modena (active c. 1362-1383)

North Italian painter recorded in Genoa and Pisa between 1362 and 1383. Barnaba is recorded in 1364 in Pisa, where he was to finish frescoes by Andrea Bonaiuti, but he did not complete the task. His work on the decorations of the ducal palace at Genoa has been destroyed. Barnaba painted in a style that combined Byzantine and Giottesque elements and used brilliant, enamel-like colors. Among his principal works are the *Coronation of the Virgin* (1374) and *Descent of the Holy Ghost*, both in National Gallery, London, and paintings in the church of San Giovanni Battista, Alba. He is also represented in the Museo Nazionale, Pisa, and in galleries in Frankfurt and Berlin, Germany, and Turin, Italy.

Barna da Siena (active c. 1350-c. 1356)

Fourteenth-century Sienese painter. Barna was the most important painter in Siena during the middle of the fourteenth century, but little is known of his career, and none of his work can be dated with certainty.

His paintings lie mainly within the iconographical tradition of Duccio di Buoninsegna, his style incorporating the forms and linear rhythms of Simone Martini and Pietro and Ambrogio Lorenzetti. Barna's principal claim to recognition is a fresco series, found in the Collegiata in San Gimignano, illustrating scenes from the *Life of Christ*. He is probably responsible for more than half of these scenes. According to Giorgio Vasari, the frescoes were begun in 1350 and finally completed by a pupil after Barna had been killed by a fall from a scaffold in 1381. However, scholars studying stylistic evidence doubt that the work continued as late as this. The series is a chronological sequel to Duccio's panel series of the *Maestà*, now in the Cathedral Museum, Siena.

The composition of Barna's work generally reflects the style of Martini, especially the angel in the *Annunciation* scene. However, other features, such as the theatrical setting of the architecture and the use of vehement gesture in the *Raising of Lazarus* and the juxtaposition of figures in the *Way of Calvary*, indicate a more individual dramatic interest in the human situation. A keen sense of nature is also to be observed in the *Baptism of Christ*, where the transparent water, in which the figure is immersed, contains several convincing representations of fish.

Other works attributed to Barna are the *Christ Carrying the Cross*, Frick Collection, New York, and the *Mystic Marriage of Saint Catherine*, Museum of Fine Arts, Boston.

see: Lorenzetti, Pietro and Ambrogio; Martini, Simone; Sienese School

Barnes Foundation

A chartered educational institution and museum in Merion, Pennsylvania, founded in 1922 by the

Barnaba da Modena: *Madonna and Child,* panel; Museo Nazionale, Pisa, Italy. Barnaba, a north Italian painter, was known for the brilliance of his color. The gilded frame and enamel-like colors give to this work the rich surface of a precious object.

gift of Dr. Alfred C. Barnes (1873-1951). The collection, one of the finest in the world, was finally opened to the public in March, 1961. It is composed of about one thousand paintings, including pictures by El Greco, Titian, Francisco Goya, and Peter Paul Rubens. About 1900, Dr. Barnes began to acquire works of the Impressionist and Post-Impressionist painters, which form the most important part of the collection. Well represented are Henri Matisse, Chaim Soutine, Pablo Picasso, Pierre Auguste Renoir, Vincent van Gogh, and especially Paul Cézanne.

Barocci (Baroccio), Federico (c. 1528-1612/1615) Italian painter, born in Urbino. Barocci received his early training first under his father, Ambrogio Barocci, then under Battista Franco, a Venetian painter working in Urbino. Later he studied under his uncle, the architect and painter Girolamo Genga, in Pesaro, where he remained, mainly engaged in copying paintings by Titian, until 1548, when he went to Rome to study the works of Raphael.

By 1552 Barocci was again in Urbino, where he executed the *Santa Cecilia* (1550-1555), and the

Barna da Siena: *The Kiss of Judas* (1350-1351), fresco; Collegiata, San Gimignano, Italy. This scene, a detail of a fresco cycle illustrating scenes from the New Testament, shows the betrayal of Christ, a subject that was extremely popular in the fourteenth century. The foreground group of Saint Peter attacking a Roman soldier and cutting off his ear balances the mass of soldiers in the background. Barna shows the scene at night with the sky dark and the soldiers carrying torches. See page 405.

Federico Barocci: *The Nativity;* Pinacoteca Ambrosiana, Milan, Italy. Barocci's treatment of light in this work was quite revolutionary. The strange, supernatural illumination of the scene, and the effect that this light has on color, was Barocci's primary concern. It was during this period that several experiments of this type were made. The soft forms seem almost to be dissolved in the light, which is the main unifying element in the painting, and which plays a major part in the creation of the quiet and tender mood.

Martyrdom of St. Sebastian (1557-1558) for the Cathedral. These established his reputation, and Pope Pius IV invited him back to Rome to assist in the decoration of his Casino in the Vatican gardens. His main contribution was a painted ceiling of the *Annunciation*. Shortly afterwards, while working in The Vatican with Federigo Zuccari, Barocci contracted an illness said to have been caused by a poisoning attempt by his rivals.

Following his return to Urbino, c. 1569 Barocci painted a *Deposition* for the Cathedral in Perugia, a Mannerist composition of crowded figures with theatrical gestures and poses and dramatic use of color. Barocci's mature style is characterized by the combination of these qualities and the influence of Antonio Correggio, which is visible in the softness of form and outline of the figures. The revolutionary treatment of light and the sense of movement and space in such later

Federico Barocci: *La Madonna del Popolo* (1579); Uffizi, Florence, Italy. Notable in this altarpiece is the rhythmic elegance of the composition with skillful grouping of the figures. Barocci's revolutionary treatment of light and his sense of movement and space influenced the development of Baroque art.

works as *La Madonna del Popolo* (1579), Uffizi, Florence, had considerable influence on Peter Paul Rubens and Gianlorenzo Bernini, and consequently on the development of Baroque art.

During the pontificate of Gregory XIII (1572-1585) Barocci again went to Rome, where he probably executed the *Last Supper* in the church of Santa Maria sopra Minerva, and the *Visitation of the Virgin to Elizabeth* in the Chiesa Nuova, before returning to Urbino, where he spent the rest of his life.

Other imortant works by Barocci are *The Circumcision* (1580), Louvre, Paris; *The Holy Family*, National Gallery, London; and *The Nativity* (1597), Prado, Madrid, Spain.

see: Baroque Art and Architecture; Correggio. Antonio; Mannerism

Baronzio, Giovanni (died 1362)

Italian painter, active in Rimini. Baronzio was possibly a pupil of Giuliano da Rimini, and also strongly influenced by Pietro Cavallini and Giotto. Paintings attributed to Baronzio include a *Crucifix* (1344) in the church of San Francesco, Mercatello, and an altarpiece of the *Madonna and Child Enthroned* (1345), Galleria Nazionale delle Marche, Urbino, although the former attribution is doubtful. Other works by Baronzio include frescoes in Ravenna and Tolentino.

Baroque Art and Architecture

The baroque period in European art spanned the years from about 1600 to about 1725 or 1750. The origin of the word baroque is uncertain. By the end of the seventeenth century, scholars were debating its meaning. Some said that it derived from a Portuguese word used to describe asymmetrical or irregularly-shaped pearls. Others explained that it meant an unevenly weighted form of argumentation. In the eighteenth century the word was used to castigate excessive freedom and any departure from the classical rules of order, simplicity, clarity, and symmetry. In all its meanings there was a clear implication of imbalance and excessive complication. However, in the late nineteenth and early twentieth centuries the term baroque overcame this pejorative meaning and is now used primarily to refer to a specific period of European art.

The most serious attempt to define the style of

(right) Giovanni Baronzio: *Madonna and Child Enthroned* (1345); Galleria Nazionale delle Marche, Urbino, Italy. At the ends of the lower section of this altarpiece the painter has represented scenes from the Life of Christ, the Adoration of the Magi, the Presentation in the Temple, and the Betrayal. Above, in the pinnacle, is the Crucifixion and in the smaller triangular sections to the sides are saints who look down toward the Madonna and Child. The gold background is typical of Italian painting of the thirteenth and fourteenth centuries.

this period was made by the Swiss art historian Heinrich Wölfflin in his work *Principles of Art History* (1915). He singled out five points as typical of all baroque artists: the tendency to concentrate on the "painterly" (broad areas of light and dark and color) rather than the linear so that the elements of a picture, sculpture, or building fuse together; the adoption of a diagonal recession in depth rather than a composition based on parallel planes in the manner of the High Renaissance; the use of "open forms" in order to give the impression that some inner, centrifugal force is driving the figures out of the framework; the determination to mold all the components of the composition into a single unit; and, consequently, the relative lack of concern with clarity and detail in the interests of an over-riding general effect.

Most historians would agree that these features singly, or in combination, do notably help to define the style.

For an understanding of the character and ideals of baroque art, some understanding of the historical background is helpful. In the second quarter of the sixteenth century, the Catholic Church was completely shaken by the impact of the Protestant Reformation. In an attempt to win back the converts to Protestantism, the Church set out to reform itself. Convened under Pope Paul III, the nineteenth Ecumenical Council met at the north Italian town of Trent from 1545 to 1563. Its main purpose was to restate Church doctrine and to bring about administrative and moral reform. One important area with which the Council dealt was the function of art in the service

(right) Caravaggio: *The Conversion of Saint Paul* (1601-1603); Cerasi Chapel, church of Santa Maria del Popolo, Rome. Caravaggio illustrates the moment when the saint, struck from his horse by a blinding vision of the resurrected Christ, converted. The artist has dramatically represented the scene with the figure of Saint Paul boldly foreshortened in the foreground and illuminated by strong light. The theme of the conversion of Saint Paul was popular during the period of the Counter Reformation (mid-sixteenth to early seventeenth centuries), when the Catholic Church was greatly concerned with reconverting Protestants.

◄ (left) Annibale Carracci: Detail of the ceiling fresco of the Farnese Gallery (1597-1604); Palazzo Farnese, Rome. Portrayed in the monochromatic roundel is the scene showing Apollo flaying Marsyas. This was the penalty Marsyas had to pay for having challenged Apollo to a music contest which he lost. The roundel is framed by *herms* (piers with half-length figures) painted to resemble sculptural details. These are in turn balanced by polychrome figures of two large nudes and two small putti. This complex framing system, especially the nude figures, derives from the design used by Michelangelo in his ceiling for the Sistine Chapel, The Vatican.

of the Church. The major notion was that, through art, the faithful could be instructed in Church teachings. One of the results of this idea was the imposition of an official iconography (acceptable religious subjects and interpretations thereof), which was an important factor in the determination of the imagery used in art representation.

A fundamental aspect of Counter-Reformation thought was the idea that the faith was not revealed through intellectual speculation or complex contemplation, but rather through a spontaneous personal experience, which was possible for everyone. This attitude is clearly reflected in an art which was designed to appeal to the emotions, to stimulate a strong spiritual reaction, and to create the setting in which the religious experience could be achieved.

Since the new baroque style was reduced to its simplest and most basic Christian message, it could appeal to Protestants as well as Catholics. This explains the fact that the style, as a Catholic invention, spread with great rapidity to the Protestant countries where it was firmly established. The result was that even in those countries which remained Protestant in the face of the Counter-Reformation, the baroque style, although modified to some degree, became the basic means of artistic expression in the seventeenth century.

Italy

The baroque style was established first in Rome. Although almost none of the artists who created the new style were native Romans, the city was the undisputed center of artistic activity during the end of the sixteenth century and the first half of the seventeenth, as the result of extensive church building and decorating activity. Artists from all over Italy and from other countries as well were attracted to Rome by the opportunities for commissions and to study.

In painting the new style was developed simultaneously by two artists—Annibale Carracci (1560-1609) from Bologna and Michelangelo Merisi (1573-1610), known as Caravaggio from the town near Milan where he was born. It was when these artists broke away from the prevailing Mannerism of the last third of the sixteenth century

(right) Caravaggio: Detail of *The Martyrdom of Saint Matthew* (*c.* 1599), oil; Contarelli Chapel, church of San Luigi dei Francesi, Rome. The artist has shown, intensified through dramatic lighting and composition, the moment just before the executioner kills Saint Matthew. The spectators shrink back in horror and an angel reaches down from a cloud to hand the saint a palm frond, the symbol of martyrdom. ►

(left) Carlo Maderno: Façade of the church of Santa Susanna (1597-1603); Rome. In this façade, the most important feature is the central section. The emphasis on the central portion of the building is achieved on the ground level through the clever design of the pilasters, which are flat at the outer edges of the façade, become columns further toward the center, and finally are doubled with the innermost columns projecting slightly at the sides of the doorway. The upper section of the façade is organized in the same way, but with flatter elements used throughout.

that the foundations were laid in Rome for the development of the baroque style. This Mannerist style was marked by a deliberate violation of the classical rules established in the High Renaissance and a tendency toward distorted forms and unclear compositions.

The Carracci based their personal anti-Mannerist style on the fusion of various elements of the works of the masters of the High Renaissance, particularly Raphael (1483-1520), Antonio Correggio (c. 1491-1534), and Michelangelo (1475-1564). The extent to which this idea was generally accepted is indicated by the contention of a contemporary critic that a perfect style could be established by fusing the drawing of Raphael and the color of Correggio, or the drawing of

Michelangelo and the color of Titian. The method was known as eclecticism. Thus, in many ways, Annibale Carracci was a reformer rather than a revolutionary, since he re-established older values and brought existing elements into a new balance.

Annibale's works in Bologna from the early 1580's to his departure for Rome in 1595 show his evolution away from Mannerist ideas. Before going to Rome, Annibale, with his brother Agostino and his cousin Ludovico Carracci, had established an academy in Bologna, but it was in Rome that his most important works were executed. The most influential of these works was the fresco cycle (1597-1604) on the ceiling of a room in the Palazzo Farnese, decorated with scenes from the lives of Hercules and Ulysses. Annibale skillfully organized the composition and turned to examples of classical sculpture for his figures. Another important Roman work was the *Assumption of the Virgin* (1601), in the Cerasi Chapel in the church of Santa Maria del Popolo.

In Rome, Carracci attracted a large number of followers, most of whom had come to the city from the Carracci academy in Bologna, and it was their common background that helped to establish a Carracci style in Rome. Foremost among these painters were Guido Reni (1575-1642) and Francesco Albani (1578-1660), who went to Rome just after 1600; Giovanni Lanfranco (1582-1647) and Domenico Zampieri (1581-1641), known as Domenichino, followed them a few years later; Francesco Barbieri (1591-1666), known as Guercino, went to Rome in 1621.

Caravaggio was more of a revolutionary figure, and his style was much more a personal invention than Annibale's. He was extremely forceful and dramatic, painting with sharp contrasts of light and dark (chiaroscuro), and much more naturalistic than Carracci. In fact, one of Caravaggio's paintings of *Saint Matthew and the Angel* (now destroyed) was rejected by the patrons because it showed the Saint with dirty feet.

Caravaggio generally placed his figures in the foreground where they are strongly lit from one side contrasting with a background that is almost always in dark shadow. This arrangement seems to force the figures out toward the viewer. Among Caravaggio's major works are *The Calling of St. Matthew* and *The Martyrdom of St. Matthew*

(1597-1599), Contarelli Chapel, church of San Luigi dei Francesi, Rome; *The Crucifixion of St. Peter* and *The Conversion of St. Paul* (1600-1601), Cerasi Chapel, church of Santa Maria del Popolo, Rome; *The Death of the Virgin* (1605-1606), Louvre, Paris; and *The Seven Acts of Mercy* (1607), church of the Monte della Misericordia, Naples, Italy.

Caravaggio's followers, unlike those of the Carracci, showed no common background, and as a result never established a group style. However, Caravaggio was one of the most influential painters in the entire history of art, and elements of his remarkably dramatic style spread across all of Europe. The Caravaggio innovations were something that an artist could take up on a completely personal basis. The most important followers of Caravaggio were Orazio Gentileschi (1563-c. 1647), Orazio Borgianni (c. 1578-1616), Bartolommeo Manfredi (c. 1580-1620/21), and Carlo Saraceni (c. 1580-1620).

The period in painting dominated by Annibale Carracci and Caravaggio is referred to as Early Baroque. In architecture, the most important figure of this period was Carlo Maderno (1556-1629). His church of Santa Susanna in Rome, completed in 1603, set the direction for the style of baroque architecture. The façade shows the build-up of forms, and the increasing density of the elements from the relatively flat areas at the sides to the thicker units around the door. This arrangement of forms established the basic pattern of rhythm and movement for the church façade of the baroque period.

In sculpture, the first clear baroque statement came a little bit later, and was made by Gianlorenzo Bernini (1598-1680), who was a member of the second generation of Roman baroque artists. His most important contemporaries were Pietro Berrettini da Cortona (1596-1669), a painter and architect, and Francesco Borromini

Gianlorenzo Bernini: The baldacchino (1624-1633); in Saint Peter's, Rome. This baldacchino shows Bernini's genius for combining an architectural framework (the thick, spiraled columns that support the huge bronze canopy above the high altar) with large-scale sculptural embellishment (the figures on the canopy itself).

Gianlorenzo Bernini: *Ecstasy of Saint Teresa* (1645-1652); Cornaro Chapel, church of Santa Maria della Vittoria, Rome. In this translation into marble of Saint Teresa's vision, in which an angel appeared to her and pierced her heart with an arrow, Bernini's incredible ability to render textures and features such as clouds, drapery, hair, skin, and feathers can be seen. The sculptor placed the group in a niche beneath a gilded sunburst and achieved a convincing sense of floating, weightless figures. This remarkable presentation of a mystical experience is one of the most famous of all baroque works.

(1599-1667), an architect. The period which was dominated by these three artists is referred to as the High Baroque.

Bernini was not only a great sculptor and architect, but also a highly accomplished painter although most of his paintings have been lost. Beyond this, he was a gifted playwright and a fine designer of sets and costumes for stage productions. As a sculptor he towered over every other practitioner of the art in the seventeenth century. In a brilliant series of sculptures including *David* (1623) and *Apollo and Daphne* (1622-1624), both in the Borghese Gallery, Rome, Bernini singlehandedly created the baroque style in sculpture. His bold and dynamic figures move with powerful energy, and are shown at the culmina-

tion of an action. A broad play of light and dark dramatizes the figures which move in an open space into which the spectator is drawn. This involvement of the viewer is a fundamental aspect of the baroque sculptural style. Bernini was also capable of the most spectacular rendering of texture, which added power to the life-like quality of the works.

With his religious statues Bernini used draperies to indicate and augment the emotional and spiritual attitude of the figures. In his later works, this tendency increased. One of his most famous works, the *Ecstasy of Saint Teresa* (1645-1652), Cornaro Chapel in the church of Santa Maria della Vittoria in Rome, is an ensemble that may be taken as typical of Bernini's sculptural and decorative style. The saint is shown in almost painful ecstasy while an angel hovers over her. The group is placed in a niche, the sides of which are composed of two theater-like rows of boxes from which members of the Cornaro family could watch the saint as she had a vision, and discuss the miracle. This frank theatricality in which the viewer participates as a witness, is an essential aspect of much of baroque art.

Bernini also executed a remarkable series of portrait busts, such as the portrait of Cardinal Scipione Borghese (1632), Borghese Gallery, Rome, in which the sitter is shown at the moment when he is about to speak, and the emphasis is on the fleeting facial expression.

In painting, Pietro da Cortona is the dominant figure in the period from about the mid-1630's to the mid-1660's. In his frescoes of the late 1620's in the church of Santa Bibiana, Rome, showing scenes from the life of that saint, Cortona created the new Roman baroque style, moving away from the eclectic manner of the immediate followers of Annibale Carracci (of which Domenichino was the dominant figure) to a more dynamic and robust style. In the mid-1630's, Cortona carried out his most ambitious work, the ceiling decoration of the Gran Salone of the Palazzo Barberini, Rome. Pope Urban VIII was a member of the Barberini family, and the ceiling was a glorification of his pontificate (1623-1644). The composition is tremendously dynamic and forceful, and the work ranks as one of the masterpieces of baroque painting. The ceiling is an illusionistic continuation of the space of the room, and large groups of figures, dramatically placed, create a powerful rhythm.

The close relationship between the spectator and the vision is seen in the great decorative frescoes such as Cortona's and others such as Andrea Pozzo's *Allegory of the Missionary Work of the Jesuits* (1691-1694), church of Sant'Ignazio, Rome, which form the best-known contribution of the baroque to painting. Ceilings appear to open up to the heavens, figures are hurtled down from the vaults above the viewer's head, and frames are broken apart by the driving forces within them. In this way the most complex allegorical subjects can achieve a dramatic impact that is immediately comprehensible even to the uninitiated.

Gianlorenzo Bernini: Detail of the *Cathedra Petri* (Chair of Peter, 1655-1666); Saint Peter's Rome. Bernini encased the original wooden chair of Saint Peter in lavishly decorated bronze and used figures of four Fathers of the Church, wrapped in fluttering drapery, as supporting elements.

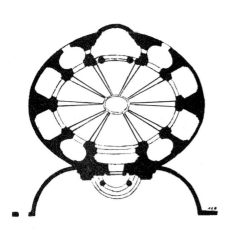

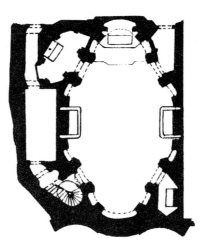

(far left) Gianlorenzo Bernini: Plan of the church of Sant'Andrea al Quirinale (1658-1670); Rome. (left) Francesco Borromini: Plan of the church of San Carlino alle Quattro Fontane (1638-1641); Rome. The oval plan was frequently employed in architecture of the baroque period, especially in church design.

(right) Gianlorenzo Bernini: Piazza of Saint Peter's (begun 1656); Rome. The wide, curved colonnades of Bernini's design for one of the most impressive piazzas in the world reach out to embrace the visitor and draw him into the church. The wide street leading out of the main area was not part of the original plan but was added between 1936 and 1950. ▶

Contemporary with the "grand manner" style of Cortona, there existed a school of genre painters who were known as Bambioccianti, after their leader, who was called Il Bamboccio. These painters produced mostly street scenes of Roman peasant life on a fairly small and intimate scale. They possess none of the didactic moralizing elements of the works of the Carracci school, and are more an outgrowth of the style of Caravaggio.

In architecture, the three major figures of the High Baroque are Bernini, Pietro da Cortona, and Francesco Borromini. The baroque style in architecture is marked by an increasingly dynamic treatment of elements. The architecture of Michelangelo was in many ways the major source of inspiration for the architects of this period, and Bernini and Borromini can be seen as following the possibilities which Michelangelo's work suggested. Borromini followed the smaller decorative elements to create a very rich and personal decorative vocabulary while the larger-scale elements of Michelangelo's style were taken up by Bernini. Both artists created rich movement; in the baldacchino (1624-1633) of St. Peter's in Rome, Bernini used huge twisted columns spiraling up to support a canopy, and in his church of San Carlino alle Quattro Fontane (1638-1646), Rome, Borromini used a complex plan with undulating walls and continuous moldings.

In Bernini's earliest architectural work, the façade of the church of Santa Bibiana (1624-1626) in Rome, rather than following the direction

Francesco Borromini: Façade of the church of Sant'Agnese (1653-1655); Piazza Navona, Rome. Although not completed according to Borromini's design the façade retains the curve and high towers that were originally intended. The skyline of this church, with the open towers balancing the dome and lantern is one of the most elegant to be found in baroque architecture.

suggested by Maderno in the façade of Santa Susanna, he opened up the ground level of the structure into a loggia. In the center, a large aedicula (niche) projects forward and up above the roof line of the two side bays.

Bernini's most famous architectural work was the colonnade (1657-1667) for the piazza in front of St. Peter's. Building on an oval plan, Bernini ingeniously worked the curved arms into the very irregularly shaped space which existed in front of the Vatican palaces. The huge colonnaded arms, reaching out to embrace the visitor and to draw him into the church, in many ways typify the baroque tendency toward large dynamic elements that control and shape large areas of space.

Pietro da Cortona's modernization of the church of Santa Maria della Pace and his new façade (1656-1657) for the church are his most important architectural works. In the shaping of the small piazza in front of the church, the church façade was treated as a theater setting or backdrop, the piazza as the orchestra level of the auditorium, and the houses around the piazza as the balcony boxes. This arrangement bears much in common with Bernini's designs for the Cornaro Chapel. The tendency to employ theatrical arrangement in the creation of a particular work and the shaping of the environment in which the work was to be seen is a basic aspect of High Baroque art.

The Late Baroque period, from about 1675 to about 1750, saw a decline in papal activity, and the gradual shift of the center of artistic activity from Rome to Paris. The architectural style of the period was one of tremendous variety, with not only the styles of Bernini, Borromini, and Cortona providing material for inspiration, but Mannerist and High Renaissance elements as well. At this time Naples, and then Turin, became centers of building activity that first rivaled, and then surpassed Rome. But it should not be imagined that all architectural activity ceased in Rome, for the last burst of building activity there during the 1720's and 1730's saw the construction of two of the most famous and beloved sites of Rome; the

Nicola Salvi: Trevi Fountain (1732-1762); Rome. In this famous fountain, a fine example of late baroque art in Rome, Salvi, who also designed the façade of the building behind the fountain, combined many diverse elements, including the water, into an organized whole.

Trevi fountain (1732-1762) designed by Nicola Salvi (1697-1751), and the so-called Spanish Steps (1723-1725), designed by Francesco de Sanctis (1693-1740).

The major architects of this period were Carlo Fontana (1634-1714), Guarino Guarini (1624-1683), Filippo Juvarra (1678-1736), and Bernardo Vittone (1704/5-1770). The works of Guarini in Turin, especially the chapel of the Holy Shroud (1667-1690), and the church of San Lorenzo (begun 1668), were immensely complex in plan and vaulting and were dominated by an apparent lack of harmony. There is often no relationship between one level and the next, and while some of the details, as well as a certain structural daring, may have been derived from Borromini, the essential order and system of Borromini's works were refuted by Guarini.

Guarini was followed in Turin by Juvarra and Vittone. Juvarra was among the most revolutionary figures in the whole history of Italian architecture. His style is in no way a development of that of Guarini; he developed a completely new open style of architecture in which walls were replaced by column screens and whole interiors begin to take on the quality of gigantic and highly complex birdcages. Juvarra's most important works were the sanctuary of the Superga (1717-1731), near Turin; the huge royal hunting lodge at Stupinigi (1729-1733); and the church of the Carmine (1732-1735), Turin.

Vittone achieved a fusion of the styles of Guarini and Juvarra. His best works are the small sanctuary (1738-1739) in Vallinoto; the church of Santa Chiara (1742) in Bra; the Ospizio di Carità (before 1749) in Carignano; and the choir of the church of Santa Maria di Piazza (1751-1754), in Turin. There is a considerable parallel in the architectural ideals of Vittone, as expressed in his written works, and the ideals which lay behind the painting of the same period. Vittone wished to delight the visitors to his buildings; he appealed to the senses. The change in Italian art from the beginning of the baroque period to the end is revealed in this shift from the desire to appeal to the emotions on a grand scale to the desire to appeal to the senses on a more elegant and refined scale. This evaporation of the heavy baroque style into a lighter and more lyrical and sensual style of the rococo is not simply an Italian phenomenon, but a general European one.

In painting, the center of activity in Italy gradually shifted from Rome to Venice. It was there that almost all of the first-rate work was done during the late baroque period, by the painters Sebastiano Ricci (1659-1734), Giovanni Battista Piazzetta (1683-1754), Antonio Canale, called Canaletto (1697-1768), Francesco Guardi (1712-1793), Jacopo Amigoni (1682-1752), and Giambattista Tiepolo (1696-1770).

During the period from about 1660 to 1680, the painters in Venice began to lighten their colors to more transparent and delicate tones, and they gradually obscured the clear outlines which had been the basis of the early baroque style of the Carracci, with its emphasis on drawing. In most other Italian centers, particularly Bologna and Rome, artists continued to use darker colors well

Pietro Passalacqua and Domenico Gregorini: The façade of the churcn of Santa Croce in Gerusalemme (1743-1744); Rome. Typical of late baroque architecture is the undulating façade and the large openings between the piers on the ground floor, the tall windows on the second level, and the broken skyline, with balustrade and statues, which climaxes in the center peak.

Giambattista Tiepolo: Detail of a sketch for a ceiling fresco of the church of the Scalzi, Venice (*c.* 1743); Gallerie dell' Accademia, Venice, Italy. The ceiling for which this sketch was made was destroyed by a bomb during World War I, but this sketch shows Tiepolo's light, pastel colors, delicate shading, and free and loose brushwork; these are typical features of late baroque painting of which Tiepolo was the most important Italian representative.

into the eighteenth century. Many of the Romans and Bolognese reacted strongly against the Venetian innovations and deliberately returned to a rather somber style. When it became clear that the reaction against the new Venetian style was only leading to a repetition of patterns, there was a reaction against the late baroque style and an attempt made to return to the great masters of the early baroque in much the same way that Annibale Carracci had returned 120 years earlier to the High Renaissance examples. This academic direction spelled the end of the outmoded baroque style, but it also set back all Italian painting, for the way of the future lay in the new direction taken by the Venetians toward a freer and looser and non-academic style. These were the directions that were taken up in eighteenth-century France. Giambattista Tiepolo, the last great painter of the Italian baroque tradition is also the greatest painter of the Italian rococo, for, in Venice, the former style eases almost imperceptibly into the latter.

In sculpture, the last phase of the baroque in Italy is marked by a great increase in French influence, and the full baroque tradition of Bernini gradually faded with the rise of French classicism.

France

In France, the nature of the seventeenth-century style was determined by the nature of the sixteenth-century style, which was more classical there than in any other country.

The baroque began to make itself felt in French painting in the 1620's, after the founders of the style in Rome had already died. The main split seen in Italian painting was clearly reflected in French painting. Caravaggio's work had a direct influence on painters such as Georges de La Tour (1593-1652). Many of his scenes, dramatically illuminated by candlelight, share similar stylistic elements with works by Caravaggio such as strong and direct lighting, obscured background, and the placement of the figures in the foreground, although de La Tour tends to reduce his figures to geometrized forms. Out of the same Caravaggesque tradition come the Le Nain brothers, Antoine (c. 1588-1648), Louis (1593-1648), and Mathieu (1607-1677), the masters of seventeenth-century French genre scenes. Their subject matter suggests the Bamboccianti, although the style is modified by the French tendency to present more solid, stoic, and dignified figures. The Caravaggio influence never spread as far as Paris and de La Tour and the Le Nain brothers were provincial painters.

Working in another direction from these Caravaggio-influenced painters is the greatest French painter of the seventeenth century, Nicolas Poussin (1593/4-1665), whose style derives from Raphael and from Annibale Carracci who was the greatest proponent of the Raphaelesque manner. Poussin spent almost his entire painting career in Rome which was at that time the undisputed center of artistic activity, whereas Paris during this period was still almost a provincial center. Poussin's style was based on the idea that art should represent human beings in their most noble and high-minded acts, and since neither nature nor human beings are perfect, it became the artist's task to perfect them according to intellectual concepts, for the instruction and inspiration of the viewer. For his perfected human types, Poussin turned to the art of Greek and Roman antiquity. This was certainly far from the naturalistic style of Caravaggio who did not hesitate to show Saint Matthew with dirty feet or the dead Virgin as a swollen and putrescent corpse in his painting *Death of the Virgin* (1605), Louvre, Paris.

Poussin's paintings are intensely rational. Every element is placed with precision for the total effect of over-all harmony and clear balance; even the landscapes show a severely rationalized and ordered quality. Among Poussin's most important works are *The Inspiration of the Poet* (1628-1629), Louvre, Paris; *The Holy Family on the Steps* (1648), National Gallery, Washington, D. C.; *Landscape with the Burial of Phocion* (1648), Louvre, Paris; and *The Arcadian Shepherds,* or *Et In Arcadia Ego* (c. 1640), Louvre, Paris. Poussin's influence in Paris was tremendous, and his classical style so fully accepted that it dominated French painting until the early eighteenth century.

The second important painter of the seventeenth century in France was Claude Lorraine (1600-1682), a landscape painter who concentrated on the soft idyllic aspects of nature. Like Poussin, Claude spent almost all of his artistic life in Rome, making many trips into the countryside south of Rome to make sketches for his paintings. Among Claude's works are *The Mill* (1631), Museum of Fine Arts, Boston, Massachusetts; *Apollo Guarding the Herds of Admetus* (1654) and *Perseus and the Medusa* (1674), both in the Collection of the Earl of Leicester, Holkham, Norfolk, England.

In architecture during the first half of the seventeenth century, the major figure in France was François Mansart (1598-1666). In architecture as well as in painting the French preferred the classical style. It appears that Mansart never visited Italy, but he was aware of the new architectural style. However, most of his works were châteaux, and the sixteenth-century French style was a more important source for such works than the new Roman baroque style.

After 1661, the artistic climate in France changed considerably. In that year, young Louis XIV came to the throne. He was an expert in the art of kingship and ran a highly organized and efficient government. The production of art works was subjected to the same control and organization as other areas of production. Louis' chief minister, Jean Baptiste Colbert (1619-1683), administered the production of art works with a view toward glorifying the king. In 1664, Colbert became Inspector of Works for Louis, and he immediately reorganized the French Academy which, founded in 1648, had been directed by Charles Lebrun (1619-1690) since 1663. In the next few years Colbert also organized an Academy of Architecture (1671), which came under the direction of Jules Hardouin-Mansart (1646-1708). Colbert's goal was to establish a system to maintain standards, to put the production of works for the king and court on a smoothly efficient basis, and to create a basis on which future works would be produced. The rules set by the French Academy for the production of art were derived from Poussin's work. In 1662, Colbert reorganized the means of production of tapestries and furniture by purchasing for the king the Gobelins tapestry works in Paris, and establishing them, with Lebrun as the director, as the center of manufacture of furniture as well as tapestries for the royal residences. He founded, as well, the French Academy in Rome (1666) for the purpose of instructing and housing French painters who had gone or been sent to Rome to study classical art.

The first of Louis XIV's great projects was the completion of the palace of the Louvre which had been begun in 1546. For this work, he had Bernini called to Paris in 1665 to see the site and to execute designs. Bernini submitted three designs, none of which satisfied the king and his projects were never followed. Instead, a committee of three was appointed to submit designs—Louis Le Vau (1612-1670), an architect; Lebrun, a painter and the head of the Academy; and Claude Perrault (1613-1688), a doctor and an amateur student of classical architecture. The fact that a committee was appointed is a further manifestation of the king's organization. The final design for the Louvre, which seems to have been primarily the work of Perrault, established clearly the classical direction of the new style. It has a flat façade and long unbroken entablatures which create a severe design, a style that is in contrast to the more rhythmical works of this period in Italy.

Louis' major project was the gigantic palace of Versailles, near Paris, which was begun in 1669 by Le Vau, and continued after his death in 1670 by Jules Hardouin-Mansart, who expanded it greatly. This project was on so vast a scale that it took almost all the available resources of the state and, again, would not have been possible without its highly efficient organization. The geometric design of the palace was extended to the surrounding garden, one of the most famous in the world for its symmetry and balanced perfection that are the equivalent in architecture and garden design of the landscape paintings of Poussin.

Hardouin-Mansart had been limited to some degree at Versailles by Le Vau's original design. He was much freer in his work on the church of the Invalides (1690-1691), Paris. The dome reflects Michelangelo's designs for the dome of St. Peter's, Rome, and the severe elements of the façade recall the Louvre designs of Perrault, but the general movement, particularly the projection of the central element and the strong play of light and shadow suggest the full baroque style of Rome. Even so, there is still a solidity and a heaviness that is French and not Italian.

In sculpture, the style was primarily classicizing, although some baroque elements such as the windblown drapery perfected by Bernini do appear. But compared to the full baroque of Bernini the style of the French is rather tame. The sculptor who most closely approached Bernini's style was Pierre Puget (1620-1694), who was decidedly out of fashion during the time that Colbert was alive and Lebrun was the director of the Academy. It was only in the mid-1680's that Puget's most important work, *Milo of Crotona* (1671-1683), was accepted by the king and placed in the gardens at Versailles, and even then after some hesitation.

Puget's increased success was indicative of the general situation in French art toward the end of the century. There was a very strong widespread reaction against the rigid rules and dictated tastes of the Academy. On the one hand were the Poussin followers who insisted that drawing was the most important element in painting because it appealed to the mind and to reason. In opposition, were the followers of the Flemish painter Peter Paul Rubens (1577-1640) who felt that color was the most important element because it appealed to the

Louis Le Nain: Detail of *The Peasants' Meal* (1630); Louvre, Paris. Louis was one of three brothers who worked together and who were among the most important genre painters in seventeenth-century France. Le Nain has given a great sense of nobility to these peasants; the tendency to dignify the humblest classes is characteristic of French genre painting.

senses and was more true to nature. This tendency toward the more sensual was precisely the same tendency that was noted in Italian art in the first decades of the eighteenth century. In France it reached even greater heights, and could be appreciated by everyone and required no special experience or education.

Antoine Watteau (1684-1721) is a pivotal figure; he is both the last artist of the baroque period in France and the first artist of the succeeding period, the rococo. The term rococo applies primarily to the art of the period of Louis XV, who reigned from 1715 to 1774. The style is gayer, lighter in color, smaller in scale, and more delicate than the baroque style of Louis XIV.

With the death of Louis XIV in 1715, Paris became the center of artistic activity in France, and the middle classes and lesser nobility became the chief patrons. It was to this new urban group that the delicate and sensuous works of Watteau appealed. His best-known works are *The Embarkation for the Isle of Cythera* (1717) and *Gilles* (1721), both in the Louvre, Paris. The colors are almost pastel and the surfaces more precious than the previous style. The style of Watteau which would have horrified Colbert or Lebrun, was sufficiently widespread and popular by 1717 for Watteau to have been accepted into the French Academy even though a whole new category had to be established to make it possible.

The new and intimate style was much more suited to small Parisian town houses than was the large-scale style of Versailles. With the shift of the artistic center from Versailles to Paris after the death of Louis XIV, baroque art in France, which had been an expression of the monarchy softened into the rococo style of the period *c.* 1715-*c.* 1770.

Flanders

In Flanders (modern Belgium), the baroque was expressed primarily in painting. The major painter of the period was unquestionably Peter Paul Rubens (1577-1640), one of the greatest painters of all time and in many ways the most perfect representative of the baroque style.

Rubens was born and trained in Antwerp, and was a master in the painters' guild by 1598; but his real artistic education began in 1600 when he made his first trip to Italy where he remained for eight years, traveling and studying extensively. Rubens completely assimilated the major elements of Italian art and fused in his own style the styles of Annibale Carracci and Caravaggio. It seems that he planned to stay in Italy and make his career there as the slightly younger Poussin and Claude Lorraine were to do. But he was called back to Antwerp in 1608 by an illness in his family and he settled there. He became increasingly successful, and his studio obtained a growing number of commissions and assistants. Among Rubens' most important works are *The Raising of the Cross* (1609-1610), Cathedral, Antwerp, Belgium; *The Rape of the Daughters of Leucippus* (c. 1610), Bayerische Staatsgemäldesammlungen, Munich, Ger-

many; *The Assumption of the Virgin* (1626), Cathedral, Antwerp, Belgium; *The Mystic Marriage of Saint Catherine* (1628), church of the Augustinians, Antwerp, Belgium; and *The Castle of Steen* (c. 1635), National Gallery, London.

Ruben's first works completed after his return to Antwerp showed a style that was clearly based on Italian prototypes. His muscular figures reveal the influence of Michelangelo, and his bold diagonal placements of figures and his lighting suggest the work of Caravaggio. His compositions are of tremendous power and of an emotional intensity that involves the spectator. This inclusion of the spectator is, as we have noted, a basic aspect of the baroque style. Rubens' most ambitious cycle of

◄ (left) Nicolas Poussin: *The Arcadian Shepherds* (c. 1640); Louvre, Paris. In this painting, the carefully placed and subtly balanced figures reveal the restrained nature of French baroque art as opposed to the intense movement of Italian baroque art. The composition, especially the outstretched arms of the kneeling figure on the left and the crouching figure on the right, lead the eye of the viewer to the inscription on the tomb, which is the focal point of the scene.

(right) Cabinet of Italian manufacture with gilt bronze and inlaid stone decoration (seventeenth century); Palazzo Pitti, Florence, Italy. Baroque taste extended beyond works in painting, sculpture, and architecture to every area of artistic production including furniture and tapestry making. This lavishly decorated piece, executed for a member of the Medici family, reveals the baroque preference for sumptuous materials and ornate style.

paintings (1622-1625) was executed for Marie de' Medici, the French Queen, and showed various episodes in her life such as birth, education, and marriage, in a highly allegorical manner. The paintings in this cycle, now in the Louvre, Paris, swirl and vibrate with overwhelming life and excitement. While Poussin's paintings often have the quality of tinted drawings, in a work by Rubens the drawing and painting are inseparable at every stage of development.

Flanders during the seventeenth century was under Spanish domination, and Rubens worked in Antwerp for the Spanish governor, and also traveled in Spain where he was to exert a strong influence on the major Spanish baroque painters, particularly Diego Velázquez (1599-1660).

Another major Flemish painter was Anthony Van Dyck (1599-1641), who was first a pupil and then an assistant of Rubens. Van Dyck's works include his *Self-Portrait* (c. 1621), Bayerische Staatsgemäldesammlungen, Munich, Germany; *Portrait of Frans Snyders* (c. 1620), Frick Collection, New York; *The Vision of the Blessed Herman Joseph* (1630), Kunsthistorisches Museum, Vienna, Austria; and *Portrait of Quinten Simons* (c. 1634), Mauritshuis, The Hague, The Netherlands. Van Dyck was a superb portraitist, and he served in England as court painter to King Charles I from 1632 until his death in 1641. He often painted his figures in somber tones against a background of dramatic sky and trees. It was this style that established the pattern for English portraiture for the next 150 years.

(Article continues in Volume 3)

Claude Lorraine: *View of the Campo Vaccino in Rome* (1636); Louvre, Paris. Claude was one of the most important French baroque artists. As a painter of idealized landscape he was one of the greatest masters of all time.